Platform Embedded Security Technology Revealed

Safeguarding the Future of Computing with Intel Embedded Security and Management Engine

Xiaoyu Ruan

Platform Embedded Security Technology Revealed

Xiaoyu Ruan

Publisher: Heinz Weinheimer
Lead Editors: Steve Weiss (Apress); Patrick Hauke (Intel)
Coordinating Editor: Melissa Maldonado
Cover Designer: Anna Ishchenko

Distributed to the book trade worldwide by Springer Science+Business Media New York, 233 Spring Street, 6th Floor, New York, NY 10013. Phone 1-800-SPRINGER, fax (201) 348-4505, e-mail orders-ny@springer-sbm.com, or visit www.springeronline.com.

For information on translations, please e-mail rights@apress.com, or visit www.apress.com.

About ApressOpen

What Is ApressOpen?

- ApressOpen is an open access book program that publishes high-quality technical and business information.

- ApressOpen eBooks are available for global, free, noncommercial use.

- ApressOpen eBooks are available in PDF, ePub, and Mobi formats.

- The user friendly ApressOpen free eBook license is presented on the copyright page of this book.

To my parents, to my wife, Gloria, and to our children, Alexander and Angelina, who have expanded the possibilities for our future.

Contents at a Glance

Contents

About the Author

Xiaoyu Ruan is a security researcher with the Platform Engineering Group at Intel Corporation. He is responsible for designing cryptography infrastructure and security applications for Intel's security and management engine. Xiaoyu obtained his Ph.D. and M.S. degrees in computer engineering from the North Dakota State University in 2007 and 2005, respectively, and his B.S. degree in electrical engineering from Fudan University of China in 2003. He is an author of 15 peer-reviewed journal and conference papers and holds three U.S. patents in the areas of cryptography, security, and information theory.

About the Technical Reviewer

Hareesh Khattri received his M.S. degree in electrical and computer engineering from North Dakota State University. He has worked as a computer security researcher at Intel Corporation since 2007. As part of his work at Intel Corporation, Hareesh has done security evaluation of multiple generations of Intel Manageability Engine technology and associated platform features.

Acknowledgments

This book would not have been possible without the strong support from my manager, Michael Berglund, and a number of colleagues, including Vincent von Bokern, William Stevens, Daniel Nemiroff, Purushottam Goel, Andrew Fry, and many others, who provided me with invaluable advice. I wholeheartedly appreciate the help.

Special thanks go to Hareesh Khattri of the Security Center of Excellence at Intel. With his unique expertise and attention to detail, Hareesh performed an extremely thorough review that significantly improved the quality of the manuscript.

I would also like to express my gratitude to editors Patrick Hauke, Corbin Collins, Melissa Maldonado, Steve Weiss, and Kimberly Burton-Weisman. I am truly impressed by their skills, dedication, and patience.

Introduction

Malware, virus, e-mail scam, identity theft, evil maid, password logger, screen scraper...

Cyber security concerns everyone. Computers can be your trusted friends or traitors. The Internet is a scary place. Going on the Internet is like walking the streets of a crime-ridden neighborhood. Cyber criminals work to steal your privacy, money, assets, and even identity. Cyber-attacks are intangible, invisible, and hard to detect. Due to the increasing popularity of mobile devices, the danger is several-fold worse today than it was seven years ago.

Technologies that created the security problem as a side effect are supposed to resolve the problem. Prevention is the key—the potential loss and cost of dealing with incidents is simply too high to afford.

However, it is more difficult to defend a castle than to build it. The mitigation against cyber-attacks is complicated and involves multiple layers of building blocks:

- *Algorithm*: An algorithm is a set of mathematical calculations that realize a specific cryptographic functionality, such as encryption, digital signature, hashing, and so forth.

- *Protocol*: A protocol is a set of rules and messages that govern the transmission of data between two entities. Security protocols are always built on cryptographic algorithms.

- *Application*: An application is a computer program that accomplishes a specific task, such as authenticating a user to a protected database. Applications are built with algorithms and protocols as the backbone.

Algorithms and protocols are often standardized and used across the industry for compatibility and interoperability. On the other hand, applications may be standardized, but in most cases they are invented and deployed by individual vendors to distinguish their products from competitors.

Algorithms, protocols, and applications can be realized in software, hardware, or combinations of both. Security measures that are rooted in hardware are more robust than those rooted in software, because attacks against well-designed hardware-based protections not only require advanced expertise, but also cost significant resources.

Intel is committed to delivering state-of-the-art solutions for supporting a safe computing environment. The embedded engine built in most Intel platforms today is a major achievement of that effort. It features hardware implementations for standard algorithms and protocols, as well as innovative applications that are exclusively available on Intel products, including:

- Privacy safeguard with EPID (enhanced privacy identification)

- Strong authentication and secure transaction with IPT (identity protection technology)

- Verified boot process

- . . . and many more

Thanks to these protections, users are largely shielded from dangers when they are surfing the Web. With peace of mind, people can enjoy all the good things that technologies have to offer.

This book takes the readers through an extensive tour of the embedded engine, exploring its internal architecture, security models, threat mitigations, and design details of algorithms, protocols, and interesting applications.

The journey begins now.

CHAPTER 1

■ ■ ■

Cyber Security in the Mobile Age

The number of new security threats identified every month continues to rise. We have concluded that security has now become the third pillar of computing, joining energy-efficient performance and Internet connectivity in importance.

—Paul S. Otellini

This book is an in-depth technical introduction to an embedded system developed and manufactured by Intel Corporation. The embedded system is not an independent product; it is a native ingredient inside most of Intel's computer product portfolio, which includes servers, desktops, workstations, laptops, tablets, and smartphones. Although not well known to most end users, the embedded system plays a critical role in many consumer applications that people use every day. As such, its architecture, implementation, and security features are worth studying.

Depending on the end product in which the embedded engine resides, the engine is denominated differently:

- For the embedded system shipped with computing devices featuring Intel Core family microprocessors, it is called the *management engine.*

- For the embedded system shipped with computing devices featuring the Intel Atom system-on-chip (SoC), it is called the *security engine.* Note that not all Atom platforms use the security engine introduced in this book.

For the sake of convenience, this book refers to it as *the security and management engine, the embedded engine,* or simply *the engine.*

Three Pillars of Mobile Computing

In August 2010, Intel announced the acquisition of security giant McAfee. Paul S. Otellini, Intel's president and CEO at the time, emphasized that "security has become the third pillar of computing" when commenting on the investment. The other two pillars of computing are energy-efficient performance and Internet connectivity.

The three pillars summarize the core characteristics for computing, especially mobile computing. Intel's security and management engine is an embedded component that serves as the backbone that supports the three pillars for multiple forms of computers, including mobile endpoints, desktops, workstations, and servers. As its name indicates, the engine's main functionalities are security and management. In the meantime, power efficiency and connectivity are also addressed in its design.

Power Efficiency

Mobile devices distinguish themselves from stationary platforms in mobility and independence of AC (alternating current) power supply. The battery life is hence an important factor for evaluating the quality of a mobile product. Before the battery technology sees a major breakthrough, computer manufacturers have to strive to deliver hardware and software with low energy consumption.

A number of general strategies can be employed to save power:

- Decrease the processor's clock frequency, with the potential tradeoff of performance. For example, the security and management engine runs at a significantly lower speed than the platform's main processor. This is possible without degrading the user experiences, because the engine is not designed to be involved in performance-critical paths.

- Dim the display screen and shut down devices that are not being used or place them in sleep states. For example, after being idle for a configurable amount of time, like 30 seconds, the security and management engine may completely power off or run in a low-power state with very low clock frequency. Events that may wake up the engine to its full-power state include device interrupts and messages received from the host operating system.

- Simplify and adjust hardware and software logic. Redundant routines should be removed. For example, applying blinding to public key operations is meaningless, because there is no secret to be secured from side-channel attacks; whenever feasible, favor performance over memory consumptions for runtime programs. These are part of the design guidelines for the security and management engine.

Internet Connectivity

Needless to say, the majority of applications running on a mobile device rely on network connections to function. Looking into the architecture, there are two models of splitting the workload between the local device and the cloud:

- The main functionality of the cloud is storage, for contents such as movies, music, and personal files. The local device carries out most of computational tasks. This model requires stronger computing capability of the mobile devices, which may imply higher prices.

- Besides storage, the cloud also performs a certain amount of computations for the device. The device is responsible for only limited computations, and its main tasks are input and output. This model is advantageous in lowering the cost of the device. However, it requires high network bandwidth and powerful servers that are able to support a large number of devices simultaneously.

Security

Security is not standalone, but closely relevant to the other two pillars. Security is becoming vitally important for computers, thanks to the increasing connectivity. While enjoying all the benefits and conveniences the Internet has to offer, connected devices are also exposed to widespread attackers, viruses, and malware on the open network. The new challenges of securing mobile platforms are originated from three characteristics of mobile computing:

- *Always connected*: Smartphones and tablets may never be turned off. Attacks can be mounted at any time and take any amount of time.

- *Large data transmission*: Because of its convenience, mobile devices are used more often for operations that involve secure data transmission with servers, for example, web site logon, financial transaction, online purchase, and so forth. This makes attacks that require collecting a large amount of data more likely to succeed.

- *Privacy*: Mobile devices hold sensitive data that would not normally appear on stationary computers. The data includes but is not limited to phonebook and location information. A security objective for mobile devices is to protect users' personal information.

To mitigate these threats, security researchers have invented and deployed various countermeasures to safeguard computers and prevent leakage and abuse of assets. They include software-based solutions, like antivirus programs, firewalls, and so on, and hardware-based solutions, such as secure boot.

Now let's take a look at the relationship between security and power. Unfortunately, improvements in security and reduction in energy consumption are largely contradictory. A security measure, although an essential element, costs power to accomplish its work that is not functionally beneficial. However, an insecure system is not practically usable. Well-designed cryptography and security implementations can provide desired protection strengths with minimum power consumption. The following are some strategies that can be considered:

- Offload intensive mathematical operations to hardware engines that operate at lower frequency. Most cryptography algorithms are built on complex mathematics. The dedicated hardware should feature specific logic for underlying operations, so the calculation can be completed faster with lower power, compared to general-purpose processors.

- Utilize efficient algorithms and parameters; for example, when designing elliptic curve cryptography, select the curves carefully, and use the ones that require the fewest operations without degrading the security strength.

- Avoid overengineering. Choose algorithms and key sizes that meet, but don't overwhelmingly exceed, robustness requirements. For example, using a public key cryptosystem with security strength of 256 bits to protect a 128-bit symmetric key is a waste of computing power.

- Store keys and other secrets in secure, nonvolatile memory if possible and avoid repeated derivations for every power cycle.

BYOD

Bring Your Own Device, or BYOD, is a fast-growing emerging application thanks to the booming mobile computing development. An increasing number of companies now support BYOD programs and allow employees to use their personal mobile devices for work, such as sending and receiving corporate e-mails and accessing work data.

According to a survey[1] conducted by Intel, the following are the three top-ranked benefits voted by corporate IT (information technology) managers across different continents:

- Improve efficiency and worker productivity

- Increase opportunities for worker mobility

- Save costs by not having to purchase as many devices for employees to use

Alongside the gains are risks and challenges. Not surprisingly, security is the number-one rated barrier of deploying BYOD in most countries, especially for heavily regulated industries. With BYOD, it is increasingly common to see malware that targets the IT infrastructures of government agencies and industrial companies. The safety level of a corporate asset is equal to the strength of the weakest link that handles the asset. Because the employees' devices are handling confidential business data, they must apply the required security enforcements per the company's IT policies.

Here are a few security considerations when converting an employee's device for BYOD:

- *Secure boot*: The system integrity must be guaranteed. Rootkits and malware that infects the boot flow place the entire operating environment at risk. It is recommended that rooted mobile devices should not be permitted for BYOD. Refer to Chapter 6 for technical insights into Intel's Boot Guard technology.

- *Hard-drive encryption*: The whole drive, or at least the partition that stores business data, should be encrypted with a standard algorithm. The encryption key may be randomly generated at the first boot and sealed in a dedicated trusted device, such as a TPM[2] (*Trusted Platform Module*). The key may also be calculated from the user's credentials using a one-way function with a salt at each boot. Regardless of how the key is generated, it should be unique per device. Deriving the key solely from a password is not a good idea, because the employee may use the same password for multiple purposes.

- *Strong authentication*: The minimal length and complexity of the login password should be enforced. A password should be a combination of characters and cannot be a four-digit number. The device memory should not contain plaintext secrets before the device is unlocked by the employee. In addition, some business applications may warrant additional multifactor authentication at runtime.

- *Isolated execution*: Sensitive applications should execute in a secure mode that is logically separated from the nonsecure mode and other irrelevant applications. Intel's proprietary features, like TXT[3] (*Trusted Execution Technology*) and the upcoming SGX[4] (*Software Guard Extensions*) technology, have built infrastructures for isolated execution.

- *Employee privacy*: Depending on the organization's BYOD policy, the employee's personal data, such as photos, videos, e-mails, documents, web browse cache, and so on, may need to be secured from access or abuse by business applications. This can be achieved by the same isolation technique mentioned earlier.

- *Remote wipe capability*: Mobile device theft is on the rise, rapidly. *Consumer Reports* projects that about 3.1 million American consumers were victims of smartphone theft in 2013, more than double the 1.4 million in 2012. Once a BYOD device is reported stolen, even though the hard drive is encrypted, it is still essential, for defense in depth, to wipe the hard drive and prevent loss of business data and personal information. In April 2014, major industry players, including Apple, Google, Microsoft, Samsung, Nokia, AT&T, Sprint, and others, signed on to the "Smartphone Anti-Theft Voluntary Commitment"[5] that pledges to implement a "kill switch" feature by 2015 that can wipe the data of a lost phone and disallow the phone from being reactivated without an authorized user's consent.

While tightening up the security of employees' mobile equipment and getting ready for BYOD, an inevitable side effect is the increased power consumption and worsening battery life. To improve employee satisfaction, the strategies discussed in the previous section should be taken into account when defining BYOD policies.

Incident Case Study

What's happening in the area of cyber security? From credit card fraud to identity theft, from data breach to remote execution, cyber security is being covered increasingly by the media—not only technical journals but also popular newspapers and magazines—and is drawing a lot of public attention. The subject of cyber security is no longer an academic matter that concerns only researchers and computer manufacturers. In the era of mobile computing, cyber security is a problem that impacts everyone's life more realistically than ever.

eBay Data Breach

In a press release from May 21, 2014, the giant Internet auction house eBay said it would ask its 145 million customers to change their passwords, due to a cyber-attack that compromised a database containing encrypted passwords and other nonfinancial data.[6]

How did it happen? According to the press release, the cyber-attack occurred between February and March of 2014. It comprised a small number of employee login credentials, allowing unauthorized access to eBay's corporate network. The company later clarified that the passwords were not only "encrypted," but also protected by eBay's "sophisticated and proprietary hashing and salting technology," and there was no evidence that the stolen data could be used in fraudulent actives.

Despite the fact that the stolen passwords were protected (encrypted and hashed), there are still a series of implications of the incident:

- Users' private information—including name, postal and e-mail addresses, phone number, date of birth, and so forth—was stored in the clear and leaked.

6

- Depending on the encryption or hashing algorithms (which are not disclosed by eBay) that are used to protect passwords, dedicated attackers may be able to reverse-engineer the algorithms and retrieve clear passwords.

- Password reuse among multiple sites is a poor but extremely popular practice. Even if a victim changes her password for eBay.com, her cyber security is still in danger if she also uses the same password for other web sites, such as Amazon.com. Therefore, an eBay user must change passwords for all web sites for which the compromised password is used, to be safe.

Target Data Breach

On December 19, 2013, Target, the second largest retail store in the United States, reported a data breach that resulted in approximately 40 million credit and debit card numbers being stolen.[7] Victims were consumers who shopped at Target stores (excluding Target.com) between November 27 and December 15, 2013 and paid with payment cards. In January 10, 2014, the company further announced that, in addition to the 40 million stolen cards, personal information, including names, phone numbers, and postal and e-mail addresses of approximately 70 million customers, was also compromised due to the incident. In other words, nearly one-third of the total population of the United States was impacted.

Following one of the most massive breaches in US history, in February 2014 Target reported that its net earnings for the holiday season had plunged 46 percent year-to-year. On March 5, the company's chief information security officer resigned from the job. Two months later, Target's chairman, president, and CEO Gregg Steinhafel also stepped down, after as many as 35 years of service at the company. The press release described that Steinhafel "held himself personally accountable" for the breach.

The company explained in January 2014 that the breach was due to login credentials being stolen from one of its vendors and then used to access Target's internal network. The attacker might have exploited vulnerabilities in the management software deployed in the internal network to access the secret data. Target did not disclose the name of the vendor or the management software.

From the brief description, one may reasonably deduce what happened: the attacker logged into Target's network using the stolen credentials. He then installed malware on the flawed management software to exploit the vulnerability. The malware scanned in the host memory for payment card numbers and then secretly uploaded to a remote server established by the attacker that harvested them. Furthermore, the fact that online purchases at Target.com were not affected suggested that the malware might have infected point-of-sale (POS) machines. A research conducted by Intel's McAfee Labs following the incident had identified a number of malware that aims at POS endpoints and transaction verification systems.[8]

The breach unfolded several problems with Target's information security management:

- Vendors' access to Target's network was not protected with a sufficiently strong authentication method. A credential that can be stolen and used without the victim's knowledge is likely a username and password. This old and simple way of authentication is very vulnerable and too weak to fortify valuable assets.

- The vendor's account was allowed to perform privileged operations after accessing Target's internal network, and the operations were not closely monitored and examined. The principle of least privilege should always be exercised as a best practice of information security, not only in computer product designs but also in enterprises' IT management.

- The third-party management software suffered critical security flaws. Either the software vendor did not know about the vulnerability until the breach took place or Target did not apply patches that fixed the vulnerability in a timely manner.

OpenSSL Heartbleed

The Request for Comments 6520 "Transport Layer Security (TLS) and Datagram Transport Layer Security (DTLS) Heartbeat Extension,"[9] published by the Internet Engineering Task Force (IETF) in February 2012, introduces and standardizes the *heartbeat extension* for the TLS/DTLS protocol. In a nutshell, it is a simple two-way protocol between a client and a server that have already established a secure TLS/DTLS session. One party sends a heartbeat request message with an arbitrary payload to its peer, who in turn sends back a heartbeat response message that echoes the payload within a certain amount of time. This extension is mainly used for checking the liveliness of the peer.

The core of the mobile computing is interconnectivity—connections between a client (laptop, smartphone, tablet, and so forth) and a server, between two servers, or between two clients. There exist various protocols that offer secure links between two entities, for example, the SIGMA (*SIGn and message authentication*) protocol introduced in Chapter 5 of this book. However, TLS/DTLS is used in the majority of secure connections over the Internet today. It provides not only one-way or mutual authentication but also encryption and integrity for messages. Most implementations of TLS/DTLS take advantage of the open-source OpenSSL cryptography library.

Heartbleed is a severe security bug in OpenSSL.[10] The vulnerability was first reported by Neel Mehta of Google's security team on April 1, 2014. The Finnish cyber security company, Codenomicon, found the same issue independently at almost the same time and named it Heartbleed. The bug was fixed promptly in an OpenSSL release on April 7.

A heartbeat request message consists of four elements:

1. Message type (1 byte)

2. *payload_length* in bytes (2 bytes)

3. Payload (length is determined by *payload_length*)

4. Padding (at least 16 bytes)

The total size of a heartbeat request message is transmitted to the receiver in variable *TLSPlaintext.length* or *DTLSPlaintext.length*, whose value must not exceed 16384 according to the protocol. Notice that the 16-bit integer *payload_length* can denote up to 65535. The bug in the vulnerable OpenSSL releases lies in the receiver side of the heartbeat implementation. The code misses bounds checking and fails to make sure that the *payload_length* is such that the total size of the four fields is not greater than the actual message size indicated by *TLSPlaintext.length* or *DTLSPlaintext.length*. The flawed implementation outputs a response heartbeat message with memory buffer of size calculated based on *payload_length*, instead of *TLSPlaintext.length* or *DTLSPlaintext.length*.

To exploit the vulnerability, a malicious TLS/DTLS client assigns a small number to *TLSPlaintext.length* or *DTLSPlaintext.length*, manipulates *payload_length* to its allowed maximum, 65535, and sends the falsified heartbeat request to a vulnerable server. On the server side, nearly 64KB of the memory beyond the payload is transmitted back to the malicious client in the heartbeat response. Although the attacker cannot choose the memory region at which he can peek, the leaked memory likely contains information used for the current TLS/DTLS session, including the server's secrets. And the attacker can iterate heartbeat requests repeatedly to gather more memory content from the server. Similar attacks can be launched from a rogue server to attack flawed clients.

Figure 1-1 shows the attack scenario. The attacker's client first establishes a TLS/DTLS connection with the target server. The client then sends a manipulated heartbeat request to the server. The message is only 28 bytes in size, but it specifies, on purpose, the payload length as 65535—the maximum value that can be represented by a 16-bit integer—although the actual payload is only 9 bytes long: {ed 15 ed 7c 05 9f 7b 99 62}. In the OpenSSL implementation, the size of the padding field is fixed at the minimum allowed by the standard, 16 bytes.

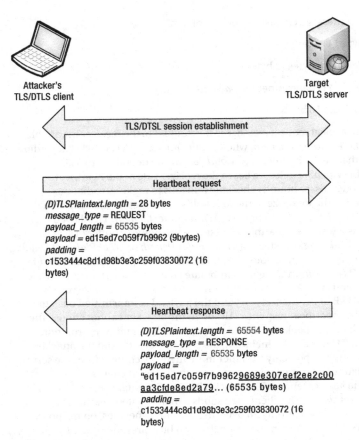

Figure 1-1. *Heartbleed attack*

The server with a buggy OpenSSL library calculates the total size of the heartbeat response buffer by adding the sizes of the message type (1 byte), *payload_length* field (2 bytes), payload (*payload_length* bytes), and padding (16 bytes), which works out to be 1+2+65535+16=65554 bytes in this case. Due to the missing bounds check, the server fails to realize that the size of its response has exceeded the maximum, 16384 bytes, defined by the specification. The size of the response also exceeds the size, 28 bytes, of the received heartbeat request. That is, as many as 65535-9=65526 bytes of the server's memory (an illustrative example is underlined in the figure: {96 89 e3 07 ee f2 ee 2c 00 aa 3c fd e8 ed 2a 79 ...}) following the payload is sent to the client in the heartbeat response. The leaked memory could contain the server's private key.

The bug had existed in OpenSSL for over two years before it was discovered. The two most popular open-source web servers, Apache and nginx, both leverage OpenSSL and are hence vulnerable. Among all active Internet web sites in the world, two out of three use Apache or nginx, as reported by Netcraft's April 2014 Web Server Survey.[11] Affected sites include popular ones such as Yahoo! and Flickr. Other than web servers, OpenSSL is the dominant library embedded in many other types of networked computer products as well, such as secure teleconferencing devices. Intel's AMT[12] (*advanced management technology*) software development kit is also affected. Famous cryptographer Bruce Schneier described the incident as "catastrophic."

Unfortunately, fixing the bug on the servers is just the beginning of the firefighting. The certificates of impacted servers must be revoked by the issuing certification authorities, and new certificates must be issued for servers' new key pairs. In the worst case, if the server's private key had been stolen before the fix was applied and the attacker was also able to obtain TLS/DTLS session caches between the server and its (potentially a large number of) clients, then secrets transmitted in those sessions were also compromised. Typically, the secrets transported over TLS/DTLS are end users' passwords, financial transactions, credit card numbers, e-mails, and other confidential information. What's worse, there is no trace of whether Heartbleed exploitations had happened and when. Therefore, it is almost impossible to accurately assess the total loss caused by the bug due to its retroactive nature.

When it rains it pours. On June 5, 2014, OpenSSL released another security advisory for six recently reported and fixed flaws.[13] These bugs were more difficult to exploit than Heartbleed, but still drew significant media attention in the wave of Heartbleed.

Key Takeaways

What can we learn from the repeated cyber security crisis? How does a company fight against cyber-attacks that make it the headlines? How to protect users' safety on the Internet? Following is a postmortem on the recent incidents.

Strong Authentication

Organizations, such as law enforcement agencies, offline and online retailers, financial institutions, medical facilities, and so on, that possess and process high-value assets should consider implementing strong authentication for access control. A strong authentication mechanism would require multiple factors of credentials for logging in. The second credential factor is usually a physical object—for example, a token—that belongs to a legitimate user.

Today, multifactor authentication is no longer an expensive investment, thanks to the emergence of innovative technologies. For many applications, the potential monetary loss due to identity theft far surpasses the cost of deploying multifactor authentication. Chapter 10 discusses strong authentication in detail and Intel's unique and cost-effective solution to the problem—IPT[14] (*Identity Protection Technology*).

Network Management

Organizations should closely monitor all network activities and flag suspicious operations. Advanced firewall devices and antivirus programs should be employed to detect malware and respond correspondingly. Intel's AMT, a core member of the vPro technology, provides a hardware-based out-of-band platform management solution that reduces cost and simplifies network administrators' work.

Boot Integrity

A platform that has been infected by virus, malware, or rootkits is running in a state that is different from its trusted and known-good state. Secure boot mechanisms, available on most new computers, examine the integrity of the platform's firmware and software components during power-on. They are designed to detect changes in platform state and identify malicious programs on the system.

In addition, secure boot can collaborate with other security measures to store secrets inside hardware, so that the confidential data is available for use only if the platform is running in a trusted state.

Hardware-Based Protection

Sophisticated viruses are capable of scanning a system's memory for signatures of interesting data, such as transactions and payment card numbers. For software-based protections, sensitive data has to appear in the system's memory in the clear at some point to be consumed by software programs. The duration of the exposure may be very short but still enough for malware to do its work. Even though the data is properly protected during transmission and at rest, attackers only need to circumvent the weakest point.

The ultimate solution is to depend on hardware for security, in which case the secrets are never exposed in the system's memory in the clear. Successful attacks against hardware launched from a remote location, if not impossible, would require extremely advanced skills to find and exploit critical hardware vulnerabilities.

State-of-the-art computers are equipped with necessary devices and hardware-based countermeasures to safeguard users' confidentiality, at rest and at runtime. For example, the TPM serves as the hardware root of trust (see Chapter 7 for more information) for a platform; Intel's SGX technology allows software programs to create and run in dedicated enclaves that are inaccessible by other components, including ring 0 drivers.

Open-Source Software Best Practice

Besides open-source operating systems such as Linux, open-source implementations of standardized protocols and functionalities have become a mainstream. Open-source software is gaining widespread popularity on endpoint devices and clouds because of many advantages it fosters: low cost, maturity, allowing faster development cycle and reduced maintenance effort, and so on. Developers simply port the functional modules they need and integrate with their products, instead of writing from scratch. They usually do not have to dig into the internal details of how the libraries structure and function. All they need is to understand the API (*application programming interface*) and invoke it.

This practice is good and bad. Although it saves engineering resources, on the other hand, it also poses risks because engineers are blind to the code that they are responsible for. One of the major disadvantages of free open-source software is that the volunteering authors provide the source code as-is and are not liable for consequences of bugs in the code, therefore the users must exercise caution during integration.

Open-source software, especially those that have been used for a long period of time by a large number of commercial products, normally enjoys high quality and performance with regard to functionality. However, the security side is a completely different story. For software development, writing working code is a relatively easier job compared to security auditing that requires dedicated resources with specialized expertise for code review and penetration testing, which, due to funding shortage, is often inadequate for open-source software.

Many adopters do not exercise comprehensive security validation for open-source modules of the products like they do for their owned components. This is usually due to lacking an in-depth understanding of the open-source modules, which renders it difficult or impossible to come up with effective test cases that are likely to identify critical vulnerabilities. Another excuse for deprioritizing security validation on open source is the presumption, and de facto an illusion, that open-source software "must be" mature because it is open and can be read and reviewed by anyone, plus it has been deployed by countless other products for so many years. In reality, the openness does not imply secure code. The security validation gap of using open-source software should be filled by individual product owners.

Eventually, the amount of resources that should be spent on comprehending and validating open-source code is a judgment call about opportunity cost. If vulnerabilities are discovered in released products, will the expense of fixing the issue and deploying the patch be higher than the investment on validation? Notice that there is an intangible price of brand name damages that must be taken into consideration as well.

In the security and management engine's firmware, only a small fraction originates from open-source domain, and it is only used in modules that do not assume security responsibilities. For example, the TLS implementation in the AMT firmware application is not ported from OpenSSL and hence not affected by OpenSSL's vulnerabilities such as the Heartbleed. The validation of the engine does not discriminate between open source and closed source. Thorough testing is performed against open-source software used by the engine.

As a good general guideline, the technical white paper "Reducing Security Risks from Open-Source Software"[15] proposes five steps that organizations should go through to take advantage of open source and lower the associative risks:

1. Identify and analyze all usages of open source.

2. Assess open source for vulnerabilities ad resolve issues.

3. Develop open-source usage policies.

4. Develop a patch management process.

5. Create a compliance gate.

Third-Party Software Best Practice

Before purchasing commercial software from for-profit vendors or outsourcing software development to external parties, buyers should ask the following:

- What is the security development process exercised by the vendor?

- What types of security auditing are preformed? Is it done by the vendor itself or external consultants?

- What is the vulnerability tracking and response process?

Security validation is a pivotal stage in software development. A vendor with a good quality control system should apply proven techniques, such as static code analysis, penetration testing, and so forth, to their product development life cycle.

Even though the third-party software has been tested for security by its vendor, in many cases it is still worth it for the adopter to conduct independent code review and end-to-end validations, either in-house or by hiring specialized security auditing firms. This is necessary especially for modules that process sensitive data.

■ **Note**   Consider performing comprehensive security validation and auditing for open-source and third-party software.

Security Development Lifecycle

The Security Development Lifecycle, or SDL, is a process consisting of activities and milestones that attempt to find and fix security problems during the development of software, firmware, or hardware. The SDL is extensively exercised by technology companies, for example, Microsoft and Intel. Different companies decide their specific procedures and requirements for SDL, but they all aim at the same goal: to produce high-quality products with regard to security and to reduce the cost of handling aftermaths for vulnerabilities found after release.

Intel is committed to securing its products and customers' privacy, secrets, and assets. To build a solid third pillar for computing, a sophisticated SDL procedure of five stages is implemented at Intel to make security and privacy an integral part of product definition, design, development, and validation:

- *Assessment*: Determine what SDL activities are applicable and will be performed.

- *Architecture review*: Set security objectives, list a threat analysis, and design corresponding mitigations.

- *Design review*: Map security objectives to low-level design artifacts. Make sure designs meet security requirements.

- *Development review*: Conduct a comprehensive code review to eliminate security vulnerabilities, such as buffer overflow.

- *Deployment review*: Perform security-focus validation and penetration testing and assure that the product is ready for release, from both the privacy and security perspectives.

The SDL process applies to hardware, firmware, and software, with small differences in different stages.

Intel takes users' privacy seriously. The privacy aspect is called out in the SDL process and evaluated separately, in parallel with the technical aspect of security, throughout all the five phases. Figure 1-2 shows the SDL phases and components. A product may ship only after the deployment privacy and security review has been accomplished and approved.

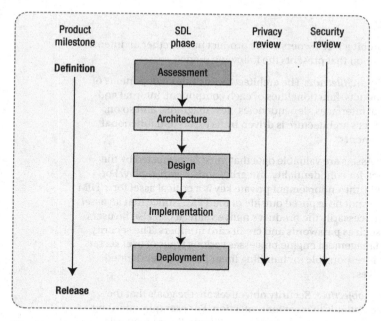

Figure 1-2. SDL phases and components

Assessment

The SDL assessment happens as part of the definition stage of a new product. The privacy assessment asks whether the product will collect users' personal information, and if so, what kinds of information, what it will be used for, and what techniques are employed to protect it from leakage and misuse. Intel has invented advanced technologies to safeguard users' fundamental right to privacy. Chapter 5 of this book is dedicated to privacy protection and Intel's EPID (*enhanced privacy identification*) scheme. The discussion in this section will focus on the security aspect of SDL.

Based on the nature and properties of the product, the assessment review concludes the set of SDL activities that must be conducted during the remainder of the product development life cycle. Generally speaking, a security feature—such as a TPM device or a cryptography engine—is subject to a complete SDL review, including architecture, design, implementation, and deployment. On the other hand, only select SDL stages may be required for those functions that are not sensitive to security per se, for example, Intel's Quiet System Technology (QST). Normally, architecture and design reviews may be skipped if the risk of waiving is deemed low; however, implementation and deployment reviews are almost always planned for all features.

Architecture

In this phase, the architecture owners of the product put together an intensive architecture description that presents the following points:

- *Security architecture*: The architecture includes components of the products, functionalities of each component, internal and external interfaces, dependencies, flow diagrams, and so on. A product's architecture is driven by its assets and functional requirements.

- *Assets*: Assets are valuable data that must be protected by the product, for confidentiality, integrity, and/or anti-replay. For example, the endorsement private key is a critical asset for a TPM and may not be exposed outside of the TPM. Notice that an asset is not necessarily the product's native value; it can also be users' data, such as passwords and credit card numbers. The security and management engine processes various types of user secrets and it is responsible for handling them properly per defined objectives.

- *Security objectives*: Security objectives are the goals that the product intends to meet for protection. For example, guarding the endorsement private key for confidentiality and integrity is a security objective for a TPM device; whereas thwarting denial of service (DoS) when an attacker is physically present is a not a security objective for the security and management engine.

- *Threat analysis*: Based on the in-scope security objectives, a list of possible attacker threats to compromise the objectives and assets are documented and analyzed. For example, in order to steal TPM's endorsement private key, an attacker may utilize side-channel attacks by accurately measuring power and time consumptions during a large number of the TPM's endorsement signing operations.

- *Mitigations against threats*: The mitigation plans detail how the architecture is designed to deter threats, protect assets, and achieve security objectives. In most cases, effective mitigations are realized through well-known and proven cryptography and security approaches. Note that security through obscurity is not a meaningful mitigation approach.

Figure 1-3 illustrates the components of the architecture review and relationships among them.

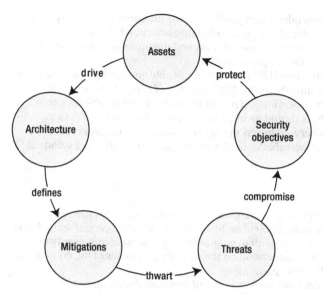

Figure 1-3. *Components of the architecture review and their relationships*

The architecture with aforementioned content is peer-reviewed and challenged by a group of architects and engineers with extensive experience and strong expertise in security. It is possible that a proposed new product be killed because one or more security objectives that are considered mandatory cannot be satisfied by a feasible and reasonable architecture. If and once the security architecture is approved, the SDL review process will move on to the design stage.

Design

During the design phase, high-level requirements are converted to prototypes. The design work for a software or firmware product contains a wide range of aspects. From the security perspective, in general, the most interesting ones are internal flows and external interfaces:

- *Internal flows*: A few security best practices should be followed in the flow design. For example: involve as few resources as possible; minimize dependency on shared objects and other modules; apply caution when consuming shared objects to prevent racing and deadlock conditions; avoid using recurrence on embedded systems.

- *External interfaces*: API must be defined with security in mind. For example: simplify parameters; do not trust the caller; always assume the minimum set of privileges that are needed to complete the tasks; verify the validity of input parameters before use; handle DoS attacks properly, if required.

Besides generic design principles, every product has its unique set of security objectives and requirements derived from the architecture review, which must be reflected in the design. The mitigations against threats and the protection mechanisms for assets are materialized in the design phase as well.

The design of cryptography should follow latest applicable government and industry standards. For example, encrypting data with AES[16] (*advanced encryption standard*); applying *blinding* to private key operations, if mitigation against timing attacks is an objective. Proprietary algorithms should be introduced only if absolutely necessary. Notice that use of nonstandard cryptography may pose difficulty in achieving security certifications such as the FIPS (*federal information processing standard*) 140-2 standard.[17]

Implementation

Engineers who implement the product in hardware or software languages should be knowledgeable about security coding practices. Members of the development team that is responsible for the security and management engine are required to complete advanced security coding classes and a training session on the security properties of the embedded engine, prior to working on the implementation.

Here are a few sample guidelines for software and firmware development:

- Use secure memory and string functions (for example, memcpy_s() instead of memcpy()) where applicable. Note that this recommendation does not apply to certain performance critical flows, such as paging.

- Comparison of two buffers should be independent of time to mitigate timing attacks. That is, memcmp() should process every byte instead of returning nonzero upon the first unmatched byte among the two buffers.

- Beware of buffer overflows.

- Make sure a pointer is valid before dereferencing it.

- Beware of dangling pointers.

- Beware that sizeof(struct) may result in a greater value than the total sizes of the structure's individual components, due to alignments.

- Set memory that contains secrets to zero immediately after use.

- Beware of integer overflows and underflows, especially in multiplication, subtraction, and addition operations.

- Remember bounds checks where applicable.

- Do not trust the caller's input if it is not in the trust boundary. Perform input parameter validation.

- When comparing the contents of two buffers, first compare their sizes. Call memcmp() only if their sizes are equal.

- Protect resources that are shared by multiple processes with mechanisms such as semaphore and mutex.

In addition, the development team that owns the security and management engine also observes a list of coding BKMs (*best known methods*) that are specific for the embedded engine. These BKMs are an executive summary of representative firmware bugs previously seen on the engine. It is crucial to learn from mistakes.

In practice, production code that is developed from scratch by an engineer with a secure coding mindset may be less of a problem. The more worrisome code in a product is usually those taken from nonproduction code. For example, proof-of-concept (POC) code created for the purpose of functional demonstration is often written with plenty of shortcuts and workarounds, but without security practice or performance considerations in mind. It is a bad practice to reuse the POC code in the final product, if and when the POC hatches to production, because in most cases, it is more difficult and resource consuming to repair poor code than to rewrite. Another source of possibly low-quality code similar to POC code is test code.

Following the completion of coding, the implementation review kicks off. The review is a three-fold effort: *static analysis, dynamic analysis,* and *manual inspection*. They may occur in tandem or in parallel.

The static analysis analyzes a software or firmware program by scanning the source code for problems without actually executing the program. A number of commercial static analysis tools are available for use for large-scale projects. If the checkers are properly configured for a project, then static analysis is often able to catch common coding errors, such as buffer overflows and memory leaks, and help improve software quality dramatically. However, despite its convenience, static analysis is not perfect. Particularly for embedded systems, because the tools in most cases do not fully comprehend the specific environments and hardware interfaces, a relatively large number of false positives may be reported. Notice that engineering resources must be allocated to review every reported issue, including those false positives. For the same reason, static analysis tools may fail to identify certain types of coding bugs.

In contrast to static analysis, dynamic analysis executes a software or firmware program on the real or a virtual environment. The analysis tests the system with a sufficiently large number of input vectors and attempts to exercise all logical paths of the product. The behavior of the system under test is observed and examined. Security coding bugs, such as a null pointer dereference, can be revealed when the system crashes or malfunctions. Such issues can be extremely hard to find without actually running the program.

The manual inspection is a source code review performed by fellow engineers that are familiar with the module, but did not write the code. The purpose is to make sure that the implementation correctly realizes the product's specific security design and architecture requirements. For example, an invocation of encryption for a secret is according to the specified algorithm, mode, and key size. Apparently, these kinds of issues cannot be found by the automatic tools. In addition, the review also checks that the generic coding guidelines are followed and tries to capture flaws in the code that were missed by the static and dynamic analysis.

As depicted in Figure 1-4, the implementation review is an iterative process. After functional or security bugs are fixed or other changes (like adding a small add-on feature) are made, the updated implementation must go through the three steps again. To conserve engineering resources, the manual code review may cover only the changed portions of the code. The two automatic analysis should be executed regularly, such as on a weekly basis, until the final product is released.

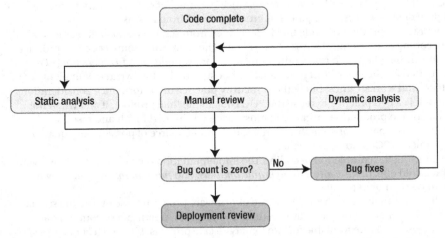

Figure 1-4. *Iterations of the implementation review. In this figure, static analysis, dynamic analysis, and manual review are performed in parallel*

Deployment

The deployment review is the last checkpoint before shipment. Sophisticated validations are performed against the product in this stage. The materials to help validation engineers create a test plan include output of the previous stages, such as security objectives of the architecture phase and the interface definition of the design phase. Comprehensive test cases aiming at validating the product's security behaviors are exercised.

Interface Testing

The first test object is the product's interface. Figure 1-5 is a graphical illustration of the interface test case design. Note that the output validation takes security objectives as input. A bug will be recorded when the behavior of the system under test violates one or more requirements.

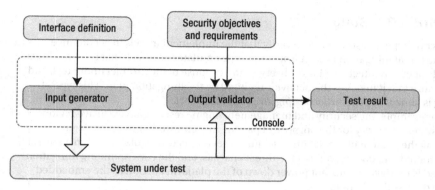

Figure 1-5. *Interface test design*

There are two categories of interface tests:

- *Positive test*: A positive test first invokes the product's interface with valid input vectors as specified in the design documents, and then verifies that the output from the system under test is correct per the security objectives and requirements. In most cases, there exist an infinite number of valid input value combinations. The test console may randomly generate valid inputs, but common cases (most frequently used values) and corner cases (extreme values) should be covered.

- *Negative test*: A negative test manipulates the input and invokes the product's interface with invalid input. The product is expected to handle the unexpected input properly and return an appropriate error code. It requires in-depth knowledge of the product in order to create good negative test cases that are able to expose security vulnerabilities.

To emphasize how pivotal the negative tests are, take the Heartbleed for example. Using the *Request for Comments 6520* as the requirement document, a simple negative test that acts like a malicious client that sends a heartbeat request with an excessive *payload_length* to the server under test would have caught the issue, because instead of notifying the client of an error (expected behavior), the flawed server would happily respond with its internal memory content of the illegitimate size requested by the client.

In addition to the scenario of "should bailout but does not," another common failure of negative tests is system crash, which can be a result of a variety of possibilities, for example, improper handling of invalid input parameters, buffer overflow, and memory leaks.

Fuzz testing, a kind of the negative testing, has become very popular in the recent years. The fuzz testing is an automated or semiautomated technique that provides a large set of invalid inputs to the product under test. The inputs are randomly generated based on predefined data models that are fine-tuned for the specific interface that will be tested. By looking for abnormal responses, such as crashing, security vulnerabilities such as buffer overflow can be uncovered.

Penetration Testing

The second type of tests intends to verify that the implementation is in accordance with the threat mitigation plan. A test of this type emulates an attack that is in the threat analysis of the architecture phase, observes the response of the product under test, and makes sure that it matches the behavior required by the mitigation plan. This type of testing is known as *penetration testing*, or *pentest* for short.

For example, the security and management engine reserves an exclusive region of the system memory for the purpose of paging. Any entity other than the engine changing the content of the region is deemed a severe security violation. Such an attack is considered and documented in the threat analysis, and the corresponding mitigation required is to trigger an instant power down of the platform as soon as the embedded engine detects the alteration.

A basic test for this case would flip a random bit in the reserved region of the host memory using a special tester and see whether the system indeed shuts down immediately as expected. Passing this basic test proves the correctness of the implementation at a certain confidence level. However, a more advanced test would understand the integrity check mechanism used for paging and replace the memory content with a calculated pattern that may have a higher chance of cheating the embedded system, and hence bypassing the protection. Obviously, design of such smart tests requires the knowledge of internal technical information of the product. This is called *white box* testing.

Before rolling out the product, a survivability plan should be drafted and archived. The survivability plan specifies roles, responsibilities, and applicable action items upon security vulnerabilities are found in the field.

CVSS

Even after going through stringent review and testing, vulnerabilities reported—either by internal teams or external sources—after the product is released are not uncommon. It is important to fairly evaluate the severity of escaped defects in order to take the right actions accordingly. For rating vulnerability, an industry standard used by the National Institute of Standards and Technology's National Vulnerability Database (NVD) is the CVSS[18] (*Common Vulnerability Scoring System*).

The CVSS defines three groups of metrics to describe vulnerability. They are base, temporal, and environmental, respectively:

- *Base group*: Represents fundamental characteristics of vulnerability. Such characteristics do not change over time or environment.

- *Temporal group*: Includes characteristics that change over time, but not environments.

- *Environmental group*: Covers characteristics that are relevant and unique to a particular environment.

Each group consists of several factors to be rated by the analysis. Figure 1-6 lists the factors under each group. The CVSS formula calculates a base score, a temporal score, and an environment score, respectively, from applicable factors. The calculation yields a score ranging from 0 to 10 inclusive, where a higher number indicates worse severity. According to NVD's standard, vulnerabilities are labeled "low" severity if they have a base score of 0.0 to 3.9, "medium" for a base score of 4.0 to 6.9, and "high" for 7.0 to 10.0.

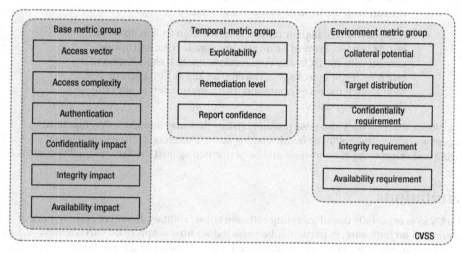

Figure 1-6. *CVSS matric groups*

Specifically for assessing severity of vulnerabilities of the security and management engine's firmware, the CVSS is slightly adjusted to better suit the nature of the engine:

- The access vector options used are *network, local,* or *physical.* Firmware bugs that can be exploited remotely via the network are more critical. "Local" means that an attacker must access the host operating system with ring 0 privilege in order to mount an attack. "Physical" refers to the capability of reading and/or writing the flash chip that holds the firmware's binary image and nonvolatile data.

- Authentication refers to authenticating to the embedded engine, not the host operating system. Some of the firmware applications, such as AMT, may require user authentication. However, authentication is not required for invoking most of the engine's features from the host operating system.

- Because the engine is a privileged device in the system, the confidentiality, integrity, and availability requirements are all rated at *high* in most cases.

Once a firmware bug is reported, the remediation plan depends on the CVSS score of the bug. The following are the general guidelines:

- If the defect is of low severity, then do not fix or fix in the next scheduled release.

- If the defect is of medium severity, then fix it in the next scheduled release. Prevent firmware downgrade from a firmware version with the fix to any vulnerable version.

- If the defect is of high or critical severity, then fix it in an ad-hoc hot-fix release. Prevent firmware downgrade from a firmware version with the fix to any vulnerable version. If exploitation of the bug may result in leakage of the chipset key or EPID private key, then launch the rekey operation with a remote server after the firmware is updated.

Notice that bug fixes also pose potential risks—they may introduce new functional bugs or security vulnerability, or break working flows. Therefore, complete functional testing and select security reviews should be performed against the fixes for quality control.

Limitations

The CVSS is especially useful for rating software vulnerabilities. However, it is not perfect when used on hardware, in particular because it does not comprehend survivability.

For example, the level of difficulty of patching a hardware bug is not taken into account. The remediation may include the following:

- Documentation and specification change

- Software workaround by remote update

- Firmware workaround by remote update

- Recall (in the worst case)

Such factors should be weighed when evaluating hardware issues.

References

1. Intel IT Center, "Insights on the Current State of BYOD," www.intel.com/content/www/us/en/mobile-computing/consumerization-enterprise-byod-peer-research-paper.html, accessed on June 10, 2014.

2. Trusted Computing Group, "Trusted Platform Module Library," www.trustedcomputinggroup.org, accessed on March 20, 2014.

3. Intel, Trusted Execution Technology, www.intel.com/txt, accessed on January 30, 2014.

4. Intel, "Software Guard Extensions Programming Reference," https://software.intel.com/sites/default/files/329298-001.pdf, accessed on May 10, 2014.

5. CTIA: The Wireless Association, "Smartphone Anti-Theft Voluntary Commitment," www.ctia.org/policy-initiatives/voluntary-guidelines/smartphone-anti-theft-voluntary-commitment, accessed on June 10, 2014.

6. eBay Inc., "eBay Inc. to Ask eBay Users to Change Passwords," http://announcements.ebay.com/2014/05/ebay-inc-to-ask-ebay-users-to-change-passwords/, accessed on June 10, 2014.

7. Target Corp., "Target Confirms Unauthorized Access to Payment Card Data in U.S. Stores," http://pressroom.target.com/news/target-confirms-unauthorized-access-to-payment-card-data-in-u-s-stores, accessed on June 10, 2014.

8. McAfee Labs, "Threat Advisory: EPOS Data Theft," https://kc.mcafee.com/resources/sites/MCAFEE/content/live/PRODUCT_DOCUMENTATION/24000/PD24927/en_US/McAfee_Labs_Threat_Advisory_EPOS_Data_Theft.pdf, accessed on June 10, 2014.

9. Internet Engineering Task Force (IETF), *Request for Comments 6520*, "Transport Layer Security (TLS) and Datagram Transport Layer Security (DTLS) Heartbeat Extension," http://tools.ietf.org/html/rfc6520, accessed on June 10, 2014.

10. OpenSSL Security Advisory, www.openssl.org/news/secadv_20140407.txt, accessed on June 10, 2014.

11. Netcraft, "April 2014 Web Server Survey," http://news.netcraft.com/archives/2014/04/02/april-2014-web-server-survey.html, accessed on June 10, 2014.

12. Kumar, Arvind, Purushottam Goel, and Ylian Saint-Hilaire, *Active Platform Management Demystified: Unleashing the Power of Intel vPro Technology*, Intel Press, 2009.

13. OpenSSL Security Advisory, www.openssl.org/news/secadv_20140605.txt, accessed on June 10, 2014.

14. Intel, Identity Protection Technology, http://ipt.intel.com/, accessed on April 20, 2014.

15. Hewlett-Packard Development Co., "Reducing Security Risks from Open Source Software," http://h20195.www2.hp.com/v2/GetPDF.aspx%2F4AAO-8061ENW.pdf, accessed on June 10, 2014.

16. National Institute of Standards and Technology, "Advanced Encryption Standard (AES)," http://csrc.nist.gov/publications/fips/fips197/fips-197.pdf, accessed on November 17, 2013.

17. National Institute of Standards and Technology, "Security Requirements for Cryptographic Modules," http://csrc.nist.gov/publications/fips/fips140-2/fips1402.pdf, accessed on April 15, 2014.

18. National Institute of Standards and Technology, Common Vulnerability Scoring System (CVSS), http://nvd.nist.gov/cvss.cfm, accessed on December 12, 2013.

CHAPTER 2

■ ■ ■

Intel's Embedded Solutions: from Management to Security

Security is, I would say, our top priority because for all the exciting things you will be able to do with computers—organizing your lives, staying in touch with people, being creative—if we don't solve these security problems, then people will hold back.

—Bill Gates

Teflon, the famous chemical, was discovered by Roy Plunkett of E. I. du Pont de Nemours and Company (commonly shortened to DuPont), in 1938 and trademarked in 1945. Teflon's major application today is in manufacturing nonstick cookware. However, it was not intended for helping grandmas make delicious pancakes when it was first discovered. For decades, it has been used in artillery shell fuses and the production of nuclear materials.

Temper foam was invented in 1966 by Chiharu Kubokawa and Charles A. Yost of NASA's Ames Research Center to protect astronauts' bodies when they are hurtling toward the earth. Today, temper foam is used to make mattresses that people sleep on every night.

The list of old inventions finding new applications in new domains goes on. The new applications benefit a much wider population and improve more people's quality of life.

When Intel's Active Management Technology (AMT) first appeared in 2005, it was marketed as an advanced system management feature for Intel 82573E series gigabit Ethernet controllers. In 2007, a new embedded coprocessor, namely the management engine, was introduced. Originally, the management engine was designed primarily for implementing the AMT rather than running security applications. At that time, the main problem that was supposed to be resolved by the embedded engine and AMT was the high expense and difficulty of system management by network administrators. The management engine was a component of Intel chipsets with vPro technology. The Intel AMT implementation was moved from gigabit Ethernet controllers to the management engine and became a feature of vPro.

Intel AMT is not the only application on the management engine. The first security application on the engine was the integrated TPM (Trusted Platform Module, see Chapter 7 for details). The number of security applications has been increasing in recent years with every release of the engine. In the latest releases, most applications running on the engine are related to security. The applications either realize "pure" security functionalities, or provide security infrastructures for other consumer features. For example, TPM and Boot Guard (refer to Chapter 6 of this book for details about Intel's Boot Guard technology) are security modules, whereas the dynamic application loader (DAL, see Chapter 9) is not implemented for security per se, but requires security as a building block.

In addition to more powerful applications and functionalities, the embedded engine has also been deployed on more platforms—not only chipsets for traditional personal computers, laptops, workstations, and servers, but also SoC (System-on-Chip) products, for example, in-vehicle infotainment, tablets, and smartphones, where security is becoming a critical infrastructure. The AMT is still widely provisioned on desktop computers and laptops, but has become an optional add-on for other mobile devices. On Intel's SoC platforms, the engine carries only security applications.

Just like Teflon and temper foam, today, the engine is realizing its greater value in the new usage model—providing robust security solutions and trusted execution environments to all forms of computer systems. The security and management engine is contributing to the promotion of people's computing experience every day and making a more substantial impact than ever before.

This book is not the first literature on the engine. Back in 2009, Intel Press published *Active Platform Management Demystified: Unleashing the Power of Intel vPro Technology*, authored by Intel's Arvind Kumar, Purushottam Goel, and Ylian Saint-Hilaire.[1] It will be referred to as the "2009 AMT book" in this chapter.

The 2009 AMT book is a systematic introduction to the management engine and AMT. It raises the platform management problems to be resolved, evaluates existing solutions, and then proposes the innovative AMT solution. It covers technical details of the management engine and the AMT, as well as instructions for setting up and configuring the AMT.

Although the engine's design has been improved in many ways since the 2009 AMT book was published, the fundamental architecture of the engine remains unchanged. A large portion of the technical descriptions in the 2009 AMT book still applies to today's security and management engine. Even after five years, it is still the best reference for infrastructures of the management engine and the AMT.

The remainder of the chapter is organized as follows. In the next section, we briefly revisit the 2009 AMT book. We will begin with a review of the hardware and firmware architectures of the management engine, and then look at the platform management problems and compare different solutions by analyzing their advantages and disadvantages. Next, a high-level introduction to the architecture of the AMT is presented. Finally, select security applications that feature on the security and management engine today are presented, with reasons for housing the applications in the embedded engine.

Management Engine vs. Intel AMT

What are the differences between the two terminologies, management engine and AMT? Do they mean the same thing?

The management engine refers to a computing environment consisting of dedicated hardware and firmware components. It has its own real-time operating system and hardware resources such as processor and memory. Just like a computer with Core CPU (central processing unit), applications can be installed and executed on the management engine. The applications are not generic software. They are implemented in firmware and designed specifically for running on the engine.

On the other hand, Intel AMT is a firmware application running on the management engine. It invokes the infrastructure and kernel application programming interfaces (APIs) provided by the management engine to build system management functionalities.

When the management engine was first introduced, Intel AMT was the primary application and it had attracted tremendous media attention. Hence some literatures use "management engine" and "active management technology" interchangeably. Today, although Intel AMT is still the most senior member of the application family, many new applications have joined the family and been deployed on the engine.

Intel AMT vs. Intel vPro Technology

Intel's vPro technology is a marketing name that covers a wide range of security and management features that are built in Intel processors and chipsets. The vPro technology resolves prevailing manageability, security, and energy efficiency problems with hardware-based protection, which is considered, when compared with software-based solutions, less vulnerable to threats such as viruses, worms, and hackers.

Many consider the AMT to be the essence of vPro. However, the vPro technology is comprised of not only AMT, but also other useful ingredients, such as:

- Intel Trusted Execution Technology[2] (TXT)

- Intel Virtualization Technology[3]

- Intel Identity Protection Technology[4] (IPT)

- Intel Anti-Theft Technology[5] (will be end of life in January 2015)

Besides AMT, some of these vPro ingredients also rely on the embedded engine to function. For example, IPT (refer to Chapter 10) and Anti-Theft.

Management Engine Overview

The management engine is made up of hardware and firmware. However, outside of its boundary, appropriate software drivers and applications must be installed on the host in order for the host to communicate with the embedded system through the dedicated host-embedded communication interface (HECI).

Hardware

The hardware is comprised of a processor, code and data caches, DMA (direct memory access) engines, cryptography engines, read-only memory (ROM), internal memory (static random-access memory, or SRAM), a timer, and other supporting devices. The devices are connected through an internal bus that is not exposed to the external world. This ensures independence, isolation, and security of the engine. The management engine's hardware devices are only accessible by the processor, the DMA engines, and the cryptography engine.

The hardware architecture is illustrated in Figure 2-1.

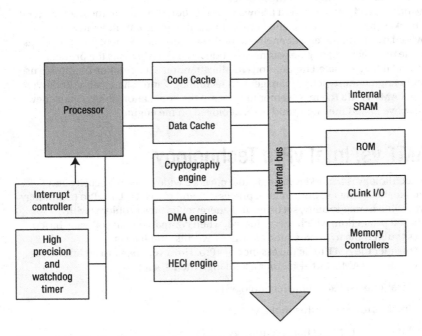

Figure 2-1. *Hardware architecture of the management engine*

Early generations of the management engine used ARC as the central processing unit. Other processors have replaced ARC in newer generations. The processor model and frequency in a specific engine depends on the form factor on which the engine is deployed. The model of the processor does not impact the engine's high-level firmware architecture.

There is a small code and data cache to help the processor reduce the number of accesses to the internal SRAM. The internal SRAM is the memory that stores firmware code and data at runtime. The capacity of SRAM varies depending on the product, but generally ranges between 256KB and 1MB.

In addition to the internal SRAM, the management engine also uses a certain amount of DRAM (dynamic random-access memory) from the main system memory. Code and data pages that are not recently accessed may be evicted from the SRAM and swapped out to the reserved memory. When a page is needed again, it will be swapped in to the SRAM. During the boot process, the DRAM region that will be used by the management engine is reserved by the BIOS (basic input/output system) for the engine's dedicated access. The reserved region, by design, is not visible to the main host operating system. That being said, the management engine's security architecture assumes that the BIOS may be compromised and the local host may be able to read and write the reserved memory region. The size of the reserved memory varies from product to product, but usually in the range between 4MB and 32MB. This is only a small fraction of the DRAM installed on today's computing devices, and hence the impact to the main operating system performance is negligible.

For many embedded applications, it is necessary to transmit bulk data between the embedded memory and the host memory. However, the engine's processor cannot address the host memory. Therefore, dedicated DMA engines are introduced for moving data between the engine's memory and the main system's memory. Notice that the reserved memory is considered the engine's memory and not the host memory. When addressing the host memory, the DMA engines can only understand physical addresses and not virtual addresses that are specific to operating systems processes. The DMA engines can only be programmed by the embedded firmware running on the management engine. The DMA engines can also be used to move a large amount of data between two buffers of the engine's internal memory. Experiments show that, when data is greater than 1KB in size, it is more efficient to invoke a DMA engine for data copying than calling memcpy() of the processor. The firmware cannot program a DMA engine to move data between two host memory locations.

The cryptography engine device offloads and accelerates heavily-used cryptography algorithms so those resource-consuming operations can be performed faster and they do not occupy the processor's clock cycles. The algorithms implemented by the cryptography engine include AES (Advanced Encryption Standard), SHA (Secure Hashing Algorithm), DRNG (Deterministic Random Number Generator), big number arithmetic, and so on. See Chapter 3 of this book for a complete list of algorithms and their API descriptions. The cryptography engine is only accessible by the engine's firmware. They are not directly available to the host, although some embedded applications implement and expose external interfaces for the host applications to take advantage of the cryptography engine. Notice that the cryptography driver in the firmware kernel not only abstracts interfaces for the cryptography engine hardware, but also implements other cryptography algorithms that are not available in the hardware.

Overlapped I/O

As shown in Figure 2-1, there are three master devices—processor, DMA, and cryptography engine—on the management engine. They all can access the embedded memory and process data. These devices are independent of each other and therefore can function at the same time without mutual interference, as long as the assets (for example, memory and global variables) that are being accessed by more than one device are properly protected against racing conditions. The protection is usually realized by employing semaphores or mutexes. By commanding multiple devices to work simultaneously, firmware applications can be optimized to minimize the system resource idle time and boost performance. The mechanism implemented by the security and management engine is de facto equivalent to overlapped I/O (input/output) or asynchronous I/O for traditional operating systems.

The idea is straightforward. After process A initializes a long cryptography operation, such as the exponentiation and modulo of RSA (a popular asymmetric-key cryptosystem invented by Ron Rivest, Adi Shamir, and Leonard Adleman) decryption, instead of sitting idle and waiting for its completion, the processor may switch to process B and perform operations that do not require the cryptography engine. In the meantime, the processor may either periodically inquire about the status register for completion of the RSA operation or watch for an interrupt signaled by the cryptography engine. Similarly, the DMA engines can also participate in the synchronization to further expedite the operations.

An interesting example of the overlapped I/O design is the flow for decrypting and parsing an H.264 video frame during movie playback. For this application, the player running on the host receives encrypted video frames from a remote content server, but the player as user-mode software is not allowed to access the content key or the clear content. The wrapped content key is sent to the security and management engine, which in turn uses its device private key to unwrap and retrieve the plaintext content key. The engine then decrypts the encrypted frames, performs slice header parsing, and sends back the resulting headers to the host. Finally, the player submits the encrypted frames and parsed headers to the GPU (graphics processing unit) through the graphics driver for playback.

Because of the limited memory capacity of the embedded memory, a large frame has to be split into chunks before it is processed. The optimal size of a chunk depends on how much embedded memory is available.

The firmware has three tasks in this usage:

1. Copy a chunk of an encrypted video frame from the host memory to the internal memory. This step is carried out by a DMA engine.

2. Decrypt the encrypted frame. For most cases, it is an AES decryption, offloaded to the cryptography engine.

3. Parse the clear frame. This step is conducted by the embedded processor.

The firmware runs the three steps repeatedly on all chunks of the frame, until the entire frame is processed.

A sequential approach would be to repeatedly exercise steps 1 to 3 for all chunks of a frame, respectively. The advantage is obviously simple firmware control logic. Figure 2-2 depicts an example of a frame that consists of four chunks. For simplicity, assume that the three tasks for a chunk— DMA copy, decryption, and parsing— take the same amount of time (denoted as one time slot in the figure). The number of time slots needed for processing a frame of n chunks is $3 \times n$. Processing all four chunks of the frame takes as many as 12 time slots.

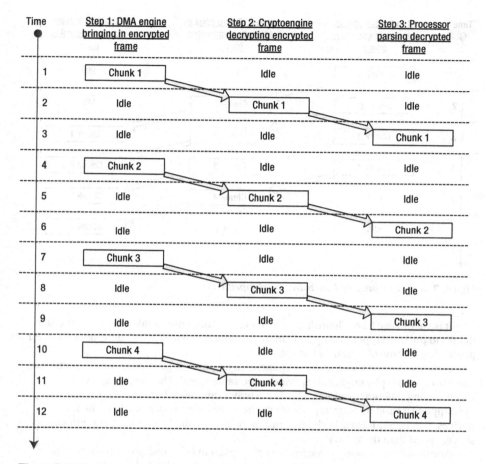

Time	Step 1: DMA engine bringing in encrypted frame	Step 2: Cryptoengine decrypting encrypted frame	Step 3: Processor parsing decrypted frame
1	Chunk 1	Idle	Idle
2	Idle	Chunk 1	Idle
3	Idle	Idle	Chunk 1
4	Chunk 2	Idle	Idle
5	Idle	Chunk 2	Idle
6	Idle	Idle	Chunk 2
7	Chunk 3	Idle	Idle
8	Idle	Chunk 3	Idle
9	Idle	Idle	Chunk 3
10	Chunk 4	Idle	Idle
11	Idle	Chunk 4	Idle
12	Idle	Idle	Chunk 4

Figure 2-2. Frame parsing flow without using overlapped I/O

Obviously, the sequential approach lacks efficiency. In this design, when step 1 is running, the DMA engine is busy; however, the cryptography engine and the processor are both idle. Similarly, in step 2 and step 3, only one device is working at any moment and the other two are not being used.

To implement an overlapped I/O optimization, the firmware must simultaneously manage three chunks of the frame (namely: previous chunk, current chunk, and next chunk) of the same size in three distinct memory buffers.

The firmware first initializes DMA for the next chunk of frame, then triggers the AES decryption for the current chunk (the current chunk has been DMA'ed into the embedded memory in the previous iteration), and finally parses the previous (decrypted) chunk of the frame (the previous chunk has been DMA'ed into the embedded memory and decrypted in the previous two iterations). When the parsing is finished, the processor waits for the completion of the AES and the DMA. Figure 2-3 explains the flow graphically.

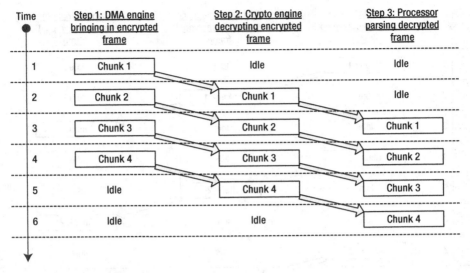

Figure 2-3. *Frame parsing flow using overlapped I/O*

It is easy to see from Figure 2-3 that processing four chunks takes only six time slots thanks to the overlapped I/O optimization. In general, the number of time slots taken for processing a frame of n chunks is $n + 2$.

Note that for the security and management engine, the processor, the DMA engines, and the cryptography engine all operate at the same speed. The exact frequency varies among different products. This is the major difference between the embedded overlapped I/O and its counterparts for the host operating systems, where the I/O devices, that is, hard drive, keyboard, and so forth, are usually operating at significantly slower speed than the main processor.

Admittedly, managing three masters may result in fairly complex firmware logic. The best practice for software engineering tells us that complicated code is more prone to bugs and errors. Therefore, such optimization strategies should be exercised with extra care. And the implementation must go through thorough testing and validation to cover all corner cases. For certain use cases, such as video frame parsing, as the throughput requirement is extremely high to guarantee smooth playback, utilizing the overlapped I/O trick is necessary.

■ **Note**　If multiple master devices are available on the embedded system, consider overlapped I/O to improve performance.

Firmware

The security and management engine's embedded firmware implements the runtime operating system, kernel, and applications.

There are numerous products and form factors of the engine. A specific version of firmware is intended for running on the corresponding engine hardware only, and a specific engine is intended for running the corresponding version of the firmware; for example:

- Intel series 5 chipset (codename IbexPeak) can load only security and management engine firmware version 6.x. It cannot load version 5.x or other firmware. It cannot load firmware from a third party or a hacker.

- Security and management engine firmware version 6.x can only execute on the Intel series 5 chipset. It cannot be executed on series 6 or other chipset generations. It cannot be executed on SoC products, nor can it run on a third-party's or a hacker's hardware platforms.

- Security and management engine firmware designed for the Bay Trail tablets cannot execute on Intel chipsets or other generations of Intel tablets.

The hardware and firmware mapping is enforced by different image signing keys. The hash values of the signing public keys are hardcoded in the ROM on different products.

Figure 2-4 shows the high-level architecture of the management engine firmware.

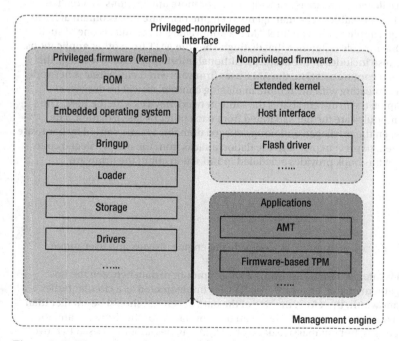

Figure 2-4. *Firmware architecture of the management engine*

There are two storage media—ROM and flash nonvolatile memory—that store the firmware's binary data and executable code. The ROM inside the management engine stores the boot loader. The code in ROM cannot be modified once manufactured. Thanks to this property, ROM is used as the root of trust of the engine. The boot loader code is usually smaller than 256KB.

The rest of the firmware is stored in flash. The flash is divided into multiple regions, for security and management engine firmware, BIOS, network controller, and so forth, respectively. Depending on which embedded applications are chosen to be included, the management engine firmware can consume from a few hundred kilobytes to 1.5 megabytes of flash space. The region for firmware is further divided into regions for executable code, configuration data, embedded applications' variable storage, and so on. The OEMs (original equipment manufacturers) are mandated to lock down the flash so it cannot be altered after the manufacturing process is completed. However, the management engine does not depend on the flash lockdown for security. The threat analysis assumes the flash can be replaced or reprogrammed by an attacker as he wishes.

As shown in Figure 2-4, firmware modules are logically divided into two categories: privileged and nonprivileged. The privileged firmware boots the engine, loads other modules, abstracts hardware devices (such as DMA engines and cryptography engines), schedules threads, manages synchronization objects (such as semaphores, timers, and mutex), and coordinates communications between embedded applications. The privileged firmware is the kernel and it implements only infrastructure for internal applications. It usually does not contain applications or expose external interfaces that are visible to the host.

The nonprivileged firmware is made up of one or more applications that realize their designed functionalities. The management engine firmware must contain at least one nonprivileged application. The Intel AMT, a nonprivileged module, is one of such applications. One notable difference that distinguishes the AMT from other applications is that the AMT also includes network stacks. Although most applications leverage the kernel for external communication, the AMT uses firmware wired and wireless network stacks for communicating with the remote managing console. As will be described later in this chapter, the firmware shares the same network devices with the host. The nonprivileged modules are further separated from each other by task isolation. The boundary between the privileged and nonprivileged domains is safeguarded by hardware and the privileged, to prevent privilege escalation attacks from the nonprivileged code.

Chapter 4 of this book provides a detailed introduction about the firmware architecture.

Software

Two classes of software programs run alongside the engine: drivers and user-mode applications.

The HECI is intended for transmitting a small amount of data between the host and the management engine firmware. The HECI is implemented as a circular buffer with limited bandwidth; therefore, the size of the data in general should be smaller than 10KB. The data transmitted through HECI can be commands for the firmware and the firmware's responses, but not massive data. The DMA engines should be used to move large amounts of data between host and firmware.

During the boot process, the BIOS can exchange messages with the firmware through HECI. On the host operating system, only ring 0 drivers may access the HECI device to send and receive messages. Together with the management engine firmware, Intel also releases HECI driver software for the HECI communication for various operating systems. The HECI driver is also called the *management engine interface (MEI) driver*. On Linux and Android, it is a device driver that supports the main kernel-based distributions.

Most firmware applications serve the role of trusted execution environments for the corresponding host applications. The firmware applications are typically used for handling sensitive secrets that must not be visible to the host and for offloading critical operations that involve the secrets. The software and firmware together realize specific functionalities. The software agents communicate with firmware applications through the HECI interface and DMA.

For example, a movie player application sends a 128-bit or 256-bit encrypted content key to firmware in a HECI message, and then the firmware uses the unique device key stored in the engine to decrypt the content key. Then the player sends another HECI command to initialize playback. Note that the device key must be securely provisioned to the engine beforehand and the device key must never be exposed to the host.

The software may also place bulk data, such as an encrypted video frame of over 1MB in size, in the host memory and notifies the firmware of the data size and the physical address thorough a HECI command. Upon receiving the HECI command, the firmware invokes its DMA engine to bring in the video frame from the host. Note that the embedded engine's DMA devices understand physical memory address only. Virtual memory must be converted to physical memory by a ring 0 driver before delivering to the firmware.

Platform and System Management

As defined in the 2009 AMT book, a *platform* is a computer system and all of its hardware components: motherboard, disk storage, network interface, and attached device, that is, everything that makes up the computer's hardware, including BIOS. On the other hand, a *system* has a broader definition. It includes both the software and the hardware of a computer.

Today, the concept of a "platform" for mobile devices should be extended to cover hardware that is not present in traditional computer systems. There is a long list of hardware that is commonly embedded in mobile platforms: GPS (global positioning system), cameras, sensors, fingerprint reader, and so forth.

The network administrator's responsibility is to make sure all computers in an enterprise are up and running normally. Even before the Intel AMT was invented, there were numerous manageability solutions available in the market to help network administrators do their jobs.

Software Solutions

There are several categories of manageability software. For example, firewalls analyze network data packets and determine whether they should be allowed or blocked, based on the rules and policies configured by network administrators. Antivirus software detects and removes malicious software programs from the system. Remote desktop control agents such as VNC (virtual network computing) and SSH (secure shell) enable IT support technicians to remotely manage a system to perform diagnosis and resolve problems.

Although very convenient and useful in daily system management, software solutions also suffer from obvious limitations:

- *Dependability*: Manageability software runs in the operating environment that they are attempting to monitor, manage, and repair. When the operating system is not booting or not configured correctly, the software manageability solutions may fail to function.

- *Availability*: Manageability software is not able to perform management tasks when the system is in low-power states (sleeping or hibernating).

- *Reliability*: Manageability software is usually launched during boot and runs quietly in the background. However, it may be accidentally or intentionally turned off by end users or other system "clean-up" utilities.

- *Security*: Software solutions are naturally less trustworthy than hardware solutions. They are vulnerable to denial of service (DoS) attacks, may be compromised to report bogus information, or may even be hijacked and become a threat to other computers in the same network.

Hardware Solutions

In contrast to software solutions, hardware solutions for manageability do not depend on the operating system or software programs; hardware solutions can be functioning when the computer is in a low-power state; and hardware-based security measures can be applied if desired.

The KVM (keyboard, video, and mouse) is a representative hardware approach. In a typical KVM setup, the computer being managed is locally connected to a network KVM device, which connects the computer's I/O devices to a remote management console over the network. A network administrator can manage numerous computers from a single console simultaneously. Sitting in his office, the administrator can see the display of the computer being serviced and control its keyboard and mouse, as if he is sitting in front of the managed computer. Figure 2-5 is a symbolic representation of the management solution based on network KVM.

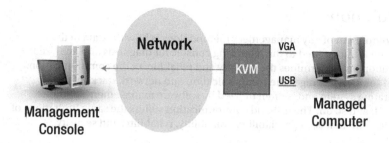

Figure 2-5. Network KVM connected to a managed computer

The equipment cost is the main factor that prevents the network KVM solution from being deployed on every computer. As can be seen in Figure 2-5, the KVM stands on the side of the computer; there must be a KVM device to support a computer (multiple computers physically located in the same location can share a multiport network KVM). The retail price of a 16-port network KVM ranges from a few hundred to over a thousand US dollars. This significantly raises the cost of network and system administration.

A more advanced hardware management solution is the baseboard management control (BMC). The BMC is a specialized embedded system that monitors various physical states, including, but not limited to, the temperature, humidity, or voltage of a computer or server. If a reported value strays out of the normal range, the administrator will be notified. A BMC combined with network KVM can realize very powerful management functionalities, including remotely power cycling, seeing displays, and controlling the keyboard and mouse. See Figure 2-6 for a symbolic representation of the BMC.

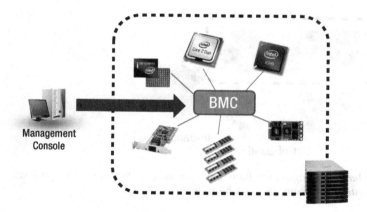

Figure 2-6. Baseboard management controller

The powerful capability and convenience of BMC comes with a price. Due to the cost, BMC is usually only justifiable for deploying on large servers that carry critical tasks.

In-Band Solutions

An important component of any management methodology is how the data of the managed machine is transmitted to the managing console for diagnosis and analyzed. The communication link determines the security and reliability of the communication.

An in-band solution leverages the communication and network stacks of the underlying operating system and is often utilized by software management solutions, such as VNC, SSH, and so on. The in-band communication suffers the same limitations of software management, that is, dependability, availability, reliability, and security.

Out-of-Band Solutions

In contrast to in-band, an out-of-band solution employs dedicated channels for communicating with the console. Generally speaking, out-of-band solutions are more robust and secure than in-band solutions, thanks to the isolation from the host being managed.

For example, a network KVM device implements a network interface separated from the network stack of the managed computer's operating system. The connections of KVM and the computer run side by side and are independent of each other.

The 2009 AMT book extends the definition of "out-of-band" for a special case, where the wired or wireless network adaptor is shared by both the operating system and an isolated management device. In this case, although the management device is located inside the chassis of the computer and it is not equipped with dedicated network hardware, it is still considered out-of-band because the management does not depend on the operating system. Figure 2-7 illustrates the sharing of a network card.

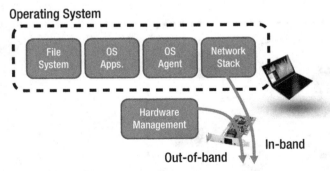

Figure 2-7. Out-of-band management: both the operating system and the hardware management traffic can use the same network hardware

Sharing a network device such as a NIC (network interface card) certainly reduces the bill of material (BOM) cost, but this slightly compromises functionality and security compared to using a dedicated network device. Functionality-wise, if the network card itself is malfunctioning and requires troubleshooting, then the communication channel between the computer and the managing console is essentially broken. Because no data can be received from the problematic computer, the administrator may have to debug the issue on site. Security-wise, for the network sharing to function properly, it is required that both the network driver on the operating system and the management device agree and obey a predefined protocol. If the driver is compromised and does not follow the protocol, it may cause a racing condition on the hardware and mount, and at a minimum, denial of service attacks, so that the system data cannot be sent to the console.

To avoid the complications of network device sharing, most security applications running on the embedded engine, unlike the AMT, do not use the firmware's network stacks to communicate with remote entities. Instead, if an application is required to exchange data with a remote server (for example, an authentication server), then it will rely on software programs running on the host operating system as the proxy.

Intel AMT Overview

We have seen different management solutions and their pros and cons. Table 2-1 gives a summary.

Table 2-1. *Comparison of Management Solutions*

Solution	Functionality	Dependability	Reliability	Availability	Security	Cost
Software, in-band	Fair	Poor	Poor	Poor	Fair	Good
Hardware, out-of-band with separate network device	Good	Good	Good	Good	Good	Poor
Hardware, out-of-band with shared network device	Good– (cannot debug NIC)	Good	Good	Good	Good	Good

As shown in Table 2-1, there is no perfect solution. However, the hardware out-of-band solution with a shared network device is the best option overall. Intel AMT is such a solution with the following desirable characteristics:

- It resides in the chipset and it is always available on all Intel vPro platforms.

- It is independent of the host operating system and power state.

- It is functional even if the host is in a lower power state or has crashed.

- It shares the network device with the host so that the hardware overhead is minimal.

The AMT ships with three software components: BIOS extension, local management service and tray icon, and remote management. They serve three configuration scenarios, respectively: through HECI before the operating system is loaded, through HECI after the operating system is loaded, and through the network.

BIOS Extension

The BIOS extension for the engine is called the Intel management engine BIOS extension (MEBX). It is a BIOS component similar to other extension ROMs. It allows the administrator and the user to perform basic configurations for the management engine and the AMT, including changing the password for authentication, turning on and off the AMT, assigning Internet Protocol (IP) addresses, configuring network protocols, selecting the engine's sleep and wake policies, and so on.

The primary reason for introducing the BIOS extension is to protect end users' privacy. By the nature of BIOS, it requires a human being's physical presence and knowledge of the correct password to authenticate to the management engine and change configurations.

The BIOS extension communicates with the embedded engine through the HECI channel. A HECI driver is implemented in the BIOS extension to facilitate the communication. The BIOS extension does not implement encryption algorithms. There is no protection applied to the HECI interface, and the messages are sent in the clear. Data sent to the engine by the BIOS extension is stored by the engine securely in nonvolatile memory with appropriate protections.

The BIOS extension executes before the BIOS delivers the end-of-POST (power-on self-test) signal to the embedded engine. The engine relies on the end-of-POST signal to determine whether a received HECI command was initialized from the BIOS extension or from the local host operating system. Select settings are deemed legitimate only if made through the BIOS extension interface. The embedded engine rejects such commands by returning an error if they are received after the end of POST.

Figure 2-8 demonstrates the flow of interactions between the host and the management engine during and after the boot process. The initial boot block is a firmware module loaded before the BIOS to facilitate the secure boot path. After the BIOS has initialized the system DRAM and reserved the exclusive region for the engine to access, it sends a DRAM-init-done HECI message to notify the engine.

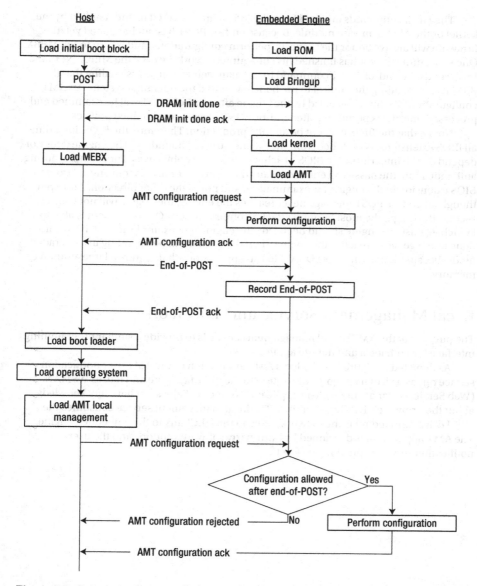

Figure 2-8. *Interaction between the host and the engine for AMT configuration, with MEBX loaded during the boot process*

The HECI commands initiated from the MEBX are delivered to and handled by the kernel or the AMT firmware module. Because end-of-POST has not happened yet, the firmware will always honor the requests, perform configurations, and return to the MEBX. Once the administrator has finished his configuration work, he exits the MEBX. Next, the BIOS sends the end-of-POST command to the management engine, signaling that the BIOS is now handing the control to the boot loader and the operating system. An AMT configuration command received by the engine after end-of-POST will be examined and processed only if it is permitted after end-of-POST, based on predefined policies.

Notice that the BIOS may not be an Intel production. Therefore, the BIOS, including all BIOS extensions, is excluded from the engine's trusted boundary. The engine does not depend on the integrity of the BIOS to achieve its security objectives. For example, during authentication, the password entered by an administrator or user is transmitted from the BIOS extension to the engine for examination, and not in the other direction. And even though an end-of-POST message never reaches the engine, the engine will not leak any secrets. By design, the most harmful attack a compromised BIOS component is able to launch against the engine should be to DoS the engine. For example, if the DRAM-init-done message never reaches the engine, then the engine will be operating in a degraded mode, because it does not have DRAM to run applications that require a large amount of memory.

Local Management Service and Tray Icon

The purpose of the AMT's local management service is to provide a similar programming interface for both local and remote applications.

As depicted in Figure 2-9, the local AMT application or the AMT user notification service opens a virtual network connection to the AMT firmware and it uses WSMAN (Web Services-Management). The application or the UNS does not have any knowledge about the firmware's HECI mechanism. The local management service consumes the HECI driver and redirects the network traffic to the HECI link to the embedded engine. The AMT application is developed by third-party software vendors, and the user notification service is provided by Intel.

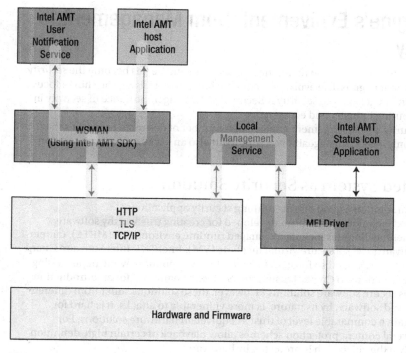

Figure 2-9. *Local software components of the AMT*

There is also a tray icon application that is developed by Intel. The tray icon application fetches status information of the management engine from the HECI interface.

Remote Management

Intel releases the AMT SDK (software development kit) to facilitate developers to interact with the AMT firmware and integrate the AMT features into their existing system management consoles and applications.

Earlier versions of AMT supported EOI (External Operations Interface) over SOAP (Simple Object Access Protocol), but the latest AMT releases only support the WS-Management interface.

Refer to the Intel AMT Implementation and Reference Guide[6] for details on the remote management development with AMT SDK.

The Engine's Evolvement: from Management to Security

Seven years since its first deployment, the management engine has become the *security* and management engine. The evolvement did not happen overnight. The shift of focus from system manageability to security reflects the increasing importance of security in today's computing industry and ecosystems.

The security and management engine has a number of desirable properties that make it not only a good manageability solution but also an excellent security solution.

Embedded System as Security Solution

What makes a solution a good one for running security applications?

Advanced techniques have been developed for creating trustworthy software solutions. These techniques include a managed runtime environment (MRTE), tamper-resistant software (TRS), a secure virtual machine (VM), Intel TXT, Intel Software Guard Extensions (Intel SGX), and so forth. Refer to the Intel Corporation white paper "Using Innovative Instructions to Create Trustworthy Software Solutions," for an introduction to the various secure software solutions.[7] However, these solutions suffer from different restrictions. And software, by its nature, is more vulnerable to attacks. It is hard for software to gain a comparable level of trust as equivalent hardware solutions. For example, several content protection schemes allow playback of certain high-definition contents only if the video path is protected by hardware.

Although it could provide very strong protection, a pure hardware solution is not preferable either. The problem of realizing security applications in hardware is the lack of flexibility and high cost. For convoluted features, it is very difficult to avoid bugs. Software programs can be patched with minimum overhead, but hardware issues may not be patchable and may require recall, which is a disaster for computer manufacturers.

A firmware/hardware hybrid is the solution that inherits the advantages of both software and hardware. On one hand, firmware runs on dedicated hardware and features hardware-level protection for security applications. On the other hand, the firmware can be stored in rewritable nonvolatile storage, and enjoys simpler deployment and the flexibility of being patched or updated at a relatively small cost.

The security and management engine is such a firmware/hardware hybrid product. Security-wise, a few highlights of the design are listed next. More details can be found in Chapter 4 of this book.

- *Independency*: The engine enjoys its own computing environment that is independent of the main operating system running on the host. The engine can run normally when the operating system crashes with a blue screen or cannot boot. Even if the host is sleeping or hibernating, the engine can also run normally. Notice that the reserved memory may not be available when the host is in a low-power state. Consequently, certain firmware features that require a large amount of memory may not function when the system is in a low-power state.

- *Isolation*: The engine does not share a processor or main memory with the host. The reserved memory is under strong confidentiality and integrity protection (see Chapter 4 of this book for details), so it is virtually isolated from the rest of the DRAM that is controlled by the host operating system. The networking devices, even if compromised, do not compromise the engine's security objectives. The DMA engine and HECI channel do not rely on the correct behavior of the host. In general, an external adversary (malware, virus, and so forth) is not able to infect the firmware.

- *Closed system*: The engine loads only firmware that is digitally signed by Intel for the engine. Attackers cannot easily change the firmware kernel or add/remove applications.

- *Small attack surface*: The only general interface that is available to all firmware modules to the host is the HECI channel. A small number of modules may invoke DMA and other low-level I/O, such as GPIO (general-purpose input/output), as needed. And only the AMT application may access the network. Data intake from these interfaces is not trusted by the security and management engine, and is fully validated before being processed. Invalid input data may cause wrong calculated responses from the engine, but will not crash the engine or compromise the security of the engine.

- *Programmability*: In addition to its native firmware applications, the engine opens its security capability to third-party host applications by exposing security APIs through HECI. See Chapter 9 of this book for more information.

- *Power efficiency*: Because the engine runs at a low frequency (from approximately 200MHz to 400MHz, depending on the product) compared to the main CPU, the power consumption is in the scale of milliwatts. In addition, the engine supports power gating. After being idle for a configurable number of seconds, it enters the sleep state to conserve power. Events that can wake up the engine include a HECI message from the host or interrupts from I/O devices.

Flexibility-wise, only a small portion (more specifically, the boot loader and standard library functions) of the engine's firmware is stored in ROM for the sake of root security and performance, and all application firmware is stored in flash. This enables a firmware update to fix or patch hardware or firmware bugs in the field.

We have seen the advantages. But is the engine perfect? What about the "cons"?

- *Cost*: The engine is a separate core and it shares few hardware devices with the main operating system. Although more isolated and secure, this adds the BOM cost of the platform, compared to security solutions that do not introduce a dedicated processor.

- *Limited computing bandwidth*: To save power and cost, the engine's processor runs at a relatively low frequency. This restricts it from serving applications that require high throughput. However, note that most security applications do not require overwhelming performance and the bandwidth is not a major concern.

- *Difficult firmware update deployment*: It is relatively easy for software to push patches and updates to end users' devices. This helps software vendors fix vulnerabilities and add new features in a timely manner. The story of a firmware update is completely different, however. Because the firmware is part of the security and management engine, and a component of the chipset or SoC, firmware hotfixes and maintenance releases must be thoroughly tested for compatibility by OEMs before being pushed to devices that are in the field. This process usually takes anywhere from a few weeks to a few months, and may not happen at all. To address the problem of firmware updates, a stringent security review process is exercised in the attempt of minimizing the need for hotfixes.

Overall, the pros of using the engine as the security solution outweigh the cons, making the engine *the* ideal place for security solutions.

Security Applications at a Glance

Realizing these attractive properties of the infrastructure, no one would be satisfied if the management engine remained just a system management tool. System manageability is an important and useful application, but it does not make use of the full potentials offered by the engine. Now that the engine is available on the system, why not make the most out of it?

First, the engine should be used as frequently as possible—not only when management service is requested on the system. After all, how often do system problems happen? They do not happen every day.

Second, a successful state-of-the-art technology should not benefit only the network administrators and the employees in enterprises. It should bring values to a larger population.

There are clearly many more possibilities and opportunities to be explored on the security and management engine. In today's mobile age, the demand for secure mobile services that involve valuable assets is gaining significant momentum. As a result, the embedded engine is reborn with new security features that are serving all end users every day.

EPID

Thanks to its direct access to hardware and isolation from the host operating system, it is convenient to leverage the security and management engine as the root of trust for the platform. The EPID (enhanced privacy identification) is a security mechanism exclusively built in the engine and serves as the hardware security root of trust for various applications running on the platform.

During Intel's manufacturing process, a unique EPID private key is retrieved from an internal key generation server and programmed to the engine's security fuses. At runtime, the engine's firmware uses the EPID private key to prove to the local host or a remote server that it is a genuine Intel platform and eligible for premium services that are available only to Intel products. Those applications rely on a hardware infrastructure that is only supported by Intel's products. For example, the CPU upgrade service, PAVP (protected audio and video path), and so on.

Leakage of an EPID private key would allow hackers to write software masquerading as Intel hardware. Such attacks may break into the applications that were built on the EPID and then steal secrets, such as user's stock brokerage passwords or copyrighted contents. To prevent the EPID key from being compromised, comprehensive protection mechanisms for the EPID private key at rest and at runtime are implemented by the engine. Of course, the EPID key generation process is also safeguarded with very strong and restrictive policies. In fact, except for the purpose of debugging, no human being is supposed to know any EPID private key value. Having said so, a key revocation scheme is supported by the engine in case of incidents.

To summarize the requirements, the EPID credential must be unique per platform; it must always be available; and the deletion, alteration, theft, or cloning of the EPID credential on one platform to another platform shall not be feasible without employing special hardware equipment and significant resources. Such a level of security strength is very difficult, if not impossible, to achieve by software solutions. The security and management engine is the ideal place to implement EPID functionalities. It offers not only ample security protection, but also flexibility in supporting EPID applications because the engine is a hardware/firmware hybrid device.

Chapter 5 of this book has more information on EPID.

PAVP

Some applications need to securely display frames and play audio to the user. The security requirement is that software running on the host operating system must not be able to peek or steal the contents being securely played back.

For example, alongside the wide deployment of the media playback feature on mobile computing devices is the problem of protecting copyrighted contents from piracy. Some content creators (such as movie studios) consider software protection insufficient and require their high-definition content, when playing back on computers, to be protected by hardware mechanisms. In other words, if a user's computer is not equipped with the required hardware capability, then that user won't be able to enjoy those contents.

Another example for the secure display usage is Intel IPT, where a sprite of keypad is displayed on the screen for the user to enter a password by mouse clicks. The sprite must be hidden from the host to prevent attacks by screen scrapers.

Intel's PAVP technology is a hardware scheme that protects video and audio assets from software attacks. Initially introduced for Blu-ray, PAVP is now used by a range of applications that rely on content protection to function.

The PAVP is realized by a few components: player software and graphics drivers on the host, the security and management engine, and the GPU. The ultimate security goal of content protection is to make sure that the content encryption key and the clear content are only visible to hardware and not exposed to any software components, including ring 0 drivers.

The responsibilities of the engine in the PAVP solution include:

- Establishing a PAVP session between the software and the GPU.

- Delivering content encryption keys to the GPU.

- Implementing the HDCP[8] (high-bandwidth digital content protection) protocol.

Chapter 8 has more information on PAVP.

IPT

Identity theft is one of the most infamous and costly cybercrimes. Anyone that uses the Internet to manage assets (such as music, photos, social life, financial accounts, and so on) can potentially be a victim. Strong authentication and transmission protection is necessary to deter identity theft. Intel IPT, backed by the security and management engine together with other components, is a cutting-edge technology for protecting end users' identities.

The IPT is an umbrella product name that comprises a numbers of features, including, as of this writing, OPT (one-time password), PTD (protected transaction display), PKI (public-key infrastructure), and NFC (near-field communication). Additional functionalities may be introduced to the IPT family in the future. These features work collaboratively to offer comprehensive identity safeguarding for the users for multiple scenarios.

- *OPT*: Implements as the second factor in a multi-factor authentication solution. The user's computer is the second factor (something you have), and the OPT is generated by the security and management engine's firmware and transmitted to the remote server for authentication. The technology eliminates the need for a physical token, meanwhile maintaining the security level.

- *PTD*: Allows a trusted entity to draw and display a secure sprite on the screen directly with the help of PAVP. The sprite is completely invisible to the host software stack. The secure display is commonly utilized for delivering sensitive information that is for the user's eyes only—for example, a keypad for authentication.

- *PKI*: Provides a robust private key management mechanism, including key generation, key storage, signature generation, and decryption. Once a private key is generated by or imported to the security and management engine, it will never be output in the clear. The engine performs private key operation under the hardware protection.

- *NFC*: Allows a user to tag his NFC-capable credit card against the NFC sensor on his computer to conveniently complete online transactions with positive identity authentication.

More technical details about the security and management engine's role and responsibility for IPT can be found in Chapter 10.

Boot Guard

Intel Boot Guard is the technology for protecting boot integrity for Intel platforms. The system's boot block is measured by hardware and the boot is allowed if and only if the measurement is successful, that is, the boot block is not altered. The hardware elements that perform the boot integrity check are the security and management engine and the CPU.

Intel Boot Guard offers two configurations: *verified boot* and *measured boot*. The engine is equipped with an array of field programmable fuses. For *verified boot*, an OEM programs the fuses with the hash value of its public key before the conclusion of the manufacturing process. The corresponding private key is used by the OEM to sign its initial boot block module, the first OEM's component that executes during boot. During the boot process, the engine and the CPU first verify the public key in the OEM's initial boot block manifest by comparing its hash with the preconfigured hash in the field programmable fuses, and then verify the OEM's signature on the initial boot block using the public key.

Alternative to using a digital signature, the *measured boot* configuration leverages the TPM on the platform. The TPM can be either a discrete TPM or a firmware-based TPM that is built in the security and management engine.

Chapter 6 of this book has more technical details on Intel Boot Guard technology.

Virtual Security Core: ARM TrustZone

ARM is an industry leader in low-cost and low-power processors, with applications in a host of mobile embedded devices, especially in the smartphones and tablet markets.

ARM deploys several security measurements among various families of products. For instance, the SecurCore family[9] provides mitigations against software, hardware, and side-channel attacks, for small form factors, such as smart cards. In particular, the SecurCore solutions enable customization of security features for a specific design and provide development process tools with added security controls.

For SoC platforms, ARM's security solution is called the TrustZone technology[10] (a.k.a. security extension). TrustZone is supported by ARM1176 and the Cortex-A series processors. In contrast to Intel's security and management engine that uses a dedicated security core, the TrustZone takes a different approach. The TrustZone splits a physical processor core and treats it as two virtual cores (or modes): one nonsecure mode and one secure mode. The nonsecure mode is also called normal mode or untrusted mode; the secure mode is also called trusted mode. The two modes share the same hardware resources but they operate independently. Some literatures refer to "mode" as "world."

Secure Mode and Nonsecure Mode

Context switch between the nonsecure mode and the secure mode is conducted through a third mode, the monitor mode, which is managed inside the secure mode. The current mode of operation is indicated by the nonsecure (NS) bit, which is bit 0 of the secure configuration register (SCR). The SCR is a read/write register that is accessible in the secure mode only, and recommended by ARM to be programmed by the monitor mode. Besides the NS bit, the SCR is also used to configure whether an interrupt—FIQ (fast interrupt request) or IRQ (interrupt request)—should be branched to the monitor mode for processing. The entry to the monitor mode can be triggered by software executing a dedicated instruction, the Secure Monitor Call (SMC) instruction, or by a subset of the hardware exception mechanisms.[11] Figure 2-10 shows the relationships among the secure mode, nonsecure mode, and the monitor mode.

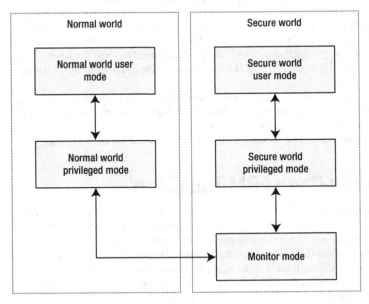

Figure 2-10. Modes in an ARM core implementing the security extensions

The switches between the two modes are strictly controlled by hardware. The secure mode is essentially another level of execution privilege. The secure mode must not leak secrets to the normal world or allow any form of privileged escalations. Applications run mostly in the normal mode, but small security-specialized code that handles secret data and sensitive operations is executed in the secure mode. For example, the key processing for content protection is run in the secure mode.

In addition to the processor, the separation of the two modes permeates all hardware, most interestingly, memory and device buses.

Memory Isolation

The memory infrastructure inside and outside of the processor core must also be isolated into two modes accordingly.

The level 1 (L1) cache in the processors is managed by the so-called memory management unit (MMU), which converts the virtual address space that is seen by the software running on the processor onto the physical address space. The MMU features an L1 memory translation table with an NS field, and entries in the TLB (translation look-aside buffer) are tagged with the NS bit. The secure mode relies on the value of the NS field to determine the value of the NS bit of the SCR when it is accessing the physical memory locations. The nonsecure mode ignores the NS field. In other words, the secure mode is always allowed to access memory belonging to both the secure mode and the nonsecure mode. Select processor models feature Tightly Coupled Memories (TCMs), which are high-performance SRAM that exist at the same level of L1 cache. There can be up to two blocks of TCM present on each instruction and data interface. Software can configure the TCMs to be accessible to the secure mode or nonsecure mode.

The Memory Protection Unit (MPU) was introduced to ARM cores starting from ARM7. This unit allows partitioning of memory into different sections and assigning them different security attributes, for example, marking the code section as read-only in order to prevent runtime alteration attack at runtime. The read/write permissions are based on two-level User and Privilege mode access; if a User mode application tries to access the Privilege mode memory, then the processor triggers an exception. The initial boot routine and interrupt handling vectors executes in the Privilege mode.

Bus Isolation

The isolation of bus interfaces and devices is required to prevent attacks from system devices. The AMBA3 (the third generation of the Advanced Microcontroller Bus Architecture) AXI (Advanced Extensible Interface) bus protocol defines controls to identify operating modes for all transactions. The AXI bus adds metadata to bus control signals and labels all read and write transactions as secure or nonsecure. The hardware logic in the TrustZone-enabled AMBA3 AXI bus fabric ensures that secure-mode resources cannot be accessed by nonsecure mode components.

The AMBA3 APB (Advanced Peripheral Bus) is used for secure peripherals and interrupts. The APB is attached to the system bus using an AXI-to-APB bridge. The APB per se is not equipped with an NS bit or its equivalent. Therefore, the AXI-to-APB bridge hardware ensures that the security of APB peripheral transactions is consistent with the AXI security signals.

Physical Isolation vs. Virtual Isolation

Conceptually, TrustZone has its similarities to Intel TXT in the sense that both achieve isolation between the secure and nonsecure modes through a trusted virtual machine or execution environment. In reality, on many Intel platforms, the security and management engine is the counterpart for security solutions that are realized by TrustZone on ARM platforms.

The obvious advantage of TrustZone over a dedicated security core is its lower BOM cost—only one core is needed for two modes of operation. But are there tradeoffs?

Although ARM's TrustZone and Intel's security and management engine both feature hardware-based security operating environments, their architectures are completely different. The isolation between the nonsecure mode and the secure mode is *virtual* for TrustZone, versus *physical* for the security and management engine. For the virtual separation mechanism, safeguarding the border of the virtually secure world and defending against threats could be a challenging task.

In addition to security, power efficiency is another important consideration for modern mobile platforms that aggressively power save. For TrustZone, the secure mode and the nonsecure mode run at the same frequency. In contrast, the security and management engine runs at a lower frequency than the main processor, resulting in less power consumption at the tradeoff of a slower operation of security tasks, which in most cases do not require high performance.

Furthermore, as described earlier in this chapter, Intel's embedded solution is also a management engine. Its many unique properties make it an excellent choice for platform management applications.

References

1. Arvind, Kumar, Purushottam Goel, and Ylian Saint-Hilaire, *Active Platform Management Demystified—Unleashing the Power of Intel vPro Technology*, Intel Press, 2009.

2. Intel Trusted Execution Technology, www.intel.com/txt, accessed on January 30, 2014.

3. Intel Virtualization Technology, www.intel.com/content/www/us/en/ virtualization/virtualization-technology/hardware-assist-virtualization-technology.html, accessed on January 30, 2014.

4. Intel Identity Protection Technology, www.intel.com/content/www/us/en/ architecture-and-technology/identity-protection/identity-protection-technology-general.html, accessed on January 30, 2014.

5. Intel Anti-Theft Technology, www.intel.com/antitheft, accessed on January 30, 2014.

6. Intel AMT Implementation and Reference Guide, http://software.intel.com/ sites/manageability/AMT_Implementation_and_Reference_Guide/default.htm, accessed on January 30, 2014.

7. Hoekstra, Matthew, Reshma Lal, Pradeep Pappachan, Carlos Rozas, Vinay Phegade, and Juan del Cuvillo, "Using Innovative Instructions to Create Trustworthy Software Solutions," http://software.intel.com/sites/default/files/article/413938/hasp-2013-innovative-instructions-for-trusted-solutions.pdf, accessed on January 30, 2014.

8. Digital Content Protection LLC, "High-bandwidth Digital Content Protection," www.digital-cp.com, accessed on May 10, 2014.

9. ARM SecurCore Processors, http://www.arm.com/products/processors/securcore/, accessed on April 1, 2014.

10. ARM TrustZone Technology, www.arm.com/products/processors/technologies/trustzone/index.php, accessed on January 30, 2014.

11. ARM Limited, "ARM Security Technology—Building a Secure System using TrustZone Technology," http://infocenter.arm.com/help/topic/com.arm.doc.prd29-genc-009492c/PRD29-GENC-009492C_trustzone_security_whitepaper.pdf, accessed on April 1, 2014.

■ ■ ■

CHAPTER 3

Building Blocks of the Security and Management Engine

Technology is nothing. What's important is that you have a faith in people, that they're basically good and smart, and if you give them tools, they'll do wonderful things with them.

— Steve Jobs

The kernel of Intel's security and management engine provides useful tools to application developers. Wonderful applications can be created on the engine with these tools.

The engine is designed to execute applications—both natively built on the engine and dynamically loaded from the host operating system. It is not a general-purpose environment per se; however, it is designed to be a foundation for various kinds of applications, especially ones that realize security functionalities.

In order to support and engage with existing and future applications, the kernel of the engine must provide a comprehensive set of basic services and tools to fulfill requirements of upper-level modules. As the number of applications running on the engine keeps growing, the number of kernel functions has grown accordingly to accommodate new functional requirements.

This chapter introduces interesting features and interfaces of the engine's kernel. Because security is the main usage of the engine and the main subject of this book, I will focus on the cryptography functions first. Besides general functionality, to address the specific requirements of embedded mobile systems, I will also review a number of design strategies and useful tricks for improving performance, saving power and memory consumption, and protecting privacy.

All cryptographic algorithms implemented by the security and management engine follow applicable US government and industry standards. There are some proprietary Intel security heuristics for the kernel's hardening measures, but they are not available to applications.

This chapter begins with a quick reference to the cryptography standards and then reveals how the engine implements them in its embedded environment. The focus is on the input and output interface of the cryptographic algorithms, rather than the mathematical details of the algorithms. Readers interested in understanding how the algorithms are designed should refer to generic cryptography lectures. D. R. Stinson's *Cryptography: Theory and Practice* (Chapman and Hall/CRC, 2005)[1] is a good introductory textbook on cryptography.

Random Number Generation

The random number generator (RNG) is the most invoked cryptography function on the engine. Except for hash, all cryptographic algorithms use keys, which are generated by a well-designed and well-implemented RNG. The security and management engine's firmware applications use the kernel's RNG for generating keys and nonces (a *nonce* is a random number that is used only once).

The RNG is a hardware device of the engine, and the kernel firmware wraps the hardware RNG and implements interface for applications to invoke. The RNG device consists of the following components:

- *Nondeterministic random bit generator (NDRBG):* This provides seeding materials to the pseudo random number generator. The entropy source consists of variations of temperature, voltage, and power. The output of the NDRBG is a derivative of the collected white noises. There is real-time health test logic associated to the NDRBG to examine the quality of its entropy output.

- *Deterministic random bit generator (DRBG):* This implements the DRBG specified in National Institute of Standards and Technology (NIST) special publication 800-90A,[2] with the Advanced Encryption Standard (AES) counter-mode option. After the (Edward) Snowden leaks, NIST strongly advised against use of the DRBG with Dual Elliptic Curve option,[3] but the AES counter-mode option is still an approved and recommended DRBG.

- *Built-in selftests (BISTs)* compliant with the Federal Information Processing Standards (FIPS) 140 standard, required BISTs are performed by the RNG, including power-on selftests and continuous selftests.

  - The power-on selftest is a known-answer test. During the boot of the security and management engine, the RNG feeds its DRBG logic with a hardcoded seed and checks if the resultant random number matches the corresponding hardcoded answer.

  - The runtime selftest runs whenever a new random number, 32 bits in size, is generated at runtime. It checks whether the current output number is identical to the immediately previous random number the RNG generated. If the two are equal, then the current output number is discarded and a new random number is generated.

The only kernel interface exposed for the RNG is a function for getting a random number with the size specified by the caller. The function does not restrict an upper limit of the size, as long as the caller has allocated sufficiently large memory to hold the random number. All applications share the same instance and state of the RNG. There are no interfaces for an individual application to reseed the DRBG or restart the RNG device. Reseeding and re-initialization are managed by the RNG internally according to the NIST DRBG specification. Figure 3-1 shows the interface of kernel RNG's API (application programming interface).

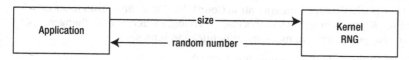

Figure 3-1. Kernel RNG API

Message Authentication

In cryptography, *message authentication*, or *secure hash*, refers to the procedure of "compressing" a large amount of data (message M) into a smaller message digest, H. For a given hash function, the size of H is a constant regardless of the size of M. The digest H generated by a good hash algorithm would look like a random string.

M can be of variable lengths, but H has a fixed size: the number of possible M values is much greater than the number of possible H values. Therefore, there may be many different M values that correspond to the same H value. Cases where two distinct messages (M and M') correspond to the same digest (H) are called "collision."

A message authentication scheme must be very "sensitive," that is, the digest H for a given M should look like a random bit string; even if only 1 bit of M has changed (been altered, added, or removed), the new digest should look like a completely different random bit string, with overwhelming probability. Because of this, the digest H can be thought of as fingerprints of a human being M.

Besides the sensitivity, a good message authentication scheme must have the following important properties:

- *One-way:* It is easy to calculate H from M, but it is computationally difficult to derive a message M from H. Because there may be multiple M values that map to the same H, the hash scheme must make sure that it is difficult to derive *any* such M from a given H.

- *Collision-free:* It is computationally difficult to find two messages M and M' that correspond to the same H. Note that the sizes of M and M' do not have to be the same.

These two facts make the secure hash algorithm useful in many cryptography and security applications. For example, an e-mail authentication server may calculate and store the digest of your password, instead of the password itself, when you set up the e-mail account. After initial setup, when you enter your password during login, the password is hashed, and the resultant digest is compared against the digest previously stored on the server at initial setup.

The hash's one-way property makes sure that no one, including the authentication server, is computationally capable of retrieving the plaintext password from its digest, even though the digest is leaked or known by an attacker. The collision-free property guarantees that it is practically impossible to find and use a string other than your password to authenticate to the e-mail server.

A hash function takes one input M, and generates one output, the message digest H. There is no secret, key, or randomness involved in the hash calculation. Anyone who knows M can derive H. Sometimes it is desirable to employ a key in the hash calculation, so that only with the key can the correct digest be obtained. This is called *keyed-hash* or HMAC (Keyed-Hash Message Authentication Code). An HMAC algorithm takes two inputs, M and key K, and generates H. In this case, H changes when M or K changes.

The engine supports standard message authentication schemes:

- MD5 (Request for Comments (RFC) 1321[4])

- SHA-1 (Federal Information Processing Standards (FIPS) Publication 180-4[5])

- SHA-224 (FIPS 180-4)

- SHA-256 (FIPS 180-4)

- SHA-384 (FIPS 180-4)

- SHA-512 (FIPS 180-4)

- HMAC keyed hash with the preceding underlying hash schemes (FIPS 198-1[6])

Figure 3-2 shows the engine's kernel interface for hash.

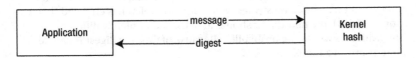

Figure 3-2. *Kernel hash API*

Figure 3-3 shows the engine's kernel interface for HMAC.

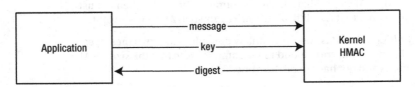

Figure 3-3. *Kernel HMAC API*

The output hash is 16 bytes long for MD5, 20 bytes for SHA-1, 28 bytes for SHA-224, 32 bytes for SHA-256, 48 bytes for SHA-384, and 64 bytes for SHA-512. As MD5 and SHA-1 have smaller output digests, there are well-known attacks against them that reduce security strength. NIST recommends against using MD5 and SHA-1 and recommends moving to SHA-256 and above. Intel's security and management engine continues to support MD5 and SHA-1 for legacy and backward compatibility.

For example, a lot of network equipment deployed in the field today still utilizes SSL/TLS crypto suites that use MD5 or SHA-1 for message authentication. The Intel AMT (*Advanced Management Technology*) application must continue to accept them. However, new firmware applications shall not use MD5 or SHA-1. Note that HMAC-MD5 and HMAC-SHA-1 are still approved algorithms by NIST and are being used in various applications for the security and management engine.

On the engine, among these secure hashing algorithms, the most frequently invoked ones—MD5, SHA-1, SHA-256, and their HMAC variants—are implemented by hardware with firmware wrappers in kernel. The others are implemented by firmware. The firmware implementation was ported from the Intel Integrated Performance Primitives crypto library.[7]

Hash with Multiple Calls

The kernel interface for message authentication allows the caller to set up a context and pass in the message to be hashed in more than one call. In general, this resume capability is required by applications that do not have the entire message data at once.

In an embedded environment where memory is a very valuable resource, even if the entire message can be available at once, it may still be preferable to call the hash function multiple times, in order to reduce runtime memory consumption. For example, to hash 1MB of data, an application can choose to allocate 64KB of memory and call the hash function 16 times—or allocate 1KB of memory and call the hash function 1024 times. Because a call to kernel API implies performance overhead (see Chapter 4 of this book for details), this is a tradeoff between memory consumption and runtime performance.

In any case, the engine's kernel is stateless, and the hash context must be maintained by the application between calls. Figure 3-4 depicts the kernel interface for resume hash/HMAC. The application should start with a "first chunk" call, followed by any number (including zero) of "middle chunk" calls, and finally a "last chunk" call. For HMAC, the context returned from the first chunk call contains a "working" derivation of the HMAC key, so that the application does not need to input HMAC key again in later middle chunk and final chunk calls.

First chunk

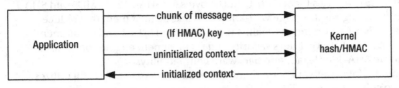

Middle chunks

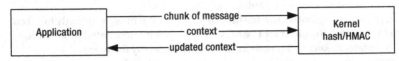

Last chunk

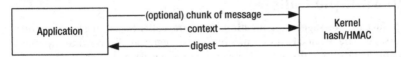

Figure 3-4. Kernel hash/HMAC resume API

Symmetric-Key Encryption

Symmetric-key encryption refers to schemes where both encryption and decryption processes use the same key, in contrast to asymmetric-key encryption where encryption and decryption use two different keys. The most popular symmetric-key scheme used in computing today is defined in AES published by NIST in 2001.[8] The algorithm specified in AES is based on the Rijndael cipher, developed by Belgian cryptographers Joan Daemen and Vincent Rijmen.

AES

AES defines three key sizes: 128, 192, and 256 bits. The kernel of the security and management engine supports all three key sizes of AES.

In general, greater key size provides stronger protection. However, it is worth noting that due to recently published related-key attacks,[9] 256-bit AES can be broken with a complexity of $2^{99.5}$, which makes it weaker than a 128-bit AES in theory (128-bit AES may be broken with a complexity of 2^{126} due to bicliques). Nevertheless, to date, no known attack against any key sizes of AES is computationally feasible.

AES is a block cipher and it has a fixed block size of 128 bits. In other words, the algorithm first splits the input data (plaintext for encryption or ciphertext for decryption) into multiple blocks, each 128 bits, and then performs a cipher operation on every block. Mode of operation describes how to repeatedly apply a single-block operation to encrypt data that is larger than a block. Various modes of operation are defined for block ciphers. The kernel of the security and management engine supports the following modes of operation:

- ECB (electronic codebook)

- ECB-CTS (ECB ciphertext stealing)

- CBC (cipher block chaining)

- CBC-CTS (CBC ciphertext stealing)

- CFB (cipher feedback)

- OFB (output feedback)

- CTR (counter)

For the engine, the most-used key sizes and modes are implemented in hardware, including 128-bit and 256-bit keys with ECB, CBC, and CTR modes. The other modes are implemented in firmware, with underlying basic AES encryption and decryption offloading to the AES hardware.

For block cipher, all the modes except ECB require an initialization vector (IV) of the block size as input to the encryption function. The same IV must be input to the decryption function.

For the CTR mode, the IV consists of two portions: a nonce and counter. The kernel allows the caller to specify sizes of the counter and nonce, as long as the counter is at least 32 bits and their total length is equal to the block size.

For AES, the plaintext and the ciphertext always have the same size, regardless of key size and mode of operation. The CTR and OFB modes have a nice native feature: the size of the data does not have to be a multiple of the block size. That means you can encrypt 2 or 31 bytes of plaintext using CTR or OFB, and the resultant ciphertext is 2 or 31 bytes. The other modes, other than ECB-CTS and CBC-CTS, require data size to be a multiple of 128 bits. Also note that for CTR and OFB modes, the same algorithm is used for both encryption and decryption.

The CTS variant of ECB and CBC applies smart tricks to the last incomplete block and the last complete block of data for the underlying mode, so that the data size does not have to be a multiple of the block size (but the data must be longer than one block). The CTS mode is widely used in network protocols such as Kerberos, which is supported by an Intel AMT application running on the engine.

There are certain requirements and best practices about which modes to use when designing an application and how to use them. Here are some critical rules that may not be very well known by all software engineers:

- For better security, avoid using the ECB mode for data that is longer than one block.

- For the CTR mode, the same key and IV combination can only be used once and must not be repeatedly used for encrypting more than one data block. If the same key and IV combination is used to encrypt more than one block of data, then the security is broken and plaintext can be easily derived from ciphertexts without knowing the key.

Let the AES key be k and IV be iv. In a typical chosen-plaintext attack scenario, the attacker chooses plaintext block p (128 bits) and calls a problematic AES-CTR oracle that uses a constant k and iv. The oracle outputs ciphertext c. According to the CTR mode definition,

```
c := AES(k, iv) XOR p
```

where AES(k, iv) denotes the ciphertext for AES block encryption with plaintext iv using key k, and a XOR b denotes result of bitwise exclusive disjunction operation for two bit strings a and b of the same size. Notice that

```
AES(k, iv) = c XOR p
```

The attacker knows both p and c. His goal is to derive the plaintext p' for another block of ciphertext c' he receives by eavesdropping. Without figuring out k or iv, p' can be easily calculated as follows:

```
p' := AES(k, iv) XOR c' = c XOR p XOR c'
```

- For the CBC mode, the IV must be "unpredictable." Unpredictability means not only that the IV cannot be a constant when encrypting multiple pieces of data, but also that an adversary must not be able to control or know the IV before the encryption happens. In practice, it is recommended to randomly generate IV for each piece of data to be encrypted.

Let the AES key be k. Consider a chosen-plaintext attack on a problematic AES-CBC oracle that uses predictable IV. The attacker has managed to acquire values of the iv and the first ciphertext block c (128 bits), and his goal is to guess the plaintext p. According to the CBC mode definition,

```
c := AES(k, iv XOR p).
```

The attack is allowed to submit his chosen plaintext p' and have the oracle perform AES-CBC encryption using the same key k. Because IV is predictable, the attacker knows the value of the IV, denoted iv', which will be used in his encryption request. Let p_guess represent the attacker's "guessed" value of p. He calculates p' and submits to the oracle:

```
P' := iv XOR iv' XOR p_guess.
```

The oracle performs encryption as follows and outputs c':

```
c' := AES(k, iv' XOR p')
    = AES(k, iv' XOR (iv XOR iv' XOR p_guess))
    = AES(k, iv XOR p_guess).
```

With c and c' in hand, the attacker just needs a simple comparison. If $c = c'$, then $p = p\_guess$. Otherwise, a new p_guess is chosen and p' submitted. The attacker repeats his guess until c' matches c. It may look an unscalable brute force effort. However, for many applications (for example, a social security number), the number of possible plaintext values is small and it is not infeasible to exhaust all possibilities. Using random IV thwarts this attack.

■ **Note** For the CTR mode, the same key and IV combination can only be used once. For the CBC mode, the IV must be unpredictable.

Before performing encryption or decryption, the AES key is first expanded using the Rijndael key schedule to generate "round keys" that are used in encryption and decryption. Most software libraries of AES provide a function for initializing and expanding the AES key into round keys. For encryption/decryption calls, the round keys are passed in, in lieu of the original AES key, to avoid repeating key expansion operations. However, this trick is not implemented by the security and management engine. Thanks to dedicated hardware, the key expansion is not a bottleneck for performance.

DES/3DES

In addition to AES, for backward compatibility, the kernel of the security and management engine also supports DES (data encryption standard),[10] an older standard for encryption that was replaced by AES.

DES has a fixed block size of 64 bits, and key sizes of 56 (DES), 112 (two-key 3DES), and 168 (three-key 3DES) bits, respectively. 56-bit DES is considered insecure because the key size is too small, but 3DES is still being used by many devices in the field today. The security and management engine supports DES and 3DES in ECB, CBC, and CTR modes. They are all implemented by firmware.

Figure 3-5 illustrates the kernel API for symmetric key encryption/decryption.

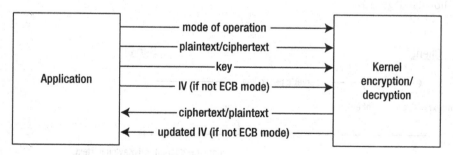

Figure 3-5. Kernel AES/DES/3DES API

Asymmetric-Key Encryption: RSA

Today, RSA[11] is the most widely deployed asymmetric-key encryption scheme. *RSA* stands for the last names of Ron Rivest, Adi Shamir, and Leonard Adleman—the three cryptographers who first invented and published the algorithm back in 1977.

For symmetric-key cryptography like AES or DES/3DES, the encrypter and decrypter must both know the same key beforehand. If the encrypter and decrypter have no prior knowledge of each other but want to communicate securely, how do they agree on the key?

Consider a real-world scenario. When making the first purchase on Amazon using your new smartphone, how does the phone transmit your credit card number and order information securely to Amazon's server so eavesdroppers on the open Internet cannot see? The solution is offered by asymmetric-key cryptography, where the encryption method uses one key, called a *public key*, and the decryption method uses another key, called a *private key*. A public key and a uniquely corresponding private key form a key pair, and they both belong to the decrypter.

The public key is not a secret. It is published and available to anyone who wishes to send encrypted messages to the decrypter. The private key is known to only the decrypter and it must be kept secret. Only the decrypter who knows the private key is able to decrypt a message encrypted with its public key. Hence, asymmetric-key cryptography is also known as *public key cryptography*.

During an online purchase, your smartphone first encrypts your credit card number with Amazon's public key and then transmits the encrypted card number. Since only Amazon knows the private key, it is the only entity that can decrypt the message and retrieve your card number. Eavesdroppers on the network can't decrypt the data.

In reality, what is encrypted using Amazon's public key may not be your credit card number, but an AES key randomly generated by your smartphone. After the encrypted AES key is transmitted to and decrypted by Amazon, your phone and Amazon can use AES to protect the credit card number and other order information. But why bother to use AES if public key encryption works? The reasons are speed and power. Symmetric-key cipher is always much faster and less resource-consuming than asymmetric-key cipher. Therefore, the latter is often only used for encrypting symmetric keys for AES and HMAC, and not the bulk data. At a high level, the interactions between the client and the server are shown in Figure 3-6.

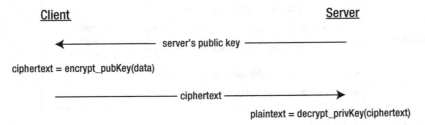

Client   **Server**

◄──────────────── server's public key ────────────────

ciphertext = encrypt_pubKey(data)

──────────────── ciphertext ────────────────►

plaintext = decrypt_privKey(ciphertext)

Figure 3-6. Asymmetric key encryption and decryption

One may question how the client can be confident that the public key indeed belongs to the server it intends to connect with, and not a man-in-the-middle. The trust is established by the PKI (public key infrastructure) system rooted to a CA (certification authority) that is trusted by both the client and the server. The book *Active Platform Management Demystified—Unleashing the Power of Intel vPro Technology* (Intel Press, 2009)[12] elaborates details on PKI and how the AMT application running on the security and management engine implements PKI.

The security and management engine implements the following functions for RSA, compliant with the PKCS #1 standard issued by the RSA Laboratories:

- Key pair generation
- Key pair validation
- Raw encryption and decryption
- Encryption and decryption with PKCS #1 v1.5 padding
- Encryption and decryption with OAEP padding

Key Pair Generation and Validation

The kernel's key pair generation for k-bit RSA, where k is an even integer, exercises the following steps:

1. The first step of generating an RSA key pair is to generate two big prime integers of length $k/2$ bits each.

   To generate a big prime number, first generate a random number and then run a primality test against the random number. The primality test ensures that the candidate has an acceptably high probability of being a prime. For k-bit RSA key pair generation, the kernel generates two distinct big random numbers. For each of the two numbers, set the most significant two bits to 1 and the least significant bit to 1. Setting the most significant two bits to 1 ensures that the product of the two numbers is exactly k bits and not fewer than k bits. Setting the least significant bit ensures the number is odd, because an even, big number cannot be prime.

2. Run a simple primality test on the two numbers (prime candidates), respectively.

   The simple primality test works as follows. The smallest 2048 primes are hardcoded in firmware. The security and management engine hardcodes only 2048 primes, but if space allows, then hardcoding more prime numbers would speed up the key generation further, because composite candidates can be eliminated sooner.

Divide the candidate by every one of the 2048 primes, one after another, and save the 2048 remainders. If any of the 2048 remainders is 0, then the candidate is composite. However, do not give up on the candidate yet. Instead, add 2 to every one of the 2048 remainders respectively, and divide the 2048 updated remainders by the 2048 corresponding small primes. Keep adding 2 to the remainders until a certain numbers of additions have been performed, or all 2048 divisions result in nonzero remainders. If a certain number of additions of 2 have been made and still some of the 2048 remainders are 0, then eliminate this candidate and generate a new random number as a candidate.

3. Run a comprehensive primality test against the candidate.

    The security and management engine uses the Miller-Rabin primality test.[13] Notice that depending on the length of the prime candidate, the number of rounds of Miller-Rabin tests varies. For example, for a 1024-bit candidate, at least three rounds of Miller-Rabin tests must be run to ensure that the error rate (falsely identifying a composite to be a prime) is[14] less than 2^{-80}. If the candidate is found a composite, then generate a new candidate.

4. After two probable prime numbers p and q are generated, calculate their product

    n = p * q

    Note that n has k bits in it. n is called *modulus*.

5. Choose a value for the public exponent e. e must be smaller than (p-1)*(q-1) and coprime to (p-1)*(q-1); that is, the greatest common divisor of e and (p-1)*(q-1) must be 1.

    The speed of the encryption operation is determined by e and the number of nonzero bits (this is also called *Hamming weight*) in the binary representation of e. Prime 65537 is a popular choice for e, as it has only two nonzero bits in its binary representation. 3 and 17 used to be popular choices but they are considered not strong enough by many applications today owing to published cryptanalysis.[15]

    If you choose a prime such as 65537 as e, then divide (p-1)*(q-1) by e. If it is exactly divisible, then e and (p-1)*(q-1) are not coprime, and a new p or q must be generated.

6. Calculate d, the multiplicative inverse of e, such that

    d·e ≡ 1 mod (p-1)*(q-1).

d is a *k*-bit integer calculated using the extended Euclidean algorithm.

7. If the application requests, calculate the following private key components for the Chinese Remainder Theorem. These key components are all *k*/2-bit long. Using them in the decryption operation proves to be more efficiently than using the *k*-bit *d*.

```
d_P := d mod (p-1)
d_Q := d mod (q-1)
q_inv := q-1 mod p
```

Among all of the preceding values, the public key consists of *n* and *e*. The private key consists of *n*, *d*, *p*, *q*, *d_P*, *d_Q*, and *q_inv*. NIST recommends using at least 2048-bit *n*, which provides equivalent security strength of 112 bits. The security and management engine supports RSA key sizes of up to 4096 bits for encryption and decryption. For key pair generation, the engine supports up to 2048 bits. Most applications running on the engine and in the mobile computing industry today use 2048-bit RSA.

The key pair generation is an expensive and lengthy operation. Generating a 2048-bit key pair takes an average of 30 seconds on the security and management engine. Most of the generation time is spent on searching for prime numbers *p* and *q*.

The simple primality test described in step 2—although not a standard step in the key generation process—is a very useful trick to expedite the prime number search. On the security and management engine, this step improves the search time for a 1024-bit prime by as much as 65%. The following illustrates its pseudo code.

Algorithm X-Y: Preliminary Primality Test

```
Input: prime candidate
Output: if candidate may be a prime, updated candidate (if it may be a prime)

SmallestPrimes[NUM_OF_SMALL_PRIMES] = {/* hardcode smallest
NUM_OF_SMALL_PRIMES primes here */}
Remainders[NUM_OF_SMALL_PRIMES] = {0}

delta = 0
for i from 0 to NUM_OF_SMALL_PRIMES-1
  remainders[i] = candidate % SmallestPrimes[i]

Loop:
for i from 0 to NUM_OF_SMALL_PRIMES-1
  If ((Remainders[i] + delta) % SmallestPrimes[i] == 0)
    delta = delta + 2
      If delta < MAX_DELTA /* upper limit of delta before giving up this
candidate */}
        goto Loop
      Else
```

```
    return COMPOSITE
candidate = candidate + delta
return MAY_BE_PRIME
```

The logic under Loop is based on the following theorem:

Theorem: If $x = k*p+r$, then $x\%p = r\%p$.
Proof: $x\%p = (k*p+r)\%p = ((k*p)\%p + r\%p)\%p = (0 + r\%p)\%p = r\%p$.

Taking advantage of this simple theorem, instead of the large candidate x, the prime search uses the small sum r of the remainder and delta in the modulus operation. This trick significantly reduces computation time.

■ **Note**   To find a big prime number from a random number, always run the preliminary primality test (prime sieve) and adjust the random number, if possible, before running the Miller-Rabin test.

The key pair generation is a blocking call. Because it takes several seconds to return, under certain circumstances, applications may prefer to abort the key generation before its completion. The kernel API provides an optional callback and abortion capability. The application may pass in a pointer to a callback function. The kernel, while performing the key pair generation, will periodically call back and see whether the application wants to stop the generation. The callback option is especially useful when a power event, such as a shutdown, happens in the middle of a key pair generation, in which case the application must not block the power event and must abort the generation as soon as possible.

Some applications running on the security and management engine need a RSA key pair during service enrollment or provisioning that is initiated by an end user. A key pair will be generated during the enrollment or provisioning operation, and the user has to wait for a key pair generation to complete. Obviously, having a customer waiting for 30 seconds or longer is not a user-friendly design.

To improve the user's experience, every time the kernel boots, it voluntarily generates a certain number of 2048-bit RSA key pairs and stores in a cache in memory. When an application invokes key generation, a pregenerated key pair is returned immediately, and then the kernel generates a new key pair in a low-priority thread to fill the cache.

■ **Note**   Consider pregenerating RSA key pairs to improve the user's experience.

The kernel's RSA key generation API is shown in Figure 3-7. The figure shows the scenario where the key generation runs to completion. Figure 3-8 shows the scenario where the generation is aborted.

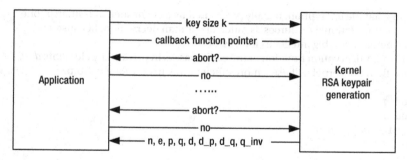

Figure 3-7. *Kernel RSA key pair generation completion flow*

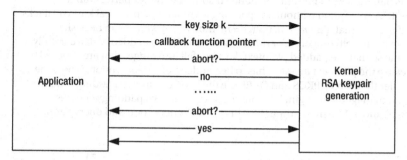

Figure 3-8. *Kernel RSA key pair generation abortion flow*

The key pair validation tests whether *p* and *q* are probable prime numbers and verifies the relationships among the key components passed in by the application (see Figure 3-9).

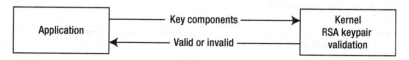

Figure 3-9. *Kernel RSA key pair validation API*

Encryption and Decryption

For encryption, first represent the plaintext as a big number *m* such that $0 <= m < n$, and then calculate ciphertext *c* as

```
c := me mod n
```

c must be smaller than *n*. For decryption, first check whether *c* is smaller than *n*. If so, recover plaintext by calculating

```
m := cd mod n
```

71

It is obvious that the encryption, usually performed by a client such as a smartphone that has limited computational resources, is much faster than decryption, because e is a small integer, whereas d is a big integer as long as k bits.

For kernel's RSA decryption function, if the caller passes in private key elements d_P, d_Q, and q_inv, then the kernel will use a more efficient way to calculate m from c:

```
m1 := c^d_P mod p
m2 := c^d_q mod q
h := q_inv·(m1 - m2) mod p
m := m2 + h·q
```

Using the Chinese Remainder Theorem, all modulo operations are with modulus p or q, which is half the size of modulus n, hence resulting in better performance.

The "raw" RSA encryption without any padding is vulnerable to several known attacks. For example, if m is so small that $m^e < n$, then $c = m^e \bmod n = m^e$ and m can be easily calculated by taking the eth root of c. For mitigation, m should be padded with a carefully designed scheme so that the padded plaintext does not fall into ranges that are exposed to attacks. Because the plaintext message has to be padded before encryption, it must be somewhat smaller than k bits. PKCS and OAEP are the two best-known padding schemes. The security and management engine's kernel supports these two padding schemes.

Figures 3-10 and 3-11 demonstrate the APIs for RSA encryption and decryption, respectively.

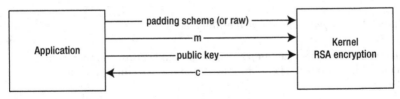

Figure 3-10. *Kernel RSA Encryption API*

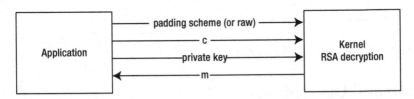

Figure 3-11. *Kernel RSA decryption API*

Digital Signature

The digital signature is realized using public key cryptography, where the *signer* (the only entity that is able to generate the signature) signs a message with its secret private key and the *verifier* (anyone) verifies the signer's signature with the signer's public key.

As seen earlier, plaintext and ciphertext, when treated as integers, in RSA encryption/decryption must be smaller than *n* in value. However, there should not be such a length restriction on the message to be signed. Therefore, the hash function is used to convert a long message to its small-size digest. What is being signed is the digest instead of the message itself. The two properties of the hash function—collision-free and one-way—make sure that the message cannot be forged, and signing the digest is as good as signing the message.

RSA

The *k*-bit RSA signature generation follows these steps:

1. Calculate h = hash(m).

2. Apply padding scheme to *h* and result in *k*-bit value, *em.*

3. Calculate signature s = em^d mod n or use the Chinese Remainder Theorem. This is a RSA raw decryption operation, though some literatures call it "private key encryption."

The Kernel API for RSA signature generation is depicted in Figure 3-12.

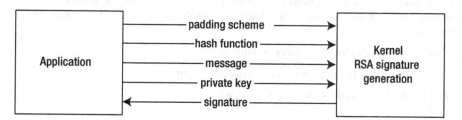

Figure 3-12. *Kernel RSA signature generation API*

RSA signature verification follows the following steps:

1. Calculate em' = s^e mod n. This is a RSA raw encryption operation, though some literatures call it "public key decryption."

2. Examine whether em' is formatted correctly according to the padding scheme. If the formatting of em' is wrong, then reject the signature.

3. Extract the message digest portion h' from em' according to the padding scheme.

4. If h' == hash(m), then accept the signature; otherwise, reject the signature.

The Kernel API for RSA signature verification is depicted in Figure 3-13.

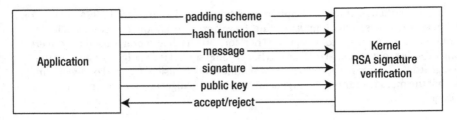

Figure 3-13. *Kernel RSA signature verification API*

The signing uses a private key, and the operation is slower. Signing is usually performed by a server with strong computational resources. The signature verification uses a public key and is usually performed by a client such as a mobile device.

The most popular signature-padding schemes are PKCS#1 and SSA-PSS. The kernel of the security and management engine supports both schemes.

ECDSA

The digital signature scheme based on elliptic curve cryptography (ECDSA) is becoming more and more popular thanks to its high security strength and smaller key sizes compared to RSA. ECDSA is especially suitable for mobile embedded devices where the following are true:

- Storage and memory space is limited
- The entire key data may not be available at once

An elliptic curve has the following definition:

$$y^2 = x^3 + ax + b$$

where *a* and *b* are predefined constants. Conceptually, an elliptic curve looks like Figure 3-14.

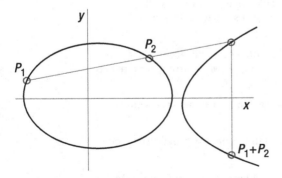

Figure 3-14. *Elliptic curve and point addition*

The ECDSA curves supported by the security and management engine are the curves defined for prime finite fields ("P curves") in NIST's DSS standard.[16] Within a finite field, all coordinates are smaller than modulo p, where p is a large prime defined in the standard. The exact shape of the curve is determined by domain parameters, including a and b. A point on the curve is denoted as (x, y), where x and y are in $[1, p-1]$ (that is, this is on a finite field). A special point called "base point" G, also a domain parameter, is defined for a given elliptic curve.

The point addition is a basic operation defined on elliptic curve. Figure 3-14 demonstrates point addition of two points, $P1$ and $P2$. To calculate the sum of two points $P1+P2$, first connect them with a straight line and then extend the line to meet the elliptic curve at the third node. The opposite point to the x axis of the third node is the sum of $P1$ and $P2$.

To add a point P to itself, draw a tangent line at the point and let the line meet the curve at the second node. Then the opposite to the x axis of the second node is the double of P.

Multiplication on an elliptic curve is realized by repeated additions. If a point P is added to itself $k-1$ times, then it becomes a scalar multiplication: an integer k multiplied by a point, denoted as $Q = k * P$. Notice that Q is also a point on the curve.

■ **Note** For a big integer k, it is easy to calculate $Q=k*P$ from k and P, but it is very difficult to derive k from Q and P.

Key Pair Generation and Validation

The mathematical foundation of ECC as an asymmetric key cryptography is the difficult problem of deriving k from Q and P in $Q = k*P$. The ECDSA key pair is defined by taking advantage of this important property. The private key PrivKey is a big number, between 1 and $n-1$ inclusive.[i] The private key is generated randomly. The corresponding public key is a point PubKey on the curve such that

```
PubKey = PrivKey * G
```

Obviously, the key pair generation of ECDSA is much faster than that of RSA, as the private key is just a random big number. On the other hand, the private keys p and q of RSA must be prime numbers, which takes significantly more resources to obtain. On the security and management engine, generating a 256-bit ECDSA key pair takes about 10 milliseconds, which is imperceptible from an end user's perspective. The engine does not implement a key pair cache for ECDSA.

A major advantage of ECDSA over RSA signature is its smaller key size (hence smaller storage space required) with strong security protection. The security strength of

---

[i] n is the order of the elliptic curve. The order of a curve is a prime integer n such that $n * G = O$, where O represents the point at infinity.

ECDSA is half of the size of the private key. So a 256-bit private key would provide 128-bit equivalent security as symmetric key cryptography. For comparison, the 2048-bit RSA provides only 112-bit of security.

This chapter does not describe the complete steps of ECDSA signature generation and verification. Instead, critical elliptic curve point operations used in ECDSA are explained, and optimization strategies for them are discussed in detail.

Scalar Multiplication

The scalar multiplication is the most intensive step in ECDSA signature generation and verification. The add-and-double algorithm is used to calculate $k*P$.

1. Represent k in its binary form with digits 0 and 1.

2. Start from result of "0" and scan the binary representation of k from left (most significant bit) to right (least significant bit).

    - For a bit that is 0, double the result. Move to the next bit.

    - For a bit that is 1, add point P to the result and double the updated result. Move to the next bit.

3. The resulting point after processing the rightmost bit is the final result.

Table 3-1 shows the computation of $198*P$ using the add-and-double algorithm. The first row in the table shows the binary representation of the scalar (198). The second row shows the result of the doubling operation from the row immediately to its left. The third row shows the result of the addition operation if the first row shows 1 in the column.

Table 3-1. Calculation of 198P Using Add-and-Double Algorithm

k=198	1	1	0	0	0	1	1	0
Double	0	2*P=2P	2*3P=6P	2*6P=12P	2*12P=24P	2*24P=48P	2*49P=98P	2*99P=**198P**
Add	P	P	2P+P=3P	6P	12P	24P	48P+P=49P	98P+P=99P	

It is easy to see from the calculation that the scalar multiplication does not require the knowledge of the entire k before calculation can begin. Calculation can start as soon as some bits of k are available, and continues simultaneously while the rest of k is received. The portion of k that has been processed can be deleted from memory. The parallel processing can save substantial time for mobile devices. The RSA signature scheme does not have such flexibility.

Let the bit length of k be m and the number of 1s in the binary representation of k be w. The scalar multiplication of $k*P$ requires $m-1$ point doublings and $w-1$ point additions. Note that doubling is in fact addition. On average $w = 0.5*m$, Therefore,

```
m + w -2 = 1.5*m -2
```

point additions are required for calculating $k*P$.

Window Method

To reduce the number of point additions and speed up ECDSA arithmetic, one may apply a precomputation trick, namely, the "window method," to the scalar multiplication. Instead of treating the binary representation of k as an m-bit string, the window method treats it as ceiling(m/t)[ii] "windows," where each window is made up of t consecutive bits (i.e., the width of a window is t bits).

1. Split the binary representation of k into windows of t bits. If m is not divisible by t, then pad (t-(m mod t)) zeros to the left of the most significant bit of k, before splitting the binary representation of k into windows.

2. Precompute 2*P, 3*P, ..., (2t-1)*P and store results in memory. The number of required precomputations is (2t-2).

3. Start from result of "0" and scan binary representation of k from left to right.

   • For a window that is 0, calculate (2t)*P' where P' is the result of previous column. Move to the next window.

   • For a window that has value of v, calculate (2t)*(v*P + P'). Move to the next window.

4. The resultant point after processing the rightmost column is the final result.

For example, the binary expression 11000110b of integer 198 can be split into four windows, with a window size of 2:

[11][00][01][10]

Here, window value $11b$ corresponds to $3P$. Window value $10b$ corresponds to $2P$. They must be precomputed before the scalar multiplication starts. Table 3-2 explains the calculation of 198P with windows size 2.

Table 3-2. *Calculation of 198P Using Window Method with Window Size 2*

k=198	11	00	01	10
Quadrupling	0	4*3P=12P	4*12P=48P	4*49P=196P
Add P			48P+P=49P	
Add 2P				196P+2P=**198P**
Add 3P	3P			

[ii] *ceiling(x)* returns the smallest integer equal to or greater than the fraction *x*.

For window size of $t = 2$, a quadrupling (multiplying by 4) is performed when moving to the next column. A quadrupling is equivalent to 2 point additions (first calculate $2*P' = P'+P'$, then $4*P' = 2*P'+2*P'$). In general, for window size of t bits, t additions are required when moving to the next column.

For window size of $t = 2$, there are 2^t possible values of a window. For windows with a nonzero value, an addition operation is required. On average, $(2^t-1)/2^t$ of all windows are nonzero.

To ramp up, using the window method to calculate $k*P$, there are three steps that need additions:

- Precomputation
  - $A = 2^t-2$
- Additions for processing a column
  - $B = \text{ceiling}((2^t-1)/2^t * \text{ceiling}(m/t)-1)$
- Additions when moving to the next column
  - $C = (\text{ceiling}(m/t)-1) * t$

The total number of additions is $A+B+C$.

Table 3-3 compares total numbers of additions with different choices of t for $m = 256$ (256-bit is one of the most commonly used ECDSA key sizes).

Table 3-3. *Numbers of Addition Operations for m=256*

t	1	2	3	4	5	6	7	8
A	0	2	6	**14**	30	62	126	254
B	127	95	74	**59**	49	41	33	31
C	255	254	253	**252**	251	250	249	248
A+B+C	382	351	333	**325**	330	353	411	533
Savings	0%	8.1%	12.8%	**14.9%**	13.6%	7.6%	-7.6%	-39.5%

From the comparison, it is obvious that for $m = 256$, the optimal window size is 4 (emphasized in bold in the table). The number of precomputations increases exponentially with t. When the window is wider than 4 bits, the precomputation cost starts to outweigh the benefit of saving of additions during the scalar multiplication.

Dual Scalar Multiplication

Besides the "single" scalar multiplication $Q = k*P$, the ECDSA signature verification also uses a "dual" scalar multiplication:

$Q = k1 * P1 + k2 * P2$

The dual scalar multiplication can be implemented by first performing two independent single scalar multiplications and then a point addition. However, this is not as fast as utilizing a smaller trick with a trivial precomputation cost of P1+P2.

Table 3-4 shows the computation of $197*P1 + 172*P2$ using the precomputation trick.

Table 3-4. *Calculation of 197*P1 + 172*P2 Using Precomputation Trick*

$k1$=197	1	1	0	0	0	1	0	1
$k2$=172	1	0	1	0	1	1	0	0
Double	0	$2P1+2P2$	$6P1+4P2$	$12P1+10P2$	$24P1+20P2$	$48P1+42P2$	$98P1+86P2$	$196P1+172P2$
Add $P1$		$3P1+2P2$						***197P1+172P2***
Add $P2$			$6P1+5P2$		$24P1+21P2$			
Add $P1$+$P2$	$P1$+$P2$					$49P1+43P2$		

For two scalars $k1$ and $k2$, there are four possibilities of their bit value combination, {0, 0}, {1, 0}, {0, 1}, and {1, 1}, corresponding to points *0*, *P1*, *P2*, and *P1+P2*, respectively. *P1* and *P2* are already available; *P1+P2* must be precomputed.

- For a column that is {0, 0}, double the result. Move to the next bit.

- For a column that is {1, 0}, add *P1* to the result and double the updated result. Move to the next bit.

- For a column that is {0, 1}, add *P2* to the result and double the updated result. Move to the next bit.

- For a column that is {1, 1}, add *P1+P2* to the result and double the updated result. Move to the next bit.

The resultant point after processing the rightmost column is the final result.

Let the bit length of $k1$ be $m1$ and that of $k2$ be $m2$; let the Hamming weight of $k1$ be $w1$ and that of $k2$ be $w2$. Using the traditional add-and-double algorithm without precomputing P1+P2, calculating k1*P1+k2*P2 requires

$$(m1-1 + m2-1) + (w1-1 + w2-1) + 1 = m1 + m2 + w1 + w2-3$$

point additions. On average, $w1 = 0.5*m1$ and $w2 = 0.5*m2$. In the ECDSA signature verification, $m1 = m2$. Let $m1 = m2 = m$. The total number of additions becomes

$$m1 + m2 + 0.5*m1 + 0.5*m2 - 3 = 1.5 (m1 + m2) - 3$$
$$= \mathbf{3*m - 3}$$

Using the method introduced in Table 3-4, one has to perform $m-1$ doublings and on average $0.75*m - 1$ additions[iii] during the scalar multiplication. Beforehand, one addition is needed for precomputing $P1+P2$. Treating doubling as addition, the total number of required additions is

$$(m - 1) + (0.75*m - 1) + 1 = \mathbf{1.75*m - 1}$$

When m is large, the trick saves approximately

$$(3 - 1.75) / 3 * 100\% = \mathbf{41.7\%}$$

of addition operations, with a tiny tradeoff of storing point $P1+P2$ in memory. Thus this is a very useful trick to speed up ECDSA on embedded systems.

The window method can also be applied to the dual scalar multiplication, in which case a window will have a height of 2 for $k1$ and $k2$. However, the amount of precomputations and memory consumption increases considerably with the increase of the window size.

Hardware Acceleration

To speed up RSA and ECDSA calls, the security and management engine has implemented hardware logic for the following big number arithmetic:

- Multiplication

- Addition

- Subtraction

- Modulo

- Exponentiation and modulo (using Montgomery multiplier)

Other Cryptography Functions

Besides the functions described earlier, the kernel supports a number of other algorithms:

- ECDH (elliptic curve Diffie-Hellman) key agreement

- AES-CMAC message authentication

- RC4 stream cipher

- DSA (digital signature algorithm)

[iii]The *joint Hamming weight* of $k1$ and $k2$ is defined as the number of nonzero columns of the binary representations of $k1$ and $k2$. A column is nonzero if at least one of the bits of $k1$ and $k2$ is nonzero for the column. There are four possible combinations of a column, $\{0, 0\}$, $\{0, 1\}$, $\{1, 0\}$, and $\{1, 1\}$, and they appear with the same probability, hence on average, 75% of all columns are nonzero columns and require addition.

The design principle of the kernel is to support any cryptography algorithms that are required by at least one application. Depending on the data throughput expectation of the application and available gate areas in hardware, the requested cipher may be implemented either wholly in firmware or partially in hardware.

To save valuable resources in the embedded system, cryptography algorithms that are not used by any applications are not included in the system.

Secure Storage

In addition to cryptography, the kernel of the security and management engine supports other infrastructural functionalities that are needed by applications.

A partition of the SPI flash chip is reserved for storing the security and management engine's nonvolatile data. As the flash size is very limited, the files cannot be too large. Generally speaking, the storage is intended for keys and credentials, such as device private keys, AMT passwords, and so on. It is not designed for storing bulk data such as video frames or network traffic.

The kernel's storage manager lets applications choose what protections are required by individual files:

- *Encryption:* 128-bit or 256-bit AES, in CTR mode

- *Integrity:* HMAC-SHA-1 or HMAC-SHA-256

- *Anti-replay:* To mitigate a physical attack of replacing the file with a previous version of the file

- *No protection:* The file will be stored in plaintext without integrity or anti-replay protection

During boot, the kernel derives a 128-bit AES key and a 256-bit AES key used for file encryption and decryption. The kernel also derives an HMAC key used for HMAC-SHA-1 and HMAC-SHA-256. These keys are referred to as *storage keys*. The storage keys are derived from security fuses that are random and unique for each instance of the part and burned into the security fuse block during manufacturing. Because the storage keys are different on every part, even if a file is copied from one part to another, it will fail the HMAC integrity check and will not be accepted by the firmware.

Although all files on the security and management engine use the same storage keys for protection, the storage manager in the kernel enforces access isolation so that a process is not able to access files that belong to other processes. The owning process of a file can also configure its file properties so the file can be shared with other specified processes with read and/or write privileges.

Debugging

For engineering firmware[iv] running on preproduction parts,[v] developers use debuggers that allow halting the processor, stepping through source code, and reviewing variable values and memory contents.

On production parts, however, the debug port is disabled by a fuse and only production-signed firmware images can execute. How to debug an application on production parts with signed firmware? The security and management engine offers two ways—debug messaging and special production-signed firmware—to facilitate debugging on production parts.

Debug Messaging

The kernel exposes a function that lets a calling application send messages through the engine's LAN interface to a debug console. Applications can call this kernel function at interesting spots and milestones. This is similar to debugging using printf in software development. Applications must be careful not to send out sensitive information. A timestamp will be appended by the kernel for all messages.

Special Production-Signed Firmware Based on Unique Part ID

Production-signed firmware has the capability of overwriting the "debug port disabled" fuse and enabling debug port on production parts. Of course, generic released firmware that is production-signed must never open the debug port—otherwise, it would be a critical vulnerability.

To enable engineers to debug on production parts, Intel may sign special firmware with a production RSA key. The special firmware

- Boots normally when running on the specific production part on which the debugging will be performed.

- Halts when running on all other production parts.

- Enables the debug port.

- Has a special version number such that attempt of updating from a released firmware to this special firmware will fail. That is, the debug engineer must physically flash this special firmware to the flash chip on the specific part.

[iv]Debug-signed firmware is signed with a debug RSA key, not one of the production RSA keys.
[v]A preproduction part has the debug port enabled and allows debug-signed firmware to run. A production part has the debug port disabled by fuse and allows only production-signed firmware to run.

The security fuses that are random and unique for each part are used to derive not only the storage keys but also a 128-bit value used as the unique part ID. Although the ID is unique, it does not pose privacy concerns because the part itself is the only entity that knows the value.

Obviously, the special firmware must hardcode the unique ID of the specific production part. During boot, the special firmware reads the unique ID from the part it is running on and compares with the hardcoded ID. If they match, it continues to boot and enables the debug port; otherwise, it is considered an attack. The firmware clears memory and halts the processor immediately.

But this method requires the knowledge of the unique ID of the part before the special firmware can be created. It means the released firmware must have an interface for outputting the unique ID to the host. Does this interface introduce privacy concerns? To avoid raising such concerns, the security and management engine invents a trick of randomization for the unique ID. With this trick, the value sent to the host is never the real unique ID, but a salted[vi] randomization of it. The host receives a different randomized ID every time it retrieves the ID from the released firmware, even if it is the same hardware part.

Algorithm 3-1 explains the procedure of generating a salted part ID. The algorithm is implemented on released firmware.

Algorithm 3-1. Salted Part ID Generation on Released Firmware

```
Input: unique ID uid (128 bits)
Output: salted ID sid (128 bits)

random_string = get_random(32 bits);
hash = SHA-256(uid || random_string);
sid = leftmost 96 bits of hash || random string;
```

The logic in the special production-signed firmware for checking the salted ID is detailed in Algorithm 3-2.

Algorithm 3-2. Checking Part ID on Special Production-Signed Firmware

```
Input: unique ID uid (128 bits), salted ID sid (128 bits)
Output: matched or mismatched

random_string = right most 32 bits of sid;
hash = SHA-256(uid || random_string);
if (left most 96 bits of hash == left most 96 bits of sid)
  return matched;
else
  return mismatched;
```

[vi]A *salt* is random data that is used as an additional input to a hash function.

In both algorithms, SHA-256 can be replaced by another one-way function such as HMAC, in which case uid can be used as a message and random_string can be used as the HMAC key. The algorithms are meant to demonstrate the idea, and the sizes of variables can be changed depending on platform.

After the debug engineer retrieves the salted part ID from his production part, he notifies the build engineer of the salted ID. The build engineer then hardcodes the salted ID, creates the special firmware, and signs it with a production RSA key. The signed firmware image is sent to the debug engineer, who then flashes to his part and launches the debugger, just like on a preproduction part.

It is worth noting that, by the security policy, a production part contains top secrets that even debug engineers are not supposed to access—for example, an EPID (*Enhanced Privacy Identification*, see Chapter 5 of this book for details) private key. The special firmware erases all such secrets from memory before enabling the debug port. Debugging critical features such as EPID must be done with test keys and not real production keys.

Once debugging is completed, the part used for debug should be destroyed. The special production-signed firmware should be destroyed also.

Secure Timer

There is a protected real-time clock in the engine. Applications can use the clock through two kernel APIs:

- *Start timer:* An application calls this function to initialize/reset its timer. A new timer is created and it immediately starts to run. A handle will be returned to the caller for identifying the timer in the future.

- *Get current timer value:* An application calls this function with a timer handle to retrieve the current value of the specific timer. The current value shows the number of seconds that have elapsed since the start timer function was called.

Notice that the secure timer in the kernel shows time that has elapsed, but does not provide current date/time information. This is because the kernel has no secure way of receiving the date/time from a time server outside of the embedded system.

Applications are responsible for getting current UTC (Universal Time Coordinated) time from a trusted external time source. For example, EPID clients use X.509 certificates for authentication and key establishment. The EPID manager firmware must validate the client's certificate before serving the client. To make sure the certificate has not expired, the firmware must always know the current date/time.

To get the current date/time information, the EPID manager requests a real-time OCSP (Online Certificate Status Protocol) response from a trusted OCSP server, which was endorsed by Intel. The response contains the current date/time. The EPID manager saves the date/time (baseline) in a file in the kernel's secure storage and calls the kernel's *Start timer* function that starts the timer. Later, when the EPID manager is verifying the validity period of a certificate, it calls the *Get current timer value* function and calculates the current date/time by adding the kernel's returned value to the baseline. The EPID manager requests a new real-time OCSP response every 30 days to calibrate its timer.

Host-Embedded Communication Interface

Almost all applications on the security and management engine need to communicate with software programs running on the host. The link between the host and the engine is called a *host-embedded communication interface*, or HECI.

There is a HECI driver that runs in ring 0 of the host operating system and manages the HECI device on the PCI bus. Individual software programs must call the HECI driver to send messages to and receive responses from the embedded engine. On the embedded side, the kernel implements a HECI driver that is the counterpart of the HECI driver on the host. It manages HECI connections for all embedded applications. The host application and its corresponding embedded application must agree on the same unique HECI client ID beforehand. The client IDs are hardcoded in both software and firmware. The host application and the embedded application must also agree on structures of predefined messages so that the sender and the recipient can understand each other. Incorrectly formatted messages should be rejected gracefully and should not cause crashes.

The HECI interface per se is not secured. No encryption is performed on messages in transit by the HECI drivers. If required, the applications must apply appropriate protection, such as an encryption and integrity check, to the messages before transmitting them.

Due to bandwidth considerations, the HECI channel is designed to carry short and simple data, rather than bulk data such as network traffic or video and audio frames. The maximum size of a HECI message is configurable per product, depending on the worst-case usage model, and ranges between 1KB and 12KB. Firmware applications usually use HECI to receive control commands from the host and to send back status information to the host. For example, an EPID client sends a HECI message to the EPID manager firmware to establish a secure session; the firmware then responds with its ephemeral Diffie-Hellman public key.

Figure 3-15 shows the HECI message data flow among software applications, the host HECI driver, the embedded HECI driver, and embedded applications.

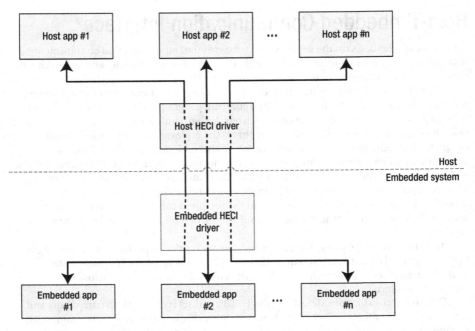

Figure 3-15. *HECI architecture overview*

Reception of messages is signaled through system interrupts. The embedded HECI driver is a dispatcher that delivers messages received from the host to the right recipient applications. The separation among different HECI clients is realized by the task isolation mechanism described in Chapter 4.

Direct Memory Access to Host Memory

The security and management engine is equipped with direct memory access (DMA) devices that allow firmware to access (read and/or write) the host's memory space by referencing its physical addresses. The kernel exposes an API for *select* applications to perform DMA operations between memory of the host and the embedded system.

Applications may use DMA to exchange large amounts of runtime data with the host. For example, AMT network traffic, video and audio frames, and so on. Such data is too large and too slow to transmit over the HECI interface.

Although DMA is certainly a convenient way to transmit data between the host and the embedded system, it grants the embedded engine with arguably dangerous privileges and creates security concerns. Vulnerability in the engine, if found by hackers, may be exploited to attack the host's memory.

At the Black Hat conference in 2009, Alexander Tereshkin and Rafal Wojtczuk demonstrated an attack that exploited a flaw of the management engine.[17] The attack manages to read and write arbitrary host memory, with certain exceptions, through the embedded DMA engine from a root kit. See Chapter 4 for more descriptions of the attack.

Although the design flaw exploited by the attack is not in the DMA component, the DMA engine is a key factor that makes the attack possible. To minimize the abuse of DMA, the firmware architecture should apply tighter control and exercise the security design principle of *least privilege*. Today, the security and management engine enforces stringent restrictions for applications accessing the host memory:

- The kernel's DMA API is only open to applications that have justifiable need to access host memory. The white list of applications that are permitted to DMA with the host is hardcoded in firmware and cannot be changed at runtime.

- For those allowed applications, the kernel enforces minimum privileges (read only from host, write only to host, or read and write). That is, an application that only needs read access is forbidden from writing to host memory.

- A small and isolated component in the kernel is responsible for determining whether DMA access requested by the calling application is legitimate, and if so, the range of host memory addresses to be accessed by the application. During development and validation, very thorough and comprehensive review and testing is performed on this component in the attempt to make it a bug-free component.

References

1. Stinson, D. R., Cryptography: Theory and Practice, Chapman & Hall/CRC, 2006.

2. National Institute of Standards and Technology, Recommendation for Random Number Generation Using Deterministic Random Bit Generators, http://csrc.nist.gov/publications/nistpubs/800-90A/SP800-90A.pdf, accessed on November 17, 2013.

3. National Institute of Standards and Technology, Supplemental ITL Bulletin for September 2013, http://csrc.nist.gov/publications/nistbul/itlbul2013_09_supplemental.pdf, accessed on November 17, 2013.

4. Rivest, R., "The MD5 Message-Digest Algorithm," RFC 1321, April 1996, http://www.ietf.org/rfc/rfc1321.txt, accessed on March 18, 2014.

5. National Institute of Standards and Technology, Secure Hash Standard (SHS), http://csrc.nist.gov/publications/fips/fips180-4/fips-180-4.pdf, accessed on November 17, 2013.

6. National Institute of Standards and Technology, The Keyed-Hash Message Authentication Code (HMAC), http://csrc.nist.gov/publications/fips/fips198-1/FIPS-198-1_final.pdf, accessed on November 17, 2013.

7. Intel® Integrated Performance Primitives (Intel® IPP), http://software.intel.com/en-us/intel-ipp, accessed on February 23, 2014.

8. National Institute of Standards and Technology, Advanced Encryption Standard (AES), http://csrc.nist.gov/publications/fips/fips197/fips-197.pdf, accessed on November 17, 2013.

9. Biryukov, Alex and Dmitry Khovratovich, "Related-key Cryptanalysis of the Full AES-192 and AES-256," Cryptology ePrint Archive: Report 2009/317, 2009, http://eprint.iacr.org/2009/317.pdf, accessed on November 17, 2013.

10. National Institute of Standards and Technology, Data Encryption Standard (DES), http://csrc.nist.gov/publications/fips/fips46-3/fips46-3.pdf, accessed on November 17, 2013.

11. RSA Laboratories, PKCS #1 v2.1: RSA Cryptography Standard, ftp://ftp.rsasecurity.com/pub/pkcs/pkcs-1/pkcs-1v2-1.pdf, accessed on November 17, 2013.

12. Kumar, Arvind, Purushottam Goel, and Ylian Saint-Hilaire, *Active Platform Management Demystified—Unleashing the Power of Intel vPro Technology*, Intel Press, 2009.

13. Rabin, M. O., "Probabilistic algorithm for testing primality," Journal of Number Theory, 1980, 12 (1), pp. 128–138.

14. Damgard, I., P. Landrock, and C. Pomerance, "Average case error estimates for the strong probable prime test," Mathematics of Computation, 1993, 61, pp. 177–194.

15. Bleichenbacher, Daniel, "Chosen Ciphertext Attacks against Protocols Based on the RSA Encryption Standard PKCS #1," CRYPTO '98, pp. 1–12.

16. National Institute of Standards and Technology, Digital Signature Standard (DSS), http://nvlpubs.nist.gov/nistpubs/FIPS/NIST.FIPS.186-4.pdf, accessed on November 17, 2013.

17. Tereshkin, Alexander and Rafal Wojtczuk, "Introducing Ring -3 Rootkits," Black Hat USA, July 29, 2009, Las Vegas, NV.

CHAPTER 4

■ ■ ■

The Engine: Safeguarding Itself before Safeguarding Others

To be a blacksmith, you must be tough yourself.

—Old Chinese Proverb

Alexander Tereshkin and Rafal Wojtczuk, from the Invisible Things Labs of Poland, introduced the concept of "Ring -3 rootkit" at the 2009 Black Hat conference in Las Vegas.[1] They presented an attack against host memory through a rootkit installed on Intel's management engine. Audiences, many hearing about the management engine for the first time, were impressed by the sophisticated attack. People asked: If the embedded system itself is buggy, how could users trust it to safeguard users' valuable assets?

The security and management engine is a small computer, with its own processor,[1] memory, and nonvolatile storage. It has the capability of performing certain tasks that do not require high bandwidth or data throughput. It acts as a helpful assistant to the main operating system, to carry security sensitive operations that are too risky to be executed on the more exposed main processing environment. In addition to security, the engine also enables platform manageability features and capabilities, such as AMT (Active Management Technology; see Chapter 2).

Due to the nature of the engine, in order to perform its assigned tasks, the engine has to communicate with the host operating system and the CPU, and access the host memory. For certain cases, the engine has even more privileges than ring 0 software.

As such, the engine itself becomes a possible security backdoor and an interesting target of hackers. Sophisticated attacks may be able to exploit the engine's vulnerabilities, if they exist, and leverage its wide range of privileges to attack against the host system.

---

[1] In this chapter, *processor* refers to the engine's processing unit. The system's main processor is referred to as a *CPU* (central processing unit).

Therefore, making it strong and robust against attacks is *the* fundamental goal when building the engine. But how is the goal achieved? This chapter reveals the techniques deployed to safeguard the security and management engine from attacks. Note that descriptions of techniques in this chapter are based on the latest engine release for 2014. Security is a progressive effort for the engine. Some of the latest safeguarding features may not be available on older versions of the engine.

The security and management engine is equipped with powerful privileges, which are necessary for the engine to perform defined security functionalities. The embedded engine is not restricted by security measures enforced by the user's operating system, Windows, Linux, or Android. The engine is able to access virtually the entire host memory space with the exception of certain system-reserved regions. The engine can also communicate with the CPU of the platform and instruct the CPU to perform specific operations. For power management, the engine has the capability to instantly power down the entire platform.

However, the security and management engine is not a black box to the host. The engine reports its status at runtime to the host via a register that is read only by ring 0 drivers of the host operating system.

Access to Host Memory

Recall that the HECI (host-embedded communication interface) introduced in Chapter 3 is a communication channel between the engine and the host. However, it suffers from narrow bandwidth—only a small amount of data can be transmitted per transaction. Due to such restrictions, HECI is commonly used for delivering control and management commands, but not bulk data.

Many applications on the engine have the need to exchange large amounts of data between the engine and its software counterparts running on the host operating system. For example, for content protection usage, the engine must first copy encrypted video and audio frames from the host to the embedded memory, and then perform decryption. A movie can have hundreds of thousands of frames, and they must be processed at high speed to ensure smoothness of the playback. Another example: the wireless LAN (WLAN) embedded application must copy network traffic data to the host memory and send it through the WLAN adapter.

To support such uses, the backbone of the engine contains dedicated DMA (direct memory access) hardware that copies data between the host memory and the embedded memory. The engine's firmware kernel is the only entity that manages DMA operations between the host and the engine through the DMA devices. Embedded applications call a kernel API (Application Programming Interface) to request DMA to and from the host memory. Host memory is referenced by its physical address.

Obviously, reading and writing arbitrary host memory is a superior privilege that, if abused, can result in serious security consequences. The attack against the engine presented by Alexander Tereshkin and Rafal Wojtczuk exploited a buffer overflow bug in the BIOS[2] and a critical design flaw in the engine, and managed to turn the engine into a rootkit that can write to arbitrary host memory.

To respond to the attack, in addition to fixing the BIOS' buffer overflow bug and correcting the engine's design flaw, several hardening measures have also been implemented on the engine.

- *Small DMA driver*: Have a small "privileged" component, named "DMA driver," in the firmware kernel manage the DMA devices. The kernel is logically isolated from other firmware modules. The kernel is subject to more stringent code review and validation to ensure it is free of bugs.

- *Restrictive access control*: The DMA access is not granted to all firmware applications. An application must show justified reasons to invoke the DMA engine. The list of applications that are allowed DMA access is predefined and hardcoded in the DMA driver. At runtime, the DMA driver identifies the caller and makes sure it is on the white list, before fulfilling the request.

- *Restrictive memory range control*: For a firmware application that is allowed DMA access, the logic for determining host memory ranges to be accessed must be a separate component that is logically isolated from the rest of the application. Just like the DMA driver, such components are subject to more stringent code review and testing to ensure they are free of bugs.

- *Integrity protection on "borrowed" memory*: The firmware reserves a portion of DRAM (dynamic random-access memory) and uses it as secondary memory at runtime. The "*borrowed*" memory is protected for integrity and confidentiality against attacks from the host.

- *Blocked access to certain system memory*: The engine's DMA devices are not allowed to read or write certain system memory; for example, the memory regions reserved for VT-d[2] (Virtualization Technology for Directed I/O) and SMM[3] (System Management Mode).

Communication with the CPU

Some firmware applications running on the security and management engine coordinate with the CPU to perform certain functionalities that involve both the engine and the CPU.

On SoC (Systems-on-Chip) systems, the data between the embedded engine and the CPU is transmitted over the Intel on-chip system fabric (IOSF). The engine's firmware was designed based on the presumption that IOSF is insecure; that is, third parties may eavesdrop the data travelled on IOSF. Therefore, no secrets or keys may be sent in the clear between the engine and the CPU. Secrets are always encrypted before transmission.

On big-core systems, the data between the engine and the CPU is transmitted over the DMI (Direct Media Interface) link. Similar to the case of IOSF, the DMI link is not trusted.

Like the DMA driver, there is a privileged "IOSF driver" and "DMI driver" in the engine's kernel that centrally manages access to the CPU. Applications that are allowed to access to the CPU are predefined, and such privilege is granted on a "need to have" basis.

Triggering Power Flow

The engine's power management unit is able to trigger power state transitions for the engine and the host. Some applications running on the engine perform power transitions at defined scenarios. For example, anti-theft[ii] must unconditionally shut down the platform without notifying the host or asking for the user's consent when it finds the system in a stolen state.

Another usage model of power transition is when an attack is detected. The engine may instantly shut down the platform to terminate the attack and prevent secrets leakage.

Security Requirements

Setting requirements is the first step for the product architecture and design. For an embedded system such as the security and management engine, security requirements are as important as, or even more important than, functional requirements.

At a high level, the engine is made up of a kernel and multiple applications running on top of the kernel. This section discusses general security requirements that must be followed by the kernel and all applications. In addition to these requirements, individual modules should define their own security requirements. For example, a basic requirement for the content protection application is never to expose its device private key or clear premium content to the host.

General security requirements used by the NIST's Common Vulnerability Scoring System[5] (CVSS) include:

- Confidentiality

- Integrity

- Availability

In addition, there is a basic guideline for realizing security: *Never rely on security through obscurity*.

When designing security hardening features for the engine, it is always assumed that all firmware source code and internal architecture documentation may be obtained by attackers. The engine's security design principle is to harden the product by applying proven cryptography and security primitives, rather than rely on hiding secrets in the code or documents.

Confidentiality

The security and management engine treats code segments and noncode segments differently when applying confidentiality protections. The code segment, also known as a text segment, is read-only and contains executable instructions. Noncode segments include data, heap, bss, stack, and so on. In this chapter, noncode segments are referred to as *data segments* for the sake of simplicity.

[ii]Anti-theft is an Intel technology for protecting data on mobile devices from being stolen. Intel has announced the termination of the service by the end of January 2015.

The engine processes many different secrets of high value in its data segment. Examples include:

- EPID (enhanced private identification) private key (see Chapter 5 for details)

- TPM (trusted platform module) endorsement key (see Chapter 7 for details)

Secret data must be kept private, at runtime and at rest. The engine has dedicated internal memory (static random-access memory or SRAM) as level-2 cache for storing runtime data and processor instructions. The memory is not accessible from the outside world.

As the internal SRAM is expensive and limited, the engine also "borrows" the system DRAM as level-3 cache and uses it to temporarily store memory pages that are not recently accessed by the processor. The DRAM is considered insecure. All data pages swapped to the DRAM, whether they contain secrets or not, are encrypted with a 128-bit AES-CBC key.

To provide confidentiality protection for secrets at rest, during manufacturing, each instance of the embedded engine is installed with unique security fuses. The kernel derives a 128-bit AES key at every boot. The key is used to encrypt nonvolatile data before the data is stored on the SPI (Serial Peripheral Interface) flash.

For applications that interact with the outside world (software programs running on the host, CPU, network, and so on), the communication channels are treated as open channels that malware can read and alter. Therefore, secrets must be protected by appropriate encryption algorithms or protocols, such as TLS[6] (Transport Layer Security). Individual applications are responsible for the protection.

What about the code segment? Due to major performance costs of encrypting code, the security and management engine does not protect confidentiality of its compiled binary image. By design, the firmware binary should not contain secrets, and hence it is not encrypted or obfuscated in any form. Note that lossless compression may be applied to the code.

The firmware binary, in its compression form, is stored on SPI flash in cleartext. At runtime, the code segment is not encrypted when it is paged out to DRAM.

Admittedly, advanced hackers have successfully reverse-engineered and disassembled the engine's firmware binary. However, knowledge of source code is not deemed a harmful threat, because no secrets or keys are ever hardcoded in the code, and the architecture and robustness of the engine does not rely on security through obscurity.

Integrity

The integrity protection makes sure that the target being protected has not been altered unexpectedly due to corruptions or attacks. Several algorithms are common choices for integrity assurance.

- *Digital signature, such as RSA and ECDSA*: The owner of the raw data signs the data with her private key. The signature is then appended to the raw data. Any entity that knows the corresponding public key can verify the owner's signature on the data. Because operations of digital signature are relatively slow, it is usually used for signing small amounts of data.

- *Keyed hash*: The owner of the raw data calculates a digest with a secret key. The digest is then appended to the data. Any entity that knows the secret key can verify the digest of the data.

- *Plain hash*: The owner of the raw data calculates a digest without a key. The digest is then appended to the data. Any entity can verify the digest of the data.

- *CRC (cyclic redundancy check)*: CRC is not a cryptography algorithm but an error-detecting scheme, which is intended to detect accidental changes to data, rather than intentional attacks. A short (for example, 32 bits) parity check value is calculated using the CRC algorithm and attached to the raw data. On retrieval, the same calculation is repeated and the result is compared with the appended parity.

The kernel of the security and management engine provides interfaces for all aforementioned algorithms for applications, to protect their data's integrity.

For an embedded system, integrity of the code segment is also a critical consideration. It is a requirement that the security and management engine's processor and hardware executes only unmodified instructions that were signed by Intel or a designated entity. The design flaw exploited by Alexander Tereshkin and Rafal Wojtczuk was lacking integrity protection for the code segment, allowing injection and execution of malicious code that is not endorsed by Intel.

More details about the approach for protecting the integrity of the engine's code segment are discussed later in this chapter.

Availability

Availability refers to the accessibility of the services provided by the embedded engine and the platform. Note that the availability requirement of the engine applies to the entire system, including the host. In other words, the engine must not cause the host to crash or become unavailable.

The exact requirement of availability varies depending on the attacker's privilege.

- If the attacker has physical access to the platform, then availability is not a consideration. With physical access, one can destroy the system with a hammer.

> ■ **Note** The anti-theft application is an exception—it must be available to function even if the attacker has physical access to the platform.

- If the attacker has local access—that is, he can install malware on the host operating system—then he shall not be able to disable, reset, or turn off the embedded engine.

- If the attacker has network access, then similarly to local access, he shall not be able to disable, reset, or turn off the embedded engine.

The general guideline regarding availability is that malware or virus on the host system or network shall not be able to mount denial of service (DoS) attacks against the engine. This requirement implies that the engine's external (such as HECI and network) interfaces must be robust. They must reject malformed input gracefully and handle large amount of requests properly. Under any circumstances, an external input should not cause the engine to crash. Note that the engine supports multiple usages and features that are running over the kernel. Security protections of one feature must be protected from compromise by users of another service. For example, an AMT administrator shall not be able to influence EPID operations.

The anti-theft application has its unique functionality, and hence, special requirement about availability. The definition of availability for anti-theft is opposite to what availability normally means. By design, it must enforce unconditional shutdown of the platform when the system is detected to be in the stolen state.

In the stolen state, the thief (attacker) possesses the platform and has physical access. In this case, anti-theft must continue to be available and function normally by enforcing the platform shutdown per defined policies. The attacker may physically destroy the platform and render it unusable, which does not violate the availability requirement of anti-theft.

Another important requirement is the availability of the host. Because the embedded engine is able to trigger instant shutdown of the system, malware may exploit firmware vulnerability to shut down the computer locally or remotely, realizing an annoying DoS attack. This is an ungraceful shutdown, and all unsaved user data will be lost. The attack may launch repeatedly right after reboot and essentially turn the computer into a brick.

The Sasser worm of 2004 is a notable example of how costly DoS attacks can be. The author of the worm reverse-engineered a patch released by Microsoft that fixed a buffer overflow bug in Windows 2000 and XP, and discovered the bug. The worm exploited the vulnerability on computers that had not installed the patch. The worm allowed remote execution of code on the host without the knowledge of the user. In the United States alone, the shutdown of computers due to the Sasser worm resulted in a damage of approximately 15 billion US dollars.[7]

Threat Analysis and Mitigation

The threat analysis involves applying the general security requirements—confidentiality, integrity, and availability—to the architecture and design of the security and management engine.

This section reviews most critical threats that are considered during the development of the engine, and the corresponding security measures and mitigation plans implemented by the engine.

Load Integrity

There are two physical locations at which the firmware image of the security and management engine are stored:

- The boot loader is stored in a ROM (read-only memory). Thanks to the nature of ROM, this small portion of code is considered intact. Mitigation against altering or injecting to the code in ROM is out of scope. The ROM is the root of trust of the embedded engine. Note that physical tampering and fault injection attacks are out of scope.

- The rest of the firmware image is stored in SPI flash together with BIOS and other firmware ingredients of the system. Different products support different sets of features and applications. Depending on the product, the size of the engine's firmware ranges from 1.5MB to 5MB.

Although the flash part is supposed to be locked down at manufacturing, in security modeling, it is assumed that the chip can be replaced and the lockdown mechanism can be circumvented by attackers. Therefore, when the boot loader in ROM is loading the image from the flash, it must be confident that the loaded code has not been modified.

The firmware image on flash is signed by Intel. The signing algorithm is 2048-bit RSA with an SHA-256 and a PKCS#1 padding scheme. The signature is not on the entire binary image of a few megabytes, but on a small manifest for the binary.

The manifest contains information for all firmware modules. A module can be the kernel or an application such as anti-theft, content protection, and so on. Among all the information of a module described in the manifest, the most critical, security-wise, is the SHA-256 digest of the module. The SHA-256 digests of all modules are digitally signed.

Here is the flow of building a firmware image:

1. Compile all modules.

2. Calculate SHA-256 digests for all compiled modules, respectively.

3. Fill in the manifest header. The header includes fields such as:

   a. Firmware version number

   b. Firmware security version number

    c.   Size of the header

    d.   Number of modules

4.   Apply compression algorithms to modules, if applicable. There are three options to choose from for a given module:

    a.   No compression

    b.   Huffman compression[8]

    c.   LZMA[9] (Lempel-Ziv–Markov chain) compression

Decompression is performed by the boot loader in ROM during loading. The engine has dedicated hardware logic to support Huffman, so the Huffman decompression is relatively fast. For an LZMA-compressed module, the decompression is carried out by firmware logic located in ROM. As it is a firmware implementation, the decompression is slower than that of the Huffman decompression. However, the adaptive LZMA enjoys a higher compression ratio than Huffman, which uses a hardcoded static dictionary. There is a tradeoff between binary image size and decompression performance at load time. In general, kernel components that impact load time choose no compression or Huffman compression for performance reasons, and applications normally use LZMA. Note that the data after decompression is still not trusted, so an attack on corrupting the decompression results is equivalent to flash corruption.

5.   Fill in all module entries in the manifest. A module entry has information such as:

    a.   Name

    b.   SHA-256 digest

    c.   Location of the compressed binary in the image

    d.   Compression algorithm

    e.   Compressed size

    f.   Uncompressed size

    g.   Entry point address

6.   Fill in the RSA public key (values of the 2048-bit n and the 32-bit e) that will be used by ROM to verify the signature during loading.

7. Sign the manifest using the RSA private key and place the signature in the manifest. The 2048-bit signature is generated on the entire manifest data exception for the RSA public key and the signature itself.

8. Append all modules after the manifest at their proper locations specified in the module entries.

The firmware security version number in the manifest header is an important field for managing firmware update or downgrade for cases where vulnerability is found and patched. Figure 4-1 illustrates the structure of the manifest.

Manifest header	Header type
	Header length
	Firmware version number
	Firmware security number
	Header size
	Number of modules (m in this example)
	Etc.
Crypto block (RSA signature does not cover this part)	RSA public key n
	RSA public key e
	RSA signature
Module #1	Module name
	SHA-256 hash value
	Address
	Compression type
	Compressed size
	Uncompressed size
	Entry point address
	Etc.
Module #2	...
...	...
Module #m	Module name
	SHA-256 hash value
	Address
	Compression type
	Compressed size
	Uncompressed size
	Entry point address
	Etc.

Figure 4-1. Manifest floor plan

During boot, the embedded engine's ROM initializes internal memory and copies the firmware image from the flash. The first thing it loads from the flash is the manifest. Here is the boot loader flow in ROM:

1. Read the RSA public key from the manifest.

2. Calculate the SHA-256 hash on the RSA public key and compare the resulting digest with the hardcoded digest in ROM. If they do not match, then the image is corrupted and will not be loaded.

   When ROM is created, the SHA-256 digest of the RSA public key is hardcoded in the code. The reason for hardcoding the 256-bit hash of the RSA public key, and not the complete 2080-bit RSA public key itself, is to save space in ROM.

3. Verify the digital signature of the manifest using the public key. If the signature verification fails, then the image is corrupted and will not be loaded.

4. Check validity of the manifest header, such as the firmware version.

5. Load the first firmware module by copying its binary from the flash. The first module is usually named "Bringup" or "Kernel". If the module is compressed, then perform decompression.

6. Calculate the SHA-256 digest on the decompressed module and compare with the corresponding hash value in the manifest. Note that at this point, the hash value in the manifest has already been verified by the RSA signature at step 3. If the digests do not match, then the image is corrupted and will not be loaded.

7. Once the first module is loaded, ROM hands the control to the "load manager" component of the first module, which will continue to load other modules listed in the manifest.

8. To load a module, the load manager copies the module's binary from the flash and performs decompression, if required. Then the load manager calculates the SHA-256 digest of the module and compares it with the digest in the manifest. If they do not match, then there are two options:

   • Stop loading this module and continue to load the next module, or

   • Unload all modules that have been loaded and halt the engine's processor

   The option taken depends on whether the module is fault-tolerant or non-fault-tolerant. Failure to load a fault-tolerant module does not break the engine's functionality or impact other modules of the engine. On the other hand, all non-fault-tolerant modules are required for the engine to function properly.

99

The ROM flow for loading the engine's firmware is depicted in Figure 4-2.

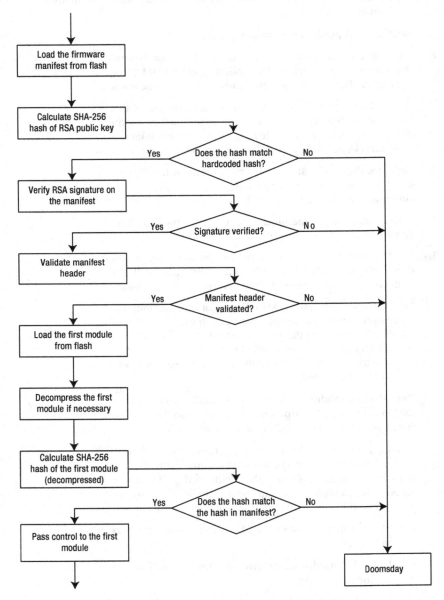

Figure 4-2. *ROM flow for loading firmware*

Note that for a compressed module, its hash in the manifest is calculated on its decompressed binary instead of the compressed binary. This means that the boot loader first decompresses the module, places the decompressed module in the engine's internal memory, and then verifies its integrity.

Does something seem suspicious? Yes. Unverified compressed binary is being placed in memory, at least temporarily. The binary is then decompressed to the internal memory. If the compressed fault-tolerant module is altered by an attacker, then it could overflow the buffer allocated for the decompressed module and overwrite other regions of the internal memory, making a code-inject attack possible. So hashing a decompressed module is arguably a poor security design practice and prone to vulnerabilities. To address the issue, the implementation must make sure that the buffer allocated for decompressed data is not overrun by the decompression algorithm.

A better design from the security perspective would be to hash the compressed form of the module. However, there is a major drawback of this option: memory consumption. The entire compressed module must be copied into internal memory before the decompression begins, and memory must be reserved for both the compressed module and the decompressed module.

On the other hand, if the hash is for the decompressed module, then there is no need to copy the compressed module into memory. The boot loader simply reads from the flash the compressed module in fixed-size chunks, and then performs decompression for the chunks as they come in. The decompressed module in the internal memory is then verified against the hash value specified in the manifest.

When architecting a computer system, there are two conflicting factors to consider, one being performance and resource consumption, and the other being security. There is almost always a tradeoff between the two sides. For systems where resources are not a major concern, it is usually better to be safe than sorry and give more weight on security. For embedded systems, however, due to the limited computing resources available, the decision is sometimes more difficult to make. It requires designers to dive deep into the threat analysis and risk assessment.

Memory Integrity

For the security and management engine, the level-1 cache is inside the processor. The engine has dedicated internal memory that serves as the level-2 cache. The capacity of the level-2 cache varies, depending on the product, and ranges from 256KB to 1MB. In the security modeling, the level-1 and level-2 cache memory is considered immune from external attacks. No encryption or integrity protection is applied.

But the embedded engine requires more runtime memory to run its applications. A small region of the system's DRAM is "borrowed" by the engine and used for the purpose of paging. The size of the borrowed memory ranges from 4MB to 32MB, depending on the product.

The embedded engine uses the borrowed DRAM for temporary volatile storage only. The engine's processor cannot directly reference addresses in DRAM, execute code from DRAM, or modify data in DRAM. When a page in DRAM needs to be accessed by the processor, the engine's paging unit has to first bring it into the internal memory.

During boot, the BIOS reserves a small portion of DRAM and notifies the security and management engine of its address and size. The BIOS hides this portion of DRAM from the operating system running on the host. From then on, the engine has exclusive control and access to this region. The host is not supposed to address, reference, or access the region.

However, hackers have shown that breaking into the reserved DRAM region is not impossible. The attack presented by Alexander Tereshkin and Rafal Wojtczuk successfully injects code into the reserved region. The injected code is later paged in by the engine and executed. This attack was possible because on Bearlake MCH (Memory Controller Hub), the management engine lacks integrity protection for the reserved region of DRAM.

How is the problem tackled in later generations of the security and management engine? Checksum is introduced for paging:

1. Before moving a page from the internal memory to the reserved DRAM region, calculate a checksum of the page and store the checksum in the internal memory.

2. The content of the page is not supposed to change while it is out in the DRAM.

3. After moving a page from the reserved DRAM region to the internal memory, calculate the checksum of the page again and compare with the stored value calculated before. If the two values do not match, then the page has been altered. Although this is possibly due to a memory corruption, for defensive security design, the security and management engine treats it as an attack and triggers an instant shutdown of the platform, which includes the engine itself and the host.

When looking for the right checksum algorithm, several conditions were considered:

-   The algorithm must be extremely simple and fast. Since paging is a very frequent runtime operation, the speed of paging plays a significant role in the engine's performance. Latency of paging must be minimized, as it negatively impacts the user's experience.

-   The checksum must be small in size, because the internal memory space is limited and expensive. The more internal space is assigned to checksum storage, the less space is available for running programs.

-   The algorithm must be able to detect alteration of pages in DRAM with a high level of confidence.

Digital signature is ruled out immediately, as it is too slow to meet the performance and storage requirements outlined.

Next candidates are hash and HMAC. Velocity-wise, they are much faster to calculate than digital signature schemes. Also, the security and management has a hardware cryptography engine for expediting hash and HMAC. Security-wise, they are NIST-approved algorithms that offer proven strength of integrity assurance. But they are still not optimal because of two reasons:

- The size of the digest is too large to fit in the internal memory. If the reserved region is 16MB and page size is 4KB, then there are 4096 entries. Using SHA-1, the size of internal memory required for storing all digests is as much as 80KB. Additionally, as will be discussed later in this section, there is other metadata that must be stored in the internal memory for a page entry.

- The speed of calculation is not fast enough to support runtime applications that require high throughput, such as AMT.

Now the only candidate is the CRC algorithm. It is simple and fast to calculate. The checksum is only 32 bits long. All that makes it a good choice from the performance perspective. What about security?

CRC is an error-detecting code. It does not use a key and it is not cryptographically strong. Imagine a naïve attack scenario: the hacker reads a page from the reserved DRAM region and calculates its CRC checksum. He then modifies the page content such that the checksum remains unchanged. For a 4KB page and 32-bit checksum, finding different pages with the same checksum is rather trivial.

So, it seems none of the standard integrity protection algorithms has characteristics to satisfy all requirements of the security and management engine. To address the problem, Intel's cryptographers have designed a proprietary algorithm specifically for paging integrity. The algorithm is based on binary polynomial operations. The input includes:

- 4KB or 1KB of raw page data

- 256-byte secret key

The output is a 32-bit integrity check value (ICV), which must be kept secret.

During the first time the security and management engine boots and before paging is enabled, the engine generates a 256-byte random number and writes it to the registers of the ICV generation hardware logic. The engine also stores the random number on flash as a secret blob. This number is used as the secret key input to the ICV algorithm.

During the following boots, the key is retrieved from the flash and reused. Although regenerating a new key randomly at every boot is apparently more secure, it is experimentally shown that generating 256 bytes of random data from the engine's hardware RNG is slower than reading a blob from the flash. For most computing systems, the boot time is a critical performance benchmark.

However, there is one case that the ICV key will be regenerated. Before moving a page out of the internal memory, the paging engine in the kernel calculates the page's ICV value and saves the resultant ICV in a preallocated region of the internal memory. The ICV calculation is performed by dedicated hardware logic. Later, when bringing a page into the internal memory, the same calculation is repeated and the result compared with the saved value.

What if the comparison fails? When the security and management engine feels that "something is wrong," several different actions can be considered as response. The firmware designers must decide what actions to take when something is wrong. The questions to ask are as follows:

- Is the error more likely a result of a firmware or hardware bug, or is the error more likely due to an active attack?

- Is it possible to recover from the error without leakage of secrets and assets?

Because of its criticality, all firmware and hardware components involved in the paging operation are reviewed and validated thoroughly. Furthermore, DRAM failure is very rare thanks to improved error-correcting and other technologies deployed in modern DRAM devices. Given these facts, when an ICV check failure occurs, the engine has very high confidence that it is due to an attack that is attempting to change the page being brought in from the DRAM. The most effective response to terminate the attack and prevent loss of assets is to shut down the platform immediately and ungracefully.

Before shutting down the platform, the engine deletes the blob that stores the ICV key from the flash. At the next boot, the engine will generate and use a new key.

Admittedly, the algorithm is not as strong as a standard hash, but it is good enough to protect the engine. With this proprietary algorithm, page alternation or replacement attacks become very difficult to mount.

As the ICV is a 32-bit secret, and the key is also secret, an attempt at random page alternation has a success probability of only 1 in 2^{32}. A random attempt will fail almost definitely, and as a result, the platform is rebooted and a new ICV key is utilized. This means that the attacker cannot learn from failures, and his prior failed attempts do not increase the chance of future success. All attempts have a success probability of 1 in 2^{32}, no matter if it is the first or the one thousandth attempt.

Another important design to make the attack even harder is that the engine keeps the ICV secretly. Furthermore, a platform reboot following a failed attempt takes at least a few seconds to complete, which substantially slows down automation. As the ICV of a page is unknown, hackers cannot simply perform the page alternation attempts "offline" without actually running the engine.

As a result, altering a page and not being detected by the embedded engine is practically impossible.

Checksums must be kept secret. A straightforward design is to keep the checksums for all pages in the internal memory. This method consumes valuable memory space. To save memory space, the security and management engine also swaps pages that store checksums to reserved DRAM region. The checksums for such pages are always stored in the internal memory.

When a page fault happens, the paging engine looks for the checksum of the page in the internal memory. If the checksum is not found, that means the checksum is out in the DRAM also. In this case, the paging engine brings the checksum page into memory first, and then brings the actual page of the page fault into memory.

For this design, handling a page fault may require two pages being swapped into memory, which seemingly will degrade performance. But the fact is, the opposite occurs. Experiments show that with comprehensive victim (a page that is selected to be swapped out to DRAM) selection heuristics, this design actually improves performance because there are fewer checksums occupying memory, and hence more memory is available as cache.

Memory Encryption

Besides integrity, confidentiality is also a requirement for data pages while they reside in the reserved DRAM region. A page is encrypted before being moved out to the DRAM. The ICV is calculated on the encrypted page. Pages that contain only code segments require protection for integrity but not confidentiality.

The algorithm used for encrypting data pages is 128-bit AES with CBC mode. During boot, the AES key for encrypting pages is derived from security fuses. The key is unique per part, as the fuses are unique. The key is stored in the internal memory and never paged out to DRAM.

Since the IV (initialization vector) for CBC mode must be unpredictable, the IV for encrypting a page is randomly generated every time the page is about to be moved to DRAM. The IV is stored together with the ICV.

Task Isolation

An *embedded system* is a computer system designed to realize dedicated and specific functions with computing constraints. The system includes hardware and firmware that runs on the hardware.

Embedded systems usually suffer from resource constraints (limited computing horsepower, memory, storage space, and so forth). An embedded system with a single-threaded or a multithreaded real-time operating system (RTOS) can run multiple processes. On the security and management engine, process is also referred to as *task*.

In an embedded system that runs multiple processes (tasks) without isolation, successful attack or compromise against one or more applications may result in the attacker gaining execution privilege and secrets of the peer applications. This is a critical security problem for embedded systems.

Process isolation as a security measure is widely supported by modern operating systems such as Windows, Linux, and Android. Is the same concept applicable to embedded systems? Intel's security and management engine resolves the problem by applying innovative task isolation techniques. The task isolation is the most involved and comprehensive security measure on the engine. This section covers the details of the technique.

Deploying task isolation on the engine has been an evolving effort. There was no task isolation for the first generation of the engine, as the size of the firmware was relatively small at that time, and all kernel and applications were developed in-house by Intel. As the number of applications running on the engine increased, isolation became a must-have security measure.

As the first step, the engine's firmware was split into two tasks—privileged and nonprivileged:

- The privileged task, also known as the *kernel*, consists of modules that manage critical system resources and handle secrets. They include the boot loader, kernel, hardware drivers, power flow management, EPID manager (see Chapter 5 for details), and so on.

- The nonprivileged task consists of the remainder of the firmware modules; for example, applications like AMT and anti-theft.

The logical separation between privileged and nonprivileged tasks is enforced by the privileged task and hardware. The hardware backbone of the engine supports two modes of operation: privileged mode and nonprivileged mode. Different access rights to hardware devices and other system resources are granted based on the mode in which the firmware is actively running.

105

In newer versions of the security and management engine, the number of embedded applications keeps growing. The number exceeds ten on the engine shipped with big core processor in 2013 (codename Haswell). With this many applications, the size of the engine's nonprivileged modules becomes considerably large. Consequently, risk of security bugs and vulnerabilities rises.

How to realize task isolation for multiple tasks in a hardware environment that supports only privileged and nonprivileged tasks? The trick is to treat and protect all nonprivileged tasks that are not actively running as privileged tasks, so that the running nonprivileged task cannot compromise them.

Asset Protection

The task isolation technique implemented by the engine makes sure that bugs in one task are restricted to its own task and do not affect any other tasks. In other words, even if the bug is exploited by attackers, other tasks are immune and safe.

The assets of a task to be protected from other tasks include but are not limited to the following:

- Memory
- Nonvolatile storage
- Hardware devices
- Synchronization objects: thread, semaphore, mutex, queues, and so forth

An asset belongs to one and only one task during its lifetime. The owner is normally the creator of the asset. The ownership cannot be transferred to another task.

The central governing component, kernel, manages all system resources. It is responsible for implementing and enforcing task isolation for nonprivileged modules. The kernel is a hybrid component of firmware and hardware. The interface of the kernel is minimized to reduce the attack surface.

The kernel provides critical and system level services to nonprivileged components. These services include: cryptography algorithms, memory management, nonvolatile storage, DMA, power management, and so on. For protected assets owned by individual tasks, the kernel exposes API for the tasks to call and manipulate.

For example, nonvolatile secrets stored on flash are assets of their owning tasks. The kernel has APIs for creating, writing, reading, and deleting the data. Another example: semaphore is an asset of its owning task. The kernel has APIs to create, get, put, and delete a semaphore.

Figure 4-3 demonstrates the kernel's flow of handling a call from a nonprivileged task for asset manipulation. A few important facts to note:

- The kernel is threadless and all kernel API functions run in the caller's thread.
- A thread is always associated with one and only one task.
- Metadata of threads and other assets for all tasks is stored in the privileged memory and cannot be modified by nonprivileged tasks. The metadata of an asset includes the ID of the owning task of this asset.

106

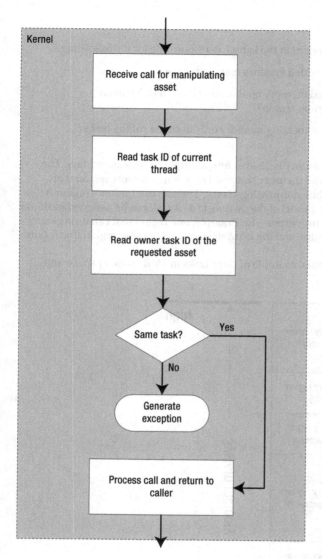

Figure 4-3. *Asset (nonvolatile data, synchronization objects, and so on) manipulation control flow*

As you can see in Figure 4-3, the kernel makes sure that the asset being accessed belongs to the same task as the caller's thread—that is, an application is not allowed to access another task's assets through kernel APIs. Such a request is considered an attack and will trigger exception. If a task has legitimate reasons to access assets of another task, then it must do so through the inter-task call mechanism.

Memory Manager

The memory manager, a component in the kernel, is responsible for the following:

- Managing the embedded system's memory space

- Creating a dedicated memory pool for each task (a task can only access its own memory region)

- For malloc() calls, allocating memory only from the calling task's memory region

The embedded engine's memory is divided into multiple regions as overlays. The kernel has read/write access to all memory regions. There is no memory region that can be accessed by more than one nonprivileged task. The size of a memory region is determined by the actual usage model of the owning task. A task can be assigned multiple memory regions with different properties—for example, one region that can be accessed by both the processor of the engine and the DMA devices, and another region that is only accessible by DMA.

Figure 4-4 shows a conceptual example of three tasks in 1MB memory space and their overlays.

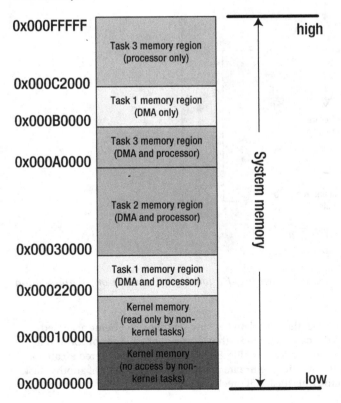

Figure 4-4. Memory overlay

Thread Manager

The single-threaded or multithreaded thread manager is also a component in the kernel. It manages threads and schedules threads to run.

One and only one thread is actively running at any moment. A thread is associated with one and only one task throughout the lifetime of the thread.

At runtime, the system determines whether requested assets/resources can be accessed based on the task of the currently running thread. At thread switch,[iii] the RTOS examines the owner tasks of the current thread and the next thread, respectively. If the two threads are owned by different tasks, then the RTOS programs the MPR (memory protection range) control register accordingly to predefined values to reflect the restriction applied to the next thread. Figure 4-5 illustrates the flow.

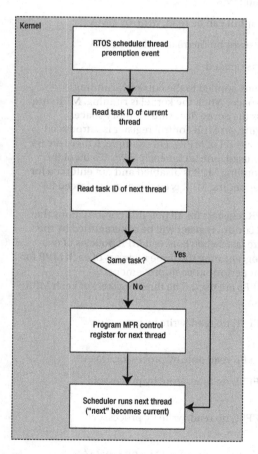

Figure 4-5. *Thread switch flow*

[iii]The scheduler decides to preempt the currently running thread with another thread.

Memory Protection Control

The security and management engine's hardware backbone supports a set of MPRs. The number of MPRs implemented in a specific product depends on the number of nonprivileged tasks. Each MPR consists of a set of three registers:

- Start address

- End address

- Access restriction (assumes one of the following values)

  - No read/write by processor or DMA

  - Read only by processor and DMA

  - No read/write by processor but can be read/write by DMA

  - Can be read/write by processor but no read/write by DMA

  - Other access restrictions as needed

The MPRs enforce the access restrictions applied to the currently running nonprivileged task for the entire memory space. When the kernel is running, MPRs are not enforced because the kernel can access the entire firmware memory space.

On the security and management engine, an MPR control register is introduced for rapidly enabling and disabling an arbitrary set of MPRs. For example, if there are 64 MPRs, then a 64-bit MPR control register is used, one bit for each MPR. If a bit of the MPR control register is 0, then the corresponding MPR is disabled and not enforced for memory access; if a bit is 1, then the corresponding MPR is enabled and enforced for memory access.

During boot, the kernel programs MPR registers for all possible combinations that may be encountered at runtime. The MPR control register will be programmed by the RTOS at runtime upon task switch to realize fast switch between MPR policies of two tasks. This trick eliminates the need for programming the three registers of each MPR for all MPRs at runtime, resulting in significant performance improvements.

For the example, in Table 4-1, nine MPRs are used. The three registers of each MPR are programmed by RTOS, at boot, as follows:

- *MPR#1:* {0x00000000, 0x0000FFFF, no read/write by processor/ DMA}

- *MPR#2:* {0x00010000, 0x00021FFF, read only by processor/DMA}

- *MPR#3:* {0x00022000, 0x0002FFFF, no read/write by processor/ DMA}

- *MPR#4:* {0x00030000, 0x0009FFFF, no read/write by processor/ DMA}

- *MPR#5:* {0x000A0000, 0x000AFFFF, no read/write by processor/ DMA}

- *MPR#6:* {0x000B0000, 0x000C1FFF, no read/write by processor/ DMA}

110

- *MPR#7:* {0x000B0000, 0x000C1FFF, no read/write by processor; RW by DMA}

- *MPR#8:* {0x000C2000, 0x000FFFFF, no read/write by processor/ DMA}

- *MPR#9:* {0x000C2000, 0x000FFFFF, read/write by processor; no read/write by DMA}

Table 4-1. *Active Task and MPR Control Setting*

Active task	MPR control register
kernel task	Don't care
Task 1	110110110
Task 2	111011010
Task 3	111101001

At runtime, the MPR register values do not change; the MPR control register is programmed to reflect memory enforcements. The actively running task and the corresponding MPR control register value (the leftmost bit represents MPR#1, and the rightmost bit represents MPR#9) are shown in Table 4-1.

When the privileged kernel is running, MPRs are not enforced.

When task 1 is running, MPR#1: {0x00000000, 0x0000FFFF, no read/write by processor/DMA} is enabled. According to Figure 4-4, memory range from 0x00000000 to 0x0000FFFF belongs to the kernel. Task 1 shall not access this range. This is why the memory access restrictions defined by MPR#1 are enabled and enforced when task 1 is active.

Similarly, MPR#5: {0x000A0000, 0x000AFFFF, no read/write by processor/DMA} is also enabled when task 1 is running. This is because the range of {0x000A0000, 0x000AFFFF} belongs to task 3, and task 1 shall not access it. Likewise, when task 1 is running, MPR#2, MPR#4, MPR#7, and MPR#8 are enforced.

However, memory access restrictions defined by MPR#3: {0x00022000, 0x0002FFFF, no read/write by processor/DMA} are disabled, because this range is owned by task 1, the running task.

Loader

The loader is responsible for loading a task to the memory region allocated by the memory manger.

Figure 4-6 shows the boot flow. The loader in the kernel loads the tasks one after another to their memory regions and initializes the tasks. The main operation that a task performs at start is to create its worker threads by calling the kernel's thread creation function. All threads created are tagged with the owning application's task ID, and it does not change for the lifetime of the thread.

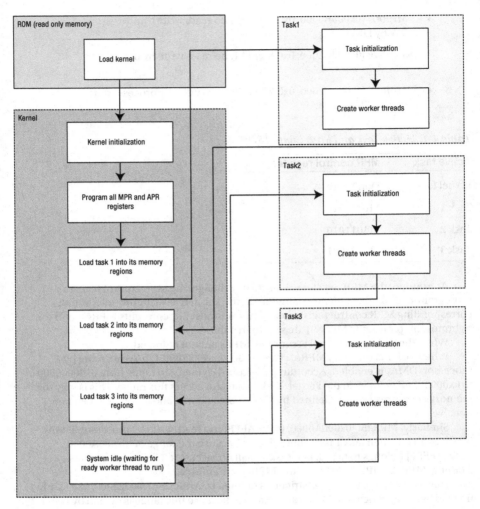

Figure 4-6. *Boot flow*

Inter-Task Call Management

On the security and management engine, a task can provide services to one or more other tasks through an indirect calling mechanism implemented by the kernel. For example, if a task needs to access assets (such as nonvolatile data) of another task, it can do so via the inter-task call mechanism.

Due to memory protection and isolation, direct calling between two tasks is a violation of task isolation and explicitly prohibited. When a task (say, task 1) needs to consume services offered by another task (say, task 2), task 1 invokes kernel's inter-task call API and specifies the function of task 2 to be called. The kernel performs the following steps for an inter-task call.

1. Copy input parameters from task 1's memory to task 2's memory.

2. Call task 2 on behalf of task 1. The kernel will notify task 2 that the caller is task 1. Task 2 can decide whether to serve task 1 or reject the call.

3. Copy the output from task 2's memory back to task 1's memory.

4. Conclude the call.

The inter-task call is a costly operation because the kernel has to copy input and output data between the caller task and the callee task. The design guideline is to minimize the use of inter-task calls and avoid calling other tasks in performance-critical flows.

In Figure 4-7, the dotted line shows that task 1 is calling task 2 through the kernel. Note that all tasks directly consume the kernel and only the kernel. Tasks cannot consume each other directly.

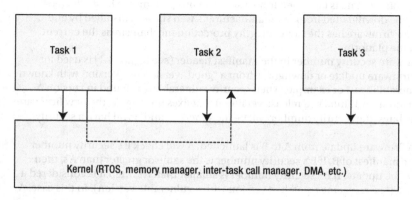

Figure 4-7. Inter-task call

Exception Handler

When the kernel firmware or hardware detects access violation, an attack is assumed to be actively undergoing. All threads belonging to the violating task shall be terminated immediately—that is, the task is stopped from running until the next power cycle.

Alternatively, a more aggressive reaction upon access violation is to reset the entire embedded system. This is the approach implemented by the security and management engine.

Nonprivileged Tasks

A nonprivileged task is an embedded application that realizes a specific set of functionalities—for example, playing back a movie.

A nonprivileged task may consume services provided by the kernel and other nonprivileged tasks. A nonprivileged task may also invoke dedicated hardware components. Multiple tasks may exist on an embedded system.

A nonprivileged task is banned from directly accessing other tasks' assets. Such access must be accomplished through the inter-task call mechanism. Access violation results in termination of the violating task or resetting the embedded system.

Firmware Update and Downgrade

The security and management engine supports firmware update and downgrade; that is, replacing the firmware that is currently installed on the platform with another version of the firmware. The firmware update replaces an older version of firmware with a newer version. It is used by Intel to deliver additional features or fix functional or security bugs to the end users. If a newer version of firmware fails to work on a platform, most commonly due to device compliance issues, then the firmware downgrade is used to rollback to an older version of firmware that works on the platform.

The firmware update is launched from a software program on the host. The new firmware can be downloaded from the manufacturer's web site and installed by end users. The new firmware has the same integrity protection mechanism as the current firmware on the platform.

The firmware security number in the manifest header (see Figure 4-1) is used for preventing firmware update or downgrade from a "good" version to a version with known security vulnerabilities. For example, when security vulnerability is found in version A with security number 1, Intel will release version B that fixes the bug. As the new firmware fixes security bugs, the security number will be incremented and B will have a security number of 2.

When a firmware update from A to B is launched, A will check B's security number as it loads the manifest of B. If B's security number is the same or greater than A's, then proceed with the update. If B's security number is smaller than A's, then it is considered a rollback attack (i.e., replacing a patched version with a vulnerable version). In this case, A immediately aborts the firmware update/downgrade flow.

Published Attacks

Ever since its birth in 2006, the management engine has been the target of many hackers and attackers in the computer security community. For white-hat hackers, trying to find and exploit bugs in the engine is an interesting academic research and challenge. For black-hat attackers, successful attacks could generate monetary profit.

To date, the most famous attack against the engine was the one mentioned at the beginning of this chapter: "Introducing Ring -3 Rootkits," published by Alexander Tereshkin and Rafal Wojtczuk of the Invisible Things Labs, at the Black Hat conference in 2009.

"Introducing Ring -3 Rootkits"

There are several components of the attack.

1. Perform literature research and find out the model of the processor used by the engine.

2. Circumvent the flash lock and dump the engine's firmware binary from the flash.

3. Use IDA disassembler[10] to disassemble and reverse-engineer the firmware code.

4. Rollback the BIOS to a version with a known bug that does not lock down memory remapping registers. This vulnerable release of BIOS allows the attack to redirect the engine's reserved DRAM region to an arbitrary location in DRAM. (The BIOS vulnerability was also found by Rafal Wojtczuk and Alexander Tereshkin and published at the Black Hat conference in 2009.)

5. Exploit the BIOS bug and redirect the reserved region to a region that can be written by attack.

6. Debug the engine's firmware and hook an application that writes data to the host memory via DMA.

7. Inject rootkit to the DRAM region. The rootkit writes to host memory through DMA.

It should be pointed out that the attack is only possible on Bearlake MCH, released in 2007. The management engine on Bearlake MCH lacks integrity protection on the reserved region of the DRAM. This is one of the vulnerabilities exploited by the attack. Intel implemented the ICV check mechanism for the reserved DRAM region in the management engine released in 2008.

The attack takes advantage of two vulnerabilities. The other one is a buffer overflow in an older version of BIOS. Although the BIOS was patched soon after the issue was reported, BIOS downgrade was not disallowed. The lesson shows how firmware rollback prevention and integrity protection are vital to computer security.

However, the attack has some limitations:

1. It must hook an application that uses DMA. The researchers did not find a way to have the rootkit program DMA directly.

2. There is no way to perform DMA without redirecting memory remapping for BIOS. The remapping clears upon reboot.

3. Not all host memory is open to the embedded engine. For example, as mentioned earlier in this chapter, the VT-d and SMM memory cannot be accessed through the embedded engine's DMA.

References

1. Tereshkin, Alexander, and Rafal Wojtczuk, "Introducing Ring -3 Rootkits," Black Hat USA, July 29, 2009, Las Vegas, NV.

2. Wojtczuk, Rafal, and Alexander Tereshkin, "Attacking Intel® BIOS," Black Hat USA, July 29, 2009, Las Vegas, NV.

3. Intel Virtualization Technology, http://www.intel.com/content/www/us/en/virtualization/virtualization-technology/hardware-assist-virtualization-technology.html, accessed on January 30, 2014.

4. Intel, "EFI System Management Mode Core Interface Spec (SMM CIS)," http://www.intel.com/content/www/us/en/architecture-and-technology/unified-extensible-firmware-interface/efi-smm-cis-v091.html, accessed on March 3, 2014.

5. National Institute of Standards and Technology, Common Vulnerability Scoring System (CVSS), http://nvd.nist.gov/cvss.cfm, accessed on December 12, 2013.

6. Request for comments 5246, "The Transport Layer Security (TLS) Protocol, Version 1.2," http://tools.ietf.org/html/rfc5246, access on December 12, 2013.

7. Brown, Rhonda, and Jackie Davenport, "Forensic Science: Advanced Investigations," Case Studies for Sasser Worm, Cengage Learning, 2012, pp. 414.

8. Huffman, D. A., "A Method for the Construction of Minimum-Redundancy Codes," Proceedings of the I.R.E., September 1952, pp. 1098–1102.

9. Pavlov, Igor, LZMA Software Development Kit, http://7-zip.org/sdk.html, accessed on December 12, 2013.

10. Hex-Rays, IDA disassembler, https://www.hex-rays.com/products/ida/, accessed on December 12, 2013.

■ ■ ■

Privacy at the Next Level: Intel's Enhanced Privacy Identification (EPID) Technology

The fantastic advances in the field of electronic communication constitute a greater danger to the privacy of the individual.

—Earl Warren, 14th Chief Justice of the United States

You've probably clicked the "I agree" button hundreds of times on privacy policy statements of service providers' web sites, from Gmail to Netflix, from Amazon to your favorite game apps. Most people simply want to enjoy the service or access contents as soon as possible, and thus do not bother to read through the privacy policy from beginning to end before giving consent. Many times, people are willing to share their private information with the service providing site/server, and they rely on the vendors' good faith to protect their privacy and not share with third parties.

To build the infrastructure for protecting the privacy of Intel's consumers, Intel invented the enhanced privacy identification (EPID) technology, which is implemented by the security and management engine on big core and systems-on-chip platforms for servers, desktops, laptops, tablets, and smartphones.

Redefining Privacy for the Mobile Age

Service providers normally promise some level of protection in their privacy policy agreements, such as not selling or renting out your personal information (name, gender, date of birth, mailing address, e-mail address, and so forth). At the same time, in exchange for the free or paid services, consumers likely have to allow service providers to archive your activities and push customized marketing correspondence to your mailbox. It may be useful information to you, or, most of the time, may be treated as spam. Notice that privacy policies and options provided to users are often subject to change. New options that have defaults as not private may be introduced. This puts even the paranoid users at a loss by having to keep up with each new feature update. In addition, it is not surprising that the Google Ads on the websites you browse are promoting products you recently showed interest in. Service providers have good incentives to make the most out of your private information. Monetization of user data is big business and a significant revenue source for many providers, especially social networking websites and apps.

The mobile computing age brings with it increasing risks to users' privacy. There are hundreds of thousands of mobile apps out there, and counting. If you are paying attention to the list of privileges that an app asks for before installation, you will find many require access to data stored on your device, such as personal information, your phone book, call history, text messages, and so forth. A paranoid user may wonder, "Hmm, why does this music app need to access my phone book?" and exit installation. But many do not bother to question. Hence, privacy is at risk.

What is the ultimate and true privacy? The nuanced answer depends on an individual's expectation, which varies based on factors such as type of data, social context, culture, and so on.

A simple answer, however, is *anonymity*. In a perfect world of anonymity, there is no identification. Everyone appears identical. In terms of computer privacy, anonymity can be realized in two ways: passively and actively.

Passive Anonymity

Imagine that an online movie service does not save the list of the contents you have watched, because you do not want others to know what kinds of movies you favor; imagine that a prescription medicine reseller does not record the history of your purchases, because you don't want to expose your health information. This is *passive* anonymity. The realization of such anonymity completely or partially relies on the attitude of the parties you are dealing with. If the movie service wants, it can save the list of titles you have streamed, and even details such as where in the titles you paused or fast-forwarded. Similarly, an online medicine vendor could derive, without much difficulty, what diseases you are suffering by examining the prescriptions you ordered.

One may argue that what types of movies a person likes is not something really secretive. However, no one knows whether such data, seemingly harmless today, could be used against you in the future. In information security, the principle of *least privilege* requires that an entity must be able to access only the information and resources that are necessary for its legitimate purpose. When talking about privacy, least privilege of the service provider is always the best interest to consumers.

An important point in the privacy discussion is the user's expectation, which varies by context. For example, an end user may be okay with sharing the list of movies he has watched with his personal friends on social networks, but not with his work colleagues. Sometimes the user may want to watch some movies privately without anyone else knowing.

Practically, end users cannot rely on the service providers' good faith to protect their privacy. The bottom line is that users' privacy is not in the providers' interest—and may even be against their interest. And even the definition of "privacy" is often up to the providers' discretion. You may choose to believe that some big names are not evil, but you simply cannot trust everyone. The privacy commitment had better be enforced by technology, and not human beings. This is *active* anonymity.

> ■ **Note** Passive anonymity relies on human beings for enforcement.

Active Anonymity

In contrast to passive anonymity, active anonymity does not depend on human beings for enforcement. The anonymity is natively built in the technology.

> ■ **Note** Active anonymity relies on technology for enforcement.

There are two fundamental and functional problems to resolve by an active anonymous authentication technology:

- *Authentication*: The user must prove to the service provider that the user is eligible to receive the service. Eligibility is established by showing that the user is a member of a group that is granted access to the specific service. There are various different criteria for becoming a member of the group—for example, possessing a specific hardware device or paying a service fee. The criteria of becoming a group member are defined by the service provider.

- *Anonymity*: The service provider must not be able to trace the user. The key words here are *not be able to* rather than *do not*. In other words, even if the service provider wants to identify a user, it should not be possible to. The user only has to show that he/she belongs to the group of eligible users, without revealing identity. Since all users in the group are allowed to receive the service, this user's request should be fulfilled after being authenticated. The technology must be designed to disable the service provider from possibly distinguishing any individual users from any other users in the same group. Furthermore, the technology must provide an option to the user so that the service provider cannot tell whether or not two or more service requests were originated from the same user.

How to achieve these two goals of anonymous authentication? A straightforward approach is to have all users that belong to the same group share the same credential for authentication. It is a feasible solution, and is in fact being used by many mobile products in the market today. But is it good enough?

The problems of this credential-sharing design are as obvious as its simplicity. Once any device is successfully compromised by attackers, and credentials are leaked, the security of the entire authentication system of the service provider is broken, and all devices with the same credential are impacted. This is a typical break-once-run-everywhere (BORE) scenario. Dealing with the aftermath is very expensive and cumbersome. To mitigate BORE, besides the two basic goals of authentication and anonymity, there is a third desired characteristic:

- *Revocation:* The technology must provide the means to revoke a select member of a group or the entire group in order to terminate services for only the select user or group without impacting nonrevoked members and groups. The reasons for revocation are determined by the providers. It could be a user's violation of the service agreement or loss or compromise of credential.

Processor Serial Number

Flashing back to 1999, Intel's Pentium III processor introduced a new feature, known as the processor serial number or PSN. The serial number is a 64-bit string programmed to processor hardware during the manufacturing process. The serial number of a processor is unique to the processor. It cannot be changed or erased during the lifetime of the processor. When the read permission is turned on, software can retrieve the PSN value by simply issuing a CPUID instruction. Note that the CPUID instruction returns other information, such as processor type and the presence of processor features, in addition to the PSN.

The read permission of the PSN can be enabled or disabled through one of two methods, as described next. The goal of restricting read permission is to make sure that the owner of the platform is aware when the PSN is available to be retrieved and by whom:

- *BIOS:* The manufacturer of the platform should provide users with an option in the BIOS configuration for disabling all software programs and websites to read PSN. Some BIOSes use *enabled* as the default value. This is a more advanced approach, because not all users know how to change BIOS configurations.

- *Control utility:* Intel released a Windows software program that lets end users configure the list of software programs and websites that are allowed to read PSN. The utility is a service that launches when Windows is booting. It is a convenient way for users of all skill levels to manage the exposure of the PSN.

Software or websites reading the PSN without the user's consent pose privacy concerns. Opponents of the PSN expressed concerns about the design of the control mechanism. For example, some BIOSes may not offer an option for users to disable the PSN. Even if such an option is offered, if it is set to *on* by default, then some consumers may not know how to enter BIOS and change the configuration. Fortunately, besides using BIOS, a user can also turn off the PSN in Intel's PSN control utility. However, the PSN may be read by software before the control utility is loaded and functional. Rogue software services that load before the control utility may read the PSN during the Windows boot process and save the value for later use, essentially bypassing the enforcement of the control utility. Furthermore, the control utility is software and may be hacked. Relying on software to protect hardware information that has implications on privacy is not a good security practice.

So why was the PSN introduced in the first place? A number of applications may benefit from the PSN. Here are some examples:

- *Secure authentication*: Take website login, for example. Traditionally, a bank's website only asks for the customer's username and password as login credentials. This is called *one-factor authentication*, where only one factor, namely, "something you know," is required. If the password is acquired by an attacker, then he can successfully log in from his computer. To enhance the authentication security, the PSN can serve as another authentication factor, that is, "something you have." To realize the two-factor authentication, the website checks the PSN of the computer in addition to the username and password. With the PSN enforcement, the attacker will not be able to log in from his computer even if he has stolen the victim's password.

- *Software piracy mitigation*: During installation, software may save the PSN of the platform. At runtime, the software checks the PSN against the stored value and functions only if they match.

- *Corporate computer management*: The PSN makes the resource management tasks of corporates' information technology (IT) departments easier. Replacing the processor on a computer is a much less frequent event than replacing other hardware and software components. Therefore, the constant PSN value allows the IT administrators to reliably identify individual platforms in the corporate network. The status of a platform can be monitored and tied to its processor PSN. Changes to the platform can be easily identified and managed.

Note that in the usages of secure authentication and software theft mitigation, the PSN protection may cause inconvenience to legitimate users. For example, if the user upgrades his processor, then he must re-register the new processor with all software vendors and websites that leverage the PSN, which could be cumbersome.

Admittedly, the PSN mechanism has its functional problems. For example, there is no infrastructure to support PSN revocation. If an attacker is able to steal the PSN of the victim's processor and exploit other vulnerabilities in software or websites, then he can possibly circumvent the two-factor authentication and log in to the victim's bank account.

However, the major concern of the PSN is privacy. Opponents argue that the mechanism for controlling the PSN access is not sufficiently robust to guarantee that the PSN is only available to software and websites that are explicitly allowed by the platform owner. In other words, unauthorized software or websites may be able to retrieve the PSN without the owner's knowledge. Even for authorized entities, there is no governance or enforcement on how they use the PSN. For example, all Internet activities of a user may be traced by misbehaving software. Abusing the PSN would compromise privacy.

Intel cares about consumers' privacy and has been dedicated to protecting it. In response to public's concerns, Intel discontinued the PSN feature in its processor products after Pentium III.

But the general demand for hardware-protected authentication still exists. How to achieve it while safeguarding users' privacy?

EPID

One of the major achievements of Intel's research effort in anonymous authentication is the enhanced privacy identification[1] (EPID). The EPID is a novel technology that resolves all aspects of the active anonymity problem: authentication, anonymity, and revocation.

Mathematically, the EPID is built on finite field arithmetic and elliptic curve cryptography (ECC). Interested readers should refer to the publications listed in the "References" section at the end of this chapter for mathematical details of the EPID.

The EPID ecosystem defines three entities:

- *EPID authority*: Responsible for generating EPID groups and private keys; also responsible for revoking members and groups. It has a root ECC key for signing group public keys, EPID predefined parameters, and revocation lists.

- *Platform*: Usually an end-consumer device that receives services.

- *Verifier*: Usually a service provider that provides premium services for the specific device.

The relationships among the three entities are shown in Figure 5-1.

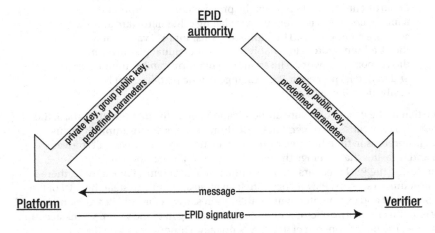

Figure 5-1. Relationships among the three EPID entities

During the setup phase, the EPID authority provides private keys for all platforms, respectively. Note that every platform has a different and unique private key. The delivery and storage of the private key must be protected (encrypted) to avoid leakage. The EPID authority also establishes and manages a server for all verifiers to retrieve EPID group public keys and EPID parameters. These materials are not secrets, are digitally signed by the EPID authority, and therefore can be delivered through open networks. Because platforms served by the verifier may belong to different groups, the verifier must obtain all group public keys used by the clients it is serving beforehand from the EPID authority.

In addition to the private key, the platform also needs the corresponding group public key and predefined parameters to generate EPID signatures. The group public key and parameters can be acquired from the EPID authority together with the private key or from a verifier.

Once the verifier and the platform are both provisioned with required information, the platform can sign messages or challenges from the verifier, and the verifier can verify whether the platform's signature is acceptable.

Like all authentication mechanisms, the prover—in this case a platform—must possess a credential and show the verifier that it knows, has, or is the credential. On the other hand, the verifier—in this case the service provider—must have sufficient knowledge beforehand to reliably verify the correctness of the credential presented by the platform.

For example, in the simple password authentication scheme, the credential is the password. The platform must know and present the password. For verification, the verifier must have the expected password or a hash fingerprint of the expected password for comparison.

In the public key authentication scheme, the credential is the private key. The verifier sends a challenge to the platform, and the platform presents a digital signature generated using its private key and the challenge. The verifier must have the platform's public key to verify the validity of the signature.

In two-factor authentication, the second factor is usually "something you have"—for example, a token device with a randomized PIN that is synchronized with the verifier's server. The PSN on a Pentium III processor is also a form of "something you have".

The credential can also be biological or "something you are," such as fingerprint or eyeball characteristics. For example, Apple's iPhone 5s features fingerprint authentication.

None of these authentication schemes is anonymous. The verifier identifies the platform with the presented *unique* credential.

Similar to traditional public key cryptography, an EPID platform owns a unique private key and must keep it secret (protecting with confidentiality). Both the EPID platform and the EPID verifier know the group public key and must maintain its integrity.

Here's what is not so similar to traditional public key cryptography:

- An EPID private key is essentially derived from a random number. The ECC private key is also a random number; but an RSA private key set is not random but a probable prime number. The key generation for EPID is thus faster than RSA.

- An EPID private key has one corresponding EPID public key—the group public key. However, a group public key corresponds to multiple EPID private keys. The number of private keys that map to the same group public key is configurable; it can be as few as several hundred or as many as tens of millions. Obviously, a group with more members, in theory, features better anonymity and offers more privacy. However, as described later in this chapter, under certain circumstances the computational cost will increase linearly with the increase of members in a group.

Intel's security and management engine is the first platform that implements EPID. Intel's chipset series 5 (released in 2008) and newer natively support the EPID platform functionality. A unique private key, in its encrypted form, is burned into security fuses for every chipset part during manufacturing.

For this EPID ecosystem, Intel acts as the EPID authority. Using the private key, the security and management engine proves that it is a genuine Intel platform, and hence eligible for premium services that are only available for Intel platforms.

Key Structures and Provisioning

The platform device must have built-in secure storage capability—at a minimum, encryption, for storing the EPID private key. Integrity and anti-reply protections for the private key storage are optional but recommended. If integrity or anti-reply is absent, attackers may be able to mount denial of service (DoS) attacks against the platform device, so services relying on EPID may not be available when requested.

For EPID version 1.1, a private key is 1312 bits in size. Its components include:

- Group ID (32 bits)

- A: An element in a predefined 512-bit elliptic curve group G1 (512 bits)

- x: An integer ranging from 0 to $p - 1$ inclusive, where p is the parameter of G1 (256 bits)

- y: An integer ranging from 0 to $p - 1$ inclusive (256 bits)

- f: An integer ranging from 0 to $p - 1$ inclusive (256 bits)

To save space, an EPID private key can also be expressed in the compressed form, which is 544 bits in size:

- Group ID (32 bits)

- $A.x$: An integer ranging from 0 to $q - 1$ inclusive, where q is the parameter of G1 (256 bits)

- *Seed*: A 256-bit string

The compressed form of a private key must be decompressed before being used for signing. The complete private key can be derived from its compressed form, together with the group's public key and values of all predefined elements such as G1.

On Intel's security and management engine, the EPID key is treated as an asset of the highest value on the engine. On Intel's manufacturing line, an EPID key, in its 544-bit compressed and encrypted form, is retrieved from Intel EPID authority's secure server that generated all keys. The manufacturing process then burns the 544-bit key to secure fuses of the engine. For security and privacy reasons, the key is then immediately and permanently deleted from the secure server. In other words, from that point on, only the part itself knows the value of its EPID private key. As the key is deleted after being burned to fuses, there is no "key retrieval" mechanism. If the part loses its EPID private key, it has to be returned to the Intel factory, and a new EPID private key has to be provisioned to it.

On Intel's security and management engine, because what the fuses store is the compressed form of the private key, EPID is not immediately available for use out of box. To save expensive fuse space, the group public key is not burned to individual platforms. In order to function as a platform, a procedure called "provisioning" must be executed first. The provisioning is a one-time effort for the life of a platform. During provisioning, the group public key and predefined parameters of EPID are sent to the platform from a verifier. The platform uses this data together with its compressed private key to derive the complete private key and then stores the complete private key in secure storage for use in future EPID sessions.

The provisioning must be done before the first invocation of the EPID on a platform. Many platform manufacturers choose to provision in their manufacturing lines for better user experience. Others perform provisioning during system initialization on the first boot. The verifier can be software running on a host operating system or a remote server. Figure 5-2 depicts the provisioning protocol.

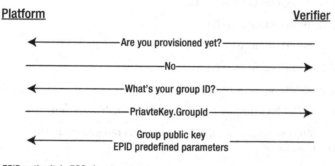

Figure 5-2. *EPID provisioning protocol*

The EPID algorithm uses four mathematical groups: G1, G2, G3, and GT. The groups G1, G2, and G3 are elliptic curve groups. The group GT is a finite field group.

- G1 is 512-bit in size. An element of G1 takes the format of (x, y) where x and y are big integers ranging from 0 to $q - 1$ inclusive.

- G2 is 1536-bit in size. An element of G2 takes the format of $(x[0], x[1], x[2], y[0], y[1], y[2])$, where $x[i]$ and $y[i]$ are big integers ranging from 0 to $q - 1$ inclusive.

- G3 is 512-bit in size. An element of G3 takes the format of (x, y) where x and y are big integers ranging from 0 to $q - 1$ inclusive.

- GT is 1536-bit in size. An element of GT takes the format of $(x[0], x[1], ..., x[5])$, where $x[i]$ is a big integer ranging from 0 to $q - 1$ inclusive.

All EPID groups share the same predefined parameters for G1, G2, G3, and GT. These groups are defined by the following parameters:

- Elliptic curve group G1. Parameters:

    - p (256-bit), a prime

    - q (256-bit), a prime

    - h (32-bit), a small integer, also denoted as cofactor

    - a (256-bit), an integer ranging from 0 to $q - 1$ inclusive

    - b (256-bit), an integer ranging from 0 to $q - 1$ inclusive

    - g1 (512-bit), a generator (an element) of G1

- Elliptic curve group G2. Parameters:

    - p (256-bit), same as in G1

    - q (256-bit), same as in G1

    - a (256-bit), same as in G1

    - b (256-bit), same as in G1

    - coeff (768-bit), the coefficients of an irreducible polynomial

    - coeff[0], coeff[1], coeff[2]: 256-bit integers ranging from 0 to $q - 1$ inclusive

    - qnr (256-bit), a quadratic nonresidue (an integer ranging from 0 to $q - 1$ inclusive)

    - orderG2 (768-bit), the total number of points in G2 elliptic curve

    - g2 (1536-bit), a generator (an element) of G2

- Elliptic curve group G3. Parameters:

    - p' (256-bit), a prime

    - q' (256-bit), a prime

    - h' (32-bit), a small integer, usually 1, also denoted as cofactor'

    - a' (256-bit), an integer between ranging from 0 to $q' - 1$ inclusive

    - b' (256-bit), an integer between ranging from 0 to $q' - 1$ inclusive

    - g3 (512-bit), a generator (an element) of G3

- Finite field group GT. Parameters:

  - q (256-bit), same as in G1

  - coeff (768-bit), same as in G2

  - qnr (256-bit), same as in G2

The public key of an EPID group consists of the following elements:

- Group ID (32 bits)

- $h1$ (512 bits): An element in G1

- $h2$ (512 bits): An element in G1

- w (1536 bits): An element in a predefined 1536-bit elliptic curve group G2

Although the group public key and predefined parameters are not secrets, the platform must verify that what is sent by the verifier is trustworthy. The EPID group pubic key and the predefined parameters are digitally signed by the EPID authority using ECDSA.[2] The EPID authority's ECC public key is hardcoded in all platform devices. The platform verifies the EPID authority's ECDSA signature before using the data sent by the verifiers to perform the private key decompression.

If the platform device has enough fuse space, the manufacturing process can provision public key and predefined parameters together with private keys for the devices, in which case the provisioning protocol can be skipped. However, because the provisioning is a one-time procedure for the lifetime of the device, and the public key and predefined parameter are not secrets, it is generally preferable to burn only the private key during manufacturing and perform provisioning before the first use of EPID. This is the design used by Intel's security and management engine to save secure fuse space.

Notice that even if a platform provisions the group public key, predefined parameters, and the private key during manufacturing, it must hardcode the ECDSA root public key of the EPID authority for verifying the verifier's signature in a SIGMA session. See the "SIGMA" section of this chapter for details.

Revocation

The EPID protocol supports revocation of members or groups. How is a platform identified for revocation? In an EPID ecosystem, the EPID authority is the only entity that has the privilege to revoke a member or a group. Once a verifier identifies a platform or group that should be revoked, it notifies the EPID authority with reasons. The authority then examines the request and executes corresponding revocation operations if the request is deemed legitimate. In certain cases, the EPID authority may decide to revoke platforms or groups without requests from verifiers.

Depending on what information is known about the entity to be revoked, a revocation request may belong to any one of three categories: private key-based revocation, signature-based revocation, or group-based revocation. The EPID authority maintains a single group revocation list (GROUP-RL), and for each group that is not on the group-based revocation list, it maintains a private key-based revocation (PRIV-RL) list and a signature-based revocation list (SIG-RL). The revocation lists are centrally managed and pushed to all verifiers of the ecosystem.

Private Key-Based Revocation

If a member's private key is proved to be possessed by any party other than the platform device itself—for example, if a valid private key is published on the Internet—then the platform device is concluded as having been compromised, and it should not receive any more services as an EPID platform. In order to revoke a member by using its private key, the EPID authority must acquire the value of the private key (in either compressed or complete form). The private key-based revocation can be initiated by a verifier or the EPID authority. Figure 5-3 shows the flows exercised by the EPID authority for revoking a private key.

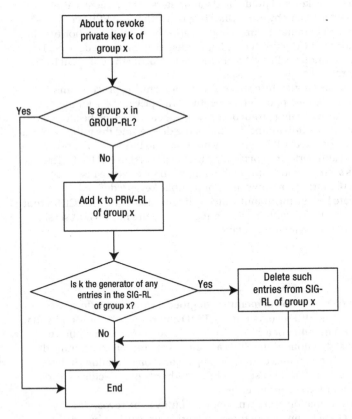

Figure 5-3. Placing a private key in the PRIV-RL

Consider a real-world scenario: the owner of a platform breaks into the device by exploiting critical vulnerability of the hardware or firmware and manages to extract the EPID private key from the device. He then shares the private key with other people so they can all enjoy services without having to buy the platform device or pay the service provider. If the provider uses the "base name" option (described later in this chapter), then it can detect such abuse and revoke the private key.

It is possible that the platform to be revoked using private key-based revocation has already been revoked by the signature-based revocation. To minimize the sizes of SIG-RL, before adding a private key to the PRIV-RL, the EPID authority first goes through the SIG-RL and checks if any revoked signatures in the SIG-RL were generated by this key. Such signatures, if any, are removed from the SIG-RL.

Signature-Based Revocation

If a member has reportedly been misbehaving, but its private key is not yet exposed or known by the EPID authority, then the EPID authority may revoke the member by identifying it using a signature the member had previously generated. Misbehaviors are defined by the verifiers and the EPID authority. For example, a platform continuously making excessive requests may be considered to be misbehaving; a platform that repeatedly generates a constant signature for the same challenge is likely compromised, because per the EPID algorithm, multiple signatures generated for the same challenge should be different.

The EPID signature allows the verifier to enforce an optional "based name" parameter so that all signatures generated by the same platform are linkable. The verifier can utilize this option to detect and identify malicious users that abuse anonymity and revoke them using the signature-based revocation mechanism.

The private key-based revocation has higher priority than the signature-based revocation. When the EPID authority receives a signature revocation request from a verifier, it first checks the signature against all entries in the private key-based revocation list. If the signature was generated by a revoked private key, then it will not be placed in the signature-based revocation list.

■ **Note**   Although a useful feature, the signature revocation is computationally expensive for both the signature generation of all platforms of this group (even if a platform is not the one that was revoked) and the verifier's signature verification, and it increases protocol traffic between the two parties. Also notice that one revoked member may have more than one signature presented in the signature revocation list.

Figure 5-4 exhibits the flows exercised by the EPID authority for revoking a signature.

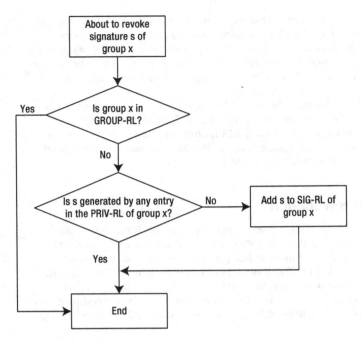

Figure 5-4. Placing a signature in the SIG-RL

Group-Based Revocation

This is the mechanism to revoke all members of a group. The reason for revoking the entire group could include termination of the service contract for a group of members, or performance—when too many members of a group have been revoked using signature revocation, the signing and verifying operations can take a very long time. At a certain point, the EPID authority can decide to revoke the group and create a new group.

Another scenario that applies to the group-based revocation is when critical vulnerability in platform implementation is found by the device manufacturer, but the vulnerability has not been exposed or exploited publicly. The vulnerability is critical because it may lead to compromise of the EPID private key. In this case, the platform manufacturer should not only push a patch that fixes the critical vulnerability to all impacted devices, but also revoke these devices using the group-based revocation.

If the group-based revocation is due to performance or platform vulnerability, then the EPID authority will create a new group and reprovision nonrevoked members of the old group. Of course, a member of the old group must show that it has not been revoked by private key and signature, in order to receive a new private key of the new group.

The group-based revocation has highest priority among the three revocation methods. Once a group is revoked, its SIG-RL and PRIV-RL will not be used by verifiers. The EPID authority does not maintain SIG-RL or PRIV-RL for revoked groups.

Figure 5-5 exhibits the flows exercised by the EPID authority for revoking a group.

130

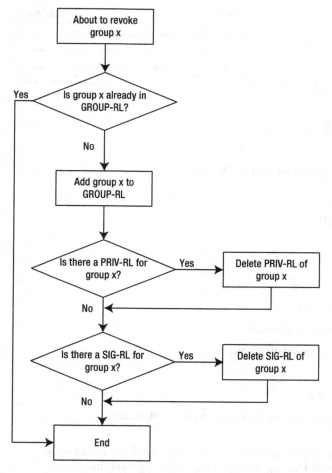

Figure 5-5. *Placing a group in the GROUP-RL*

Signature Generation and Verification

The EPID signature generation is the algorithm implemented by a platform. The EPID signature verification is the algorithm implemented by a verifier. This section gives an interface overview of the two algorithms but does not discuss mathematical details. Readers interested in the detailed steps of the signature generation and verification algorithms should refer to publications listed on the "Reference" section at the end of this chapter.

Figure 5-6 exhibits the communications between EPID entities during an authentication session.

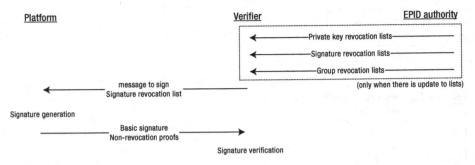

Figure 5-6. EPID signature generation and verification

Signature Generation

Input:

- EPID private key

- Corresponding EPID group public key

- Message to be signed

- Verifier's base name (optional)

- Signature revocation list of this group

Output:

- Basic EPID signature

- Non-revocation proofs, one for each entry in the signature revocation list

The basic signature generation is a very intensive operation—it takes as long as two seconds on the security and management engine, which negatively impacts the user's experience. Fortunately, most of the steps of the basic signature generation can be performed without the knowledge of the message to be signed.

The "pregenerating and caching" optimization is utilized widely in the security and management engine by many applications to expedite real-time operation. For the EPID, the engine creates and caches a certain number of "presignatures" without using the message to be signed. The presignatures are stored securely in the engine's internal memory. The presignature generation is performed right after every time the engine is powered on. Alternatively, the unused presignatures in the cache can be stored in nonvolatile memory before power-off, and loaded and reused at the next power-on. Due to the very limited storage space and large size of the presignatures, the first option is deemed more efficient for the engine.

When a signing request is received, the engine fetches a presignature from the cache and completes the final signature using the message from the verifier. The engine then kicks off generation of a new presignature in a low-priority thread, to fill the used slot of the presignature cache. Experiments show that the presignature generation contributes to about 95% of total basic signature generation time. In other words, the caching optimization reduces the EPID signing time by about 95%.

In addition to the basic EPID signature, the platform has to generate a non-revocation proof for every signature in the SIG-RL. The data transmission and computation time become noticeably long as the number of entries in the SIG-RL increases. Unfortunately, the non-revocation proof cannot be precomputed because the calculation uses the basic EPID signature as input.

If the platform's private key was used to generate at least one signature on the SOG-RL, then the non-revocation proof calculation will fail, and the platform, if not compromised, should abort and notify the verifier of the revocation of itself. Even if the platform is malicious and returns an invalid non-revocation proof for the revoked signature, the verifier will be able to detect it because the signature verification will fail.

Base Name

The base name is an optional input to the signature generation and verification algorithms. It is the verifier that decides whether to require it or not. The platform has the right to deny using a base name. If used, all signatures generated by a platform with the verifier's base name are linkable to the verifier. That is, the verifier is able to identity which signatures come from the same platform. The verifier cannot tell which platform it is, though.

Apparently, this option degrades the privacy protection for the platform. Therefore, the design guideline for the platform is to reject signature requests with base name by default and only use a base name with trusted verifiers. The platform should hardcode a list of trusted verifiers. The SIGMA protocol, introduced in the next section, provides a way to identify the verifier.

But why does a verifier want to use the base name option? The main reason is to prevent rogue platform users from abusing the anonymity of EPID. Consider a scenario where an online movie subscription service sets a limit of 100 movies per month. The base name signature can help the service provider keep track of usage for all platform subscribers, identify excessive usages, and revoke rogue platforms if necessary.

Signature Verification

Input:

- EPID group public key
- Private key revocation list
- Signature revocation list
- Group revocation list
- Message that was signed

- Verifier's base name (optional)

- Basic EPID signature

- Non-revocation proofs

Output:

- Signature valid or invalid

As shown in the input and output parameter lists, the amount of data transmitted between the platform and the verifier for signature revocation is proportional to the number of entries in the signature revocation list. This is because the verifier must send all signatures in the SIG-RL to the platform, and the platform must prove that it is not the generator of any signature in the list.

A lengthy SIG-RL is not only affecting the volume of data transmission, but also increasing the computational cost. The platform must calculate a non-revocation proof for each revoked signature; the verifier must verify the validity of each non-revocation proof sent by the platform.

For Intel's EPID ecosystem, the threshold for the number of entries in the signature revocation list of a group is set to 50 and enforced by Intel's EPID authority. The number was chosen based on performance measurement of the security and management engine, and the capacity and bandwidth of the communication channel between the engine and the verifier host software or the remote verifier server. When the number of revoked signatures exceeds 50, the group will be revoked, and a new group will be assigned to replace the old group.

The verifier must validate the platform against all three revocation lists, in the following order:

- Is the platform's group ID in the group-based revocation list? If so, abort.

- Is the platform's basic signature generated by any private key in the private key-based revocation list? If so, abort.

- Are the platform's non-revocation proofs valid against all entries in the signature-based revocation list? If not, abort. The signature revocation is checked last because its operation is much slower than the other two revocations.

The signature verification is also a mathematically intensive operation. Because the verifier usually is equipped with strong computational capability (faster CPU and more memory), though, it does not introduce significant latency from an end user's perspective.

SIGMA

The EPID provides a solution for a platform to authenticate itself anonymously to a verifier. The EPID is a one-way authentication protocol, because the verifier is not authenticating to the platform. However, for many use cases, the platform has to identify and trust the verifier.

One application of the security and management engine was the Intel Upgrade Service[i] that allowed customers to enable advanced CPU features by purchasing a $50 upgrade card. In this usage model, the engine is the EPID platform, and a remote server set up by Intel is the verifier.

On the one hand, the remote server must be assured that the target platform is indeed an eligible Intel security and management engine. On the other hand, the engine must verify that the upgrade request indeed came from a legitimate Intel server after payment was cleared, and not from a hacker's forgery. Notice that in this case there is no privacy requirement on the verifier. So the authentication method of this direction can be realized by traditional public key cryptography.

In addition to mutual authentication for each other, the platform and the verifier have to perform further secure message exchanges for application-specific protocols. The EPID algorithm per se does not establish session keys for encryption or integrity.

On top of EPID, ECDSA, and the Diffie-Hellman[3] key exchange scheme, Intel designed a protocol called SIGMA (SIGn and Message Authentication) that enables two-way authentication, one direction anonymously and the other distinctively, as well as session key agreement. The security and management engine implements the platform side of the SIGMA protocol.

Verifier's Certificate

The SIGMA protocol is built on a public key infrastructure (PKI). In this PKI, the EPID authority also serves as the root CA (certification authority) of verifiers and issues X.509 certificates to qualified verifier applications. For example, a DAL (dynamic application loader; see Chapter 9) applet that invokes EPID on the security and management engine should obtain its verifier certificate chain rooted to the Intel EPID authority CA. The server for the Intel Upgrade Service obtained its X.509 verifier certificate from the EPID authority as well.

As the root CA, the EPID authority may issue a leaf certificate for a verifier program or issue intermediate CA certificates, which then sign and issue other intermediate CA certificates or verifier certificates. Nevertheless, the verifier's certificate chain must be rooted to the self-signed certificate of the EPID authority. Recall that the platform device with compressed private key must hardcode the EPID authority's root ECDSA public key for verifying the EPID group public key and predefined EPID parameters sent from the verifier. The same ECDSA public key is also used by the platforms to validate the certificate chain of the verifier.

The SIGMA PKI supports revocation of the verifier. When a verifier is no longer qualified as an EPID verifier, and its X.509 certificate has not yet expired, then its certificate can be revoked by the EPID authority. The criteria of a qualified verifier are defined by and at the discretion of the EPID authority. For example, upon end of life, the certificate of Intel Upgrade Service was revoked.

One or more online certificate status protocol (OCSP) servers are employed to enforce the revocation. The EPID authority issues X.509 certificates to OCSP servers. The EPID authority pushes the revocation lists of intermediate CAs and/or verifiers to all OCSP servers whenever new certificates are revoked.

---

[i]Intel Upgrade Service was end-of-life in 2011 and no longer available to customers.

Upon request, the authorized OCSP servers issue signed non-revocation proofs for all intermediate CA certificates and verifier certificates to the requesting verifiers. The non-revocation proofs include timestamps that will be used by the platform. The verifier can then present the non-revocation proofs together with its certificate chain to the EPID platform.

As an embedded system, the security and management engine does not have convenient network access. Therefore, the SIGMA protocol is designed such that the platform does not communicate with the OCSP server directly but only connects with the verifier.

Let's summarize all materials signed by the EPID authority's root ECDSA key:

- EPID group certificates that contain group public keys

- EPID predefined parameters

- Verifier's certificates and intermediate CAs' certificates

- OCSP servers' certificates

Messages Breakdown

A high-level overview of the SIGMA protocol is given in Figure 5-7. Detailed descriptions follow.

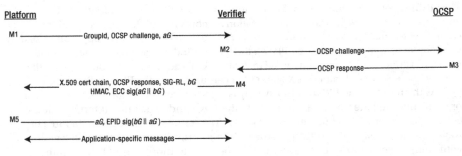

Figure 5-7. *SIGMA protocol*

To begin a SIGMA session, the platform randomly generates an elliptic curve Diffie-Hellman private key a and calculates public key $a \cdot G$. The base point G is predefined by the EPID authority. The verifier similarly generates b and calculates $b \cdot G$.

In M1, the platform sends its EPID group ID and Diffie-Hellman pubic key $a \cdot G$ to the verifier. The group ID is for the verifier to look up and send back corresponding SIG-RL for that group in M4.

Under certain cases, the platform can also send a random OCSP challenge in M1, if it wants to receive a real-time "noncached" OCSP response (non-revocation proof). If an OCSP challenge is not sent, then the verifier is allowed to provide a "cached" OCSP response that was previously generated by the OCSP server. It is up to the platform implementation to decide the maximum age of a cached OCSP response that is considered acceptable. The security and management engine accepts an OCSP response that was generated within the last 24 hours. In other words, the verifier program may vulnerably retrieve a non-revocation proof from the OCSP server every 24 hours, for example at midnight. In the case of a cached OCSP response, the challenge is not material and will not be checked by the platform.

Obviously, if the platform decides to request for a noncached OCSP response, the SIGMA session will take significantly longer because the platform has to communicate with the OCSP server via the verifier during the SIGMA session (messages M2 and M3). If the platform accepts cached OCSP response, then M2 and M3 can be skipped. Another more problematic scenario with noncached OCSP response is when the OCSP server is temporally unavailable or unreachable by the verifier, in which case the SIGMA session has to be aborted, resulting in a poor user experience.

So under what conditions should a platform request a noncached OCSP response? The answer is application specific. Intel's security and management engine requests for noncached OCSP responses only when

- *The engine has not been provisioned date/time yet.* As a platform, the engine must have the current date/time to confirm validity periods of verifiers' X.509 certificates and other PKI elements. If the engine has no date/time information, then it has to ask for a noncached OCSP response and use the timestamp in the OCSP response as the current date/time. The engine's kernel has a secure clocking capability (refer to Chapter 3 for details) and will maintain the trusted date/time, even if the device is powered off.

- *The date/time was provisioned more than 30 days ago.* Every 30 days, the engine requests for a noncached OCSP response to calibrate its date/time. This eliminates the influences of possible glitches of the internal clock.

M4 is a heavily loaded message that deserves more attention. M4 contains the following:

- *M4.1*: Verifier's Diffie-Hellman public key $b \cdot G$

- *M4.2*: SIG-RL

- *M4.3*: Verifier's X.509 certificate chain

- *M4.4*: OCSP response

- *M4.5*: HMAC on M4.1 to M4.4

- *M4.6*: Verifier's ECDSA signature on $a \cdot G \parallel b \cdot G$

Before sending M4, the verifier uses its ECC private key to sign "$a \cdot G$ concatenated with $b \cdot G$." It also derives the Diffie-Hellman shared secret s from b and $a \cdot G$. The HMAC on M4.1 to M4.4 are calculated using s.

The platform verifies validity of the certificate chain and the OCSP response, including checking the nonce if it is noncached, and then verifies the ECC signature. The platform then calculates the Diffie-Hellman shared secret s from a and $b \cdot G$ and verifies the HMAC. Once everything checks out, the platform proceeds with EPID signature generation on message $b \cdot G \parallel a \cdot G$, and sends to the verifier in M5 with $a \cdot G$. $a \cdot G$ is sent again in M5, so the verifier is able to match the $a \cdot G$ values in M1 and M5 and confirm they belong to the same SIGMA session, when there are multiple concurrent SIGMA sessions.

After the verifier verifies the platform's EPID signature (including non-revocation proofs) that has been sent in M5, the two parties have completed mutual authentication and session key agreement. The subsequent messages between the platform and the verifier are application specific. Derived values from the shared secret s are used as an encryption key and an HMAC key, respectively, to safeguard the application-specific communication.

The lifetime of a SIGMA session is determined by the platform and the verifier. Though a maximum lifetime does not have to be enforced, it is recommended that a new SIGMA session be established periodically. For performance considerations, a SIGMA session should not be renewed too frequently, because EPID is a relatively slow algorithm.

Implementation of EPID

This section discusses the best-known methods for implementing EPID infrastructure.

Key Recovery

Due to its nature of anonymity, the EPID must be a native built-in functionality of the device. The EPID private keys should be provisioned to platform devices during manufacturing, instead of in the field. This is because as soon as a consumer purchases the device, the device is associated to the consumer and is no longer anonymous. Any key provisioning in the field would have to involve the device owner's identity and actions; for example, using a credit card to purchase an EPID-based service.

Reprovisioning an EPID private key requires a "super verifier" that has access to the EPID key generation server; hence the super verifier must be set up by the EPID authority. During a SIGMA session, if a verifier finds that the platform's group is revoked, then it should direct the platform to the super verifier and the platform should check whether EPID reprovisioning is available for this platform.

As briefly discussed earlier, Intel's security and management engine supports reprovision of EPID private key in the field for one of the following two reasons:

- Performance due to too many signatures revoked by the signature-based revocation

- Critical vulnerability in firmware

In the first case, the platform presents a signature generated using its current EPID private key in a SIGMA session with the super verifier. Once the SIGMA session is established, the super verifier will send the new group ID and a complete private key to the platform. The platform then replaces the old key with the new key in its secure nonvolatile storage.

The second case is more complicated. If vulnerability is found in firmware that may leak the EPID private key, and there is no known exploit against the vulnerability yet, then the manufacturer should release a firmware hotfix and push the firmware update to all platforms that have the vulnerability. In the SIGMA session (established using the old private key from the platform's perspective), the super verifier must first confirm the platform has the latest firmware installed, and then send a new private key to the platform. From then on, the old private key is obsoleted, and the platform must use the new EPID key in all future SIGMA sessions.

■ **Note**   The firmware hotfix must also replace the secret keys that are used to protect nonvolatile files.

It is always tricky and costly to deal with consequences of critical bugs found in released products. For some cases, a recovery may not be an ideal solution. For example, if there were already published exploits against the vulnerability, then those rogue end users that had exercised the exploit and retrieved the private keys would be eligible for reprovision with a new private key and continue to enjoy premium services that they were not supposed to receive.

If the vulnerability also allowed compromised firmware to cheat the super verifier by sending an arbitrary firmware version number in the SIGMA session, then the super verifier would happily send the new private key to the vulnerable firmware.

Attack Mitigation

Like all cryptography protocols, attackers target two aspects: algorithm and implementation. To date, there are no known attacks against the EPID algorithm.

To protect an asset, the requirement of the implementation is to make the cost of successful attacks higher than the value of the asset. If an asset can be compromised on one device and used on all devices (BORE attack), then it is a high-value asset and must be afforded the strongest protection. For example, global keys that are stored in all devices fall into this category. On the other hand, device-specific secrets are of less value than global secrets. The attack must be repeated on an individual device to retrieve the secret from the device. This is impractical, especially if the attack requires special hardware, setup, and expertise to mount.

The EPID private key is a highly valuable asset because it grants access to premium services offered exclusively to the platform. The implementation of the security and management engine attempts to ensure that the EPID key cannot be revealed from a device without special and expensive equipment and advanced expertise in hacking. The following mechanisms to protect EPID private keys are applied:

- The EPID keys in fuses are in encrypted form.

- Anti-cloning: The decompressed private key is stored in secure nonvolatile storage and protected with AES for encryption and HMAC-SHA-256 for integrity. The AES and HMAC keys are unique per part. Therefore, copying the EPID key file on the flash from one part to another will not work.

- At runtime, the EPID key is handled in the engine's internal memory and is never exposed in the clear to the host.

Applications of EPID

The services and applications that are built on the EPID always have dependency on certain features of the device. Intel's security and management engine features premium applications that are only available on the engine and should not be executed by other products. These features require specific hardware and/or environment support to function. The EPID is used to prove it is *a* genuine Intel platform with such support and is eligible to enjoy the premium services, but not *which* individual Intel platform.

Examples of such premium services include:

- *Intel upgrade service*: Consumers could purchase an upgrade code from Intel and unlock advanced CPU features. This was the first application of EPID, which was dropped in 2011.

- *Anti-theft technology*: Shut down a mobile device when the owner reports it as stolen.

- *Premium content playback*: Intel platforms feature proprietary PAVP (protected audio video path) technology that offers robust hardware protection for contents (see Chapter 8 for details). Once a platform is authenticated via EPID to be a genuine Intel platform, the user can enjoy premium contents (such as high-definition movies) that are only allowed, as required by the content creators, on platforms with hardware-level content protection.

- *Identity protection technology*: Intel's identity protection technology[4] provides a simple and tamper-resistant method for protecting access to customer and business data from threats and fraud. EPID is used to authenticate the Intel platform.

Next Generation of EPID

Intel continues working on improving the EPID scheme and exploring new deployments for the EPID.

Two-way EPID

The two ways in SIGMA's two-way authentication are not equal—one direction is anonymous, and the other is not. As more applications deploy EPID, it is likely that for some applications, both sides of the protocol must remain anonymous. In that case, both parties will implement platform and verifier functionalities, and two EPID sessions must be established to realize mutual anonymous authentication.

Optimization

Intel's chipset series 5, 6, 7, and 8 and Bay Trail systems-on-chip products feature the second version of EPID: EPID 1.1. The sizes of its elements (keys, parameters, signature, revocation lists, and so forth) are not small. The algorithms require a relatively large amount of computational resources.

Performance, memory consumption, storage space, and power consumption are all critical measures for mobile devices. The new EPID 2.0 standard strives to reduce computational cost by choosing more efficient curves and reducing key sizes while maintaining the same security level. The EPID 2.0 is published as ISO/IEC standard 20008.[5]

References

1. Brickell, Ernie, and Jiangtao Li, "Enhanced Privacy ID: A Direct Anonymous Attestation Scheme with Enhanced Revocation Capabilities," *IEEE Transactions on Dependable and Secure Computing*, May/June 2012, pp. 345–360.

2. National Institute of Standards and Technology, Digital Signature Standard (DSS), http://nvlpubs.nist.gov/nistpubs/FIPS/NIST.FIPS.186-4.pdf, accessed on November 10, 2013.

3. Network Working Group, "Diffie-Hellman Key Agreement Method," http://tools.ietf.org/html/rfc2631, accessed on November 10, 2013.

4. Identity Protection Technology, http://ipt.intel.com/, accessed on April 20, 2014.

5. ISO/IEC JTC 1, "Anonymous digital signatures", ISO/IEC 20008-2, 2013.

■ ■ ■

CHAPTER 6

Boot with Integrity, or Don't Boot

You can't build a great building on a weak foundation. You must have a solid foundation if you're going to have a strong superstructure.

—Gordon B. Hinckley

You are on a business trip and staying in a nice hotel. You leave your laptop in the room while going out for a dinner appointment. The laptop has its full disk-encryption feature enabled. Being reasonably paranoid, you even turned off the laptop. You believe that the laptop and your confidential files stored in it are safe and secure. However, that may not be true. An "evil maid" who can physically access the laptop on the sly for just two minutes may be able to steal your drive encryption password without a trace. Consequently, the confidentiality of all encrypted data on the laptop is in danger.

How does the evil maid do it? The trick is the boot process. End-to-end security is essential. The boot security is as critical as, if not more critical than, runtime security.

For the past decade, the effort of securing computers has been focused largely on mitigating *runtime* threats. Numerous solutions have been developed to safeguard the integrity of computer systems and protect users' assets. These solutions include but are not limited to antivirus, network firewalls, and password managers. Some of these solutions are software-based; others are either dedicated hardware devices or hybrid designs made up of software and hardware. Most of these solutions mean to thwart certain types of security threats at runtime of the system. Drive encryption programs including TrueCrypt, PGP, and BitLocker) adopt a preboot authentication that is launched during the boot process as an extension of the BIOS before the operating system (such as Windows, Linux, Android, iOS, and so forth) is loaded.

The problem is the lack of end-to-end protection. Most software solutions are available only after being loaded by the operating system. In other words, during the boot process—that is, from the moment a user presses the power button to when the operating system takes control and finishes loading the security solutions—the computer is not benefiting from the services offered by the security measures and is hence vulnerable. Drive encryption schemes that start during the boot do not depend on the operating system to function, but they do rely on the integrity of the boot loader that loads them.

Admittedly, runtime protection is pivotal. The amount of time a computer typically spends on boot today is fairly small compared to how long the operating system is running. Operating systems have extensive interfaces and connectivity that make the attack surface wide and open. In contrast, the boot is a relatively short and contained process. As a result, attacks against the boot are more difficult to mount and succeed.

But a building is only as strong as its foundation. Hacking a computer's boot loader is similar to replacing a mansion's concrete foundation with sand. The components that are involved in the boot process comprise the root of trust for the entire system. A compromised boot loader renders the operating system—and all programs running on it—untrustworthy, including the antivirus, firewalls, and even drive encryption utilities.

Boot Attack

The boot process and components participating in the process vary, depending on the architecture of the system. How a computer boots today is significantly different and more complex than it was a decade ago. At a high level, most computers follow the boot sequence shown in Figure 6-1.

CPU reset → bootrom → BIOS → boot loader → operating system → applications

Figure 6-1. Boot flow

The BIOS (basic input/output system) is a firmware component stored in nonvolatile memory, usually a flash chip. The BIOS loads the boot loader, which is the first software component loaded during the boot process. The boot loader is stored in the hard drive, together with the operating system and applications.

For attackers, it is preferable to compromise a component that is loaded earlier than one loaded later, because taking control at an early stage enables control over all subsequent components. Successful attacks against user-mode software programs may not be glorious accomplishments in the security community nowadays. Instead, the BIOS and boot loader are becoming more interesting targets. A number of such attacks were published in the recent years. Here are two examples:

- *Attacking BIOS*: This type of attack replaces an authentic BIOS with an attacker's BIOS that contains malicious code. There have been attacks against the UEFI (Unified Extensible Firmware Interface) secure boot.

- *Attacking boot loader*: This type of attack usually installs a boot kit (a variant of root kits that runs in the kernel mode) under an attacker's control that infects the boot loader. The boot kit can be used to steal secrets during the boot path; for example, logging the user's drive encryption password.

If an adversary manages to modify the BIOS or boot loader code without authorization, then a straightforward damage he can realize is to corrupt the BIOS or boot loader and render the computer unbootable and inoperable (this category of attack is called *bricking*). The most famous example of this kind is the CIH virus, which resulted in reportedly millions of computers failing to boot in the late 1990s. The CIH virus, named after its author Chen Ing-Hau, a student at Taiwan's Tatung University, flashes and rewrites the BIOS region with junk so the infected computers can no longer start. Generally speaking, bricking the attacker's own device yields no benefits to the attacker. But if such bricking attacks can be mounted remotely and widely spread with viruses like CIH, it will cause substantial monetary loss.

In today's operating system, writing to flash or a boot loader without physical access is an incredibly privileged operation and hence more difficult to implement than 20 years ago. The bricking attacks against the boot path cause little or no harm on newer computers that are shipped with backup BIOS images on the flash and recoverable boot loaders on a special region of the hard drive or from the manufacturer-provided recovery disc. Most reputable antivirus utilities are capable of monitoring the integrity of the boot loader and of killing viruses that infect the boot loader. Pure bricking attacks against the boot path are considered out of scope in the remainder of this chapter.

Evil Maid

Joanna Rutkowska of the Invisible Things Lab was the first to describe the "Evil Maid" attack[1] in October 2009. In the Evil Maid attack, the maid attacker boots the victim's unattended laptop with her USB stick, which contains a bootable and stripped Linux operating system. The USB stick then uses the POSIX command dd to install a malicious boot kit, which changes the legitimate boot loader with a hook for recognizing and recording the full drive encryption passphrase later when the victim turns on his laptop and types in the passphrase on the keyboard. The malicious boot kit also recalculates certain fields of the MBR (master boot record), including the boot loader hash and size, in order to make it look like a legitimate MBR. The recorded passphrase is stored on the hard drive and it can be sent over the network to the attacker, or simply be retrieved by the evil maid the next day, when she can access the laptop and boot to her USB stick again. Once the encryption passphrase is acquired, the maid can just clone the victim's encrypted drive so she can steal all data on it.

Notice that the Evil Maid attack works only on a laptop that is turned off, because the attack takes advantage of the lack of boot integrity protection, and the drive encryption passphrase is entered by the user only during boot. If the maid deliberately turned off a sleeping or hibernating computer in order to mount her attack, then the victim would notice that something was wrong and suspect that someone had done something to his laptop. However, why would the victim power off his laptop in the first place, while he is going out for just an hour for dinner? The average user may not do so.

As a matter of fact, a paranoid professional user who has heard of the "cold boot" attack[2] may actually turn off his laptop even if he will be away for a short time. The researchers that presented the cold boot attack reports found that, based on experiments, the DRAM (dynamic random-access memory) still retains its content within a certain amount of time after the power is removed, even at the room temperature. Colder environments prolong the duration of the memory remanence. This observation is contrary to the popular assumption that DRAM would lose its data almost instantly when not being refreshed. The time period for which data resides in DRAM after power removal is generally long enough for an experienced attacker to figure out the drive encryption key from the DRAM. To counter such attacks, it is advisable to power down a laptop before leaving it unattended.

As you can see from the scenarios of the Evil Maid attack, without boot integrity protection, drive encryption techniques are able to safeguard your data only for cases where a thief steals and possesses your computer for good and attempts to retrieve plaintext data from it. If an attacker can secretly and physically access your computer for some period of time without you knowing, and then return it back to you, then the drive encryption cannot protect your data. This is not the fault of any specific drive encryption solution, but the limitation of the technology defined by its security model. The Evil Maid attack is simply out of scope if the user temporarily gives up the physical control of his laptop, that is, this scenario is not something that the encryption itself is intended or capable to mitigate.

To address this loophole, the security protection must start from the very beginning and cover the entire boot process. If the boot path is secured on the platform, then an evil maid will not be able to easily alter the MBR, so full drive encryption schemes can survive the attack.

BIOS and UEFI

The BIOS is the first piece of firmware that executes upon computer power-on. It is stored in nonvolatile memory, such as a flash chip on the motherboard. The fundamental functionality of the BIOS firmware is to initialize and self-test low-level hardware components of the computer, such as the CPU, keyboard, display, DRAM, and so forth, as well as to load the boot loader for the operating system from the hard drive. For a system with the security and management engine enabled, the BIOS is also responsible for communicating with the engine for basic configuration and reserving a predefined size of DRAM for the engine's dedicated access.

In fact, the BIOS is a standard that defines the platform firmware interface to the operating system. The term BIOS also refers to the firmware that implements the standard. In recent years, the UEFI standard[3] has been replacing the conventional BIOS standard, which has several limitations (such as a 16-bit real mode and a 1MB addressable memory) that are posing difficulty in meeting the needs of modern computers. Like the BIOS, the UEFI specification defines an interface between the operating system and the platform firmware, and the interface is designed to communicate only necessary information in order for the operating system to start. Besides supporting larger memory and a disk boot, the UEFI also introduces useful add-on features such as secure boot. Notice that the UEFI is backward-compatible with the BIOS standard. In this chapter, the term *BIOS* refers to the platform firmware that runs at boot, which may be either a conventional BIOS or a UEFI-compatible one.

Everything starts with BIOS on a computer, including security. If the BIOS is compromised, then all security countermeasures deployed after BIOS are essentially at risk. The era of the CIH virus—when a Windows application could program the flash and corrupt the BIOS—is long gone. Nevertheless, security researchers have reported BIOS alteration attacks using advanced techniques in recent years.

BIOS Alteration

At the Black Hat Europe conference in 2006, John Heasman presented a rootkit made possible by altering BIOS's ACPI (advanced configuration and power interface) table[4] The rootkit can infect Windows during Windows installation. This attack requires the capability of reflashing the flash chip where the BIOS is stored. At the 2009 CanSecWest Security conference, Anibal Sacco and Alfredo Ortega demonstrated patching malicious code into the decompression routines of the BIOS.[5] Similar to Heasman's finding, physical access and reflashing capability is required to mount the attack.

Requiring physical access and reflashing BIOS firmware with an attacker's code significantly limits the value of the proposed attacks, because nowadays, most manufacturers do not allow arbitrary programming of the BIOS. When manufacturers issue BIOS updates for adding hardware support and fixing bugs, the new BIOS images are usually digitally signed with the manufacturer's private key. Only if the signature checks out by the operating system will the BIOS update be scheduled to launch after reboot.

At the Black Hat USA conference in 2009, Rafal Wojtczuk and Alexander Tereshkin presented an attack against certain vulnerable BIOS.[6] The attack exploits a buffer overflow bug in these BIOSes to subvert the integrity protection (digital signature) on the BIOS update. The attack is more sophisticated than the ones introduced by Heasman, Sacco, and Ortega, because it does not require physical access, making remote and wide deployment possible.

Software Replacement

Attacks can be classified into various models according to the intension. With the exception of the CIH virus, the attacks discussed so far in this chapter target taking control of victims' computers and stealing secrets or performing other harmful operations.

In other models, however, attackers are playing with and hacking their owner devices, in the attempt to achieve certain goals:

- *Install adversary's software system on a low-end device*: The software shipped with low-end hardware by its OEM (original equipment manufacturer) may come with limited functionalities. It is to the user's interest to replace the original software stack with unauthorized software, where more powerful functionalities are available; for example, installing Android on a GPS (Global Positioning System) or media player device. Notice that the low-end device may not be equipped with premium hardware features, which limits what the adversary's software is able to accomplish.

- *Install adversary's software system on a high-end device*: The high-end device features hardware capabilities to support premium functionalities, such as enhanced high-definition movie playback, near field communication (NFC), and so forth. The adversary's software can bypass certain restrictions. For example, content protection may be deployed by an OEM's software to enforce a movie rental period. The adversary's software may remove such policy so that the user can own the movie permanently.

Jailbreaking

Jailbreaking or *rooting* refers to the action of overcoming certain restrictions of the firmware and software stack that are installed on the device by the device OEM or carrier (in the case of a smartphone). Essentially, jailbreaking is a form of privilege escalation that allows the user to gain the root privilege and full control of his device.

It is common practice for OEMs and wireless carriers to implement restrictions in the firmware and software that is shipped with the hardware. There are a number of reasons for this practice. For example, here are a few:

- Selling applications and additional services to users after they purchase the device

- Protecting the device from malware and viruses

- Promoting the OEM's software products by preinstalling and locking them down in the operating system

- Preventing the wireless device under service contract from being used with other carriers

- Collecting usage data from wireless subscribers

Jailbreaking would invalidate all aforementioned purposes; hence it is against the OEM and carrier's interest. For example, a jailbroken iPhone or iPad may be able to run third-party applications that are not authorized by or purchased from the official Apple App Store. It is also possible to jailbreak a smartphone, unlock premium services, and enjoy them for free, while the carrier intended to collect extra charges for these services. For example, tethering or Hotspot is usually a paid function charged by the amount of 4G data shared between the smartphone and other non-4G platforms, such as a laptop. Software of a jailbroken phone may cheat the carrier by reporting tethering or Hotspot traffic as regular 4G data, hence avoiding extra charges.

Besides circumventing restrictions in the existing firmware and software stack, a more sophisticated form of jailbreaking is to install a completely different software system and possibly repurpose the device. This is especially interesting for devices that are equipped with powerful hardware capabilities but limited software functionalities. HP's TouchPad is such an example.

Launched in July 2011, the TouchPad was discontinued less than two months later. Remaining inventories were sold at extremely low prices to clear the stock. The TouchPad was made of state-of-the-art hardware specifications for that time, including a 1024×768–pixel touch screen, 16GB or 32GB of storage, and 1GB of memory. The operating system preinstalled on the TouchPad was the webOS, which suffers several limitations, such as very small number of available apps, compared to its competitors, iOS and Android. Obviously, it is to the users' interest if a "better" operating system can be installed to run on the TouchPad hardware. In October 2011, the first Android-based jailbreak was released by CyanogenMod.[i] The CyanogenMod converts the TouchPad to a dual-boot system that supports both webOS and Android.

---

[i]CyanogenMod is a free open source operating system for smartphones and tablets, based on the Android mobile platform.

In most cases, jailbreaking is made possible by exploiting design flaws or vulnerabilities in the firmware or software. For example, if a manufacturer's firmware is not digitally signed, then it is convenient to replace it with an adversary's firmware. Even if the architecture and design are sound, bugs in implementation may be exploited to allow jailbreaking.

Now, when the device owner is the hacker, how does the device protect itself from being broken? Clearly, a meaningful integrity protection scheme would have to depend on a root of trust that is in hardware and intact from alteration. How do Intel's CPU and security and management engine help with this matter?

Trusted Platform Module (TPM)

Discussions regarding the integrity of firmware and software on a platform always involve trusted platform module[7] (TPM). The TPM is a public standard that defines the interfaces of a security coprocessor. A TPM implementation is a hardware device that provides cryptographic functionalities for the software to invoke.

Because the TPM is hardware, it is more difficult for attackers to break its security and protections. Attacks against hardware are usually attempted through side channel analysis; for example, timing information, power consumption, and electromagnetic emissions. These attacks require not only physical access, but also special equipment and advanced skills. These requirements limit the scope of the damage of successful attacks, because the hardware attacks cannot be reproduced widely and easily by spreading viruses or malware.

Beside its hardware nature, another important feature of the TPM is its independence. The TPM is a module isolated from the main operating system. Its operations do not rely on and is not impacted by the operating system or the software running on it. This makes the TPM a trustworthy "third-party" for examining the integrity of the software stack.

TPM may be implemented as a physically discrete device or as a logical component inside a security coprocessor. Recent generations of Intel's secure and management engine features a firmware TPM, which is used to support secure boot designs as well as other purposes defined in the TPM standard. For more information about the TPM on the embedded engine, refer to Chapter 7 of this book. Despite the existence of the firmware TPM, it is also possible to include a discrete TPM in the platform. Intel's secure boot architecture, Intel Boot Guard, can work with either the firmware TPM or a discrete TPM.

Platform Configuration Register

The primary goal of the TPM is to protect the integrity of the platform. As such, it is equipped with implementations of hash algorithms and one or more banks of platform configuration registers (PCRs). During the boot process, the PCRs can be used to store and report the hash results for every firmware and software component. The operation of hashing a boot component is often referred to as a *measure*. The operation of measuring the next component is often referred to as an *extend*, because the measurement of the next component is against not only the next component, but also all components that have been measured before it. In other words, the measurement is always incremental. This is defined in the following formula:

$$\text{digest}_{new} := H_{hashAlg}\left(\text{digest}_{old} \,\|\, \text{data}_{new}\right)$$

In this formula, $\|$ means concatenation and **data**$_{new}$ refers to the binary data of the component being measured. **H**$_{hashAlg}$ is the chosen hash algorithm, like SHA-256. From the formula, it is easy to understand that an altered component that is loaded during the boot process will result in incorrect or unexpected measurements for not only itself, but also all components loaded after it, even though those components are intact. Typically, the measurements are checked later locally or reported to remote servers for attestation. The TPM serves as secure storage only and does not perform the comparison for measurements.

Notice the PCR is not specific for the boot time measurement. Rather, supporting the integrity of boot components is just one of many usage models of the PCR. Per the TPM specification, the PCRs are designed for generalized representation of a platform state, and platform-specific specifications may define additional PCR behaviors. In general, a platform specification may define a PCR to represent any value that is authoritatively known by the TPM or has been securely communicated to the TPM.

Many secure boot architectures take advantage of the TPM's measurement capability. However, the TPM has other useful ingredients in addition to the PCR, and the TPM is not just about protecting boot integrity. The TPM has a range of cryptographic capabilities, such as sealing and binding data, to help secure the platform not only during boot but also at runtime.

Field Programmable Fuses

Newer security and management engines shipped with select Intel platforms in and after 2013 support a feature called *field programmable fuses*. As its name indicates, it allows fuses to be burned after leaving Intel's manufacturing facility, in the OEM's factory or in the field. The field programmable fuses are essentially another nonvolatile storage medium. However, it is not the only nonvolatile storage in the engine.

Field Programmable Fuses vs. Flash Storage

The security and management engine's kernel contains a storage manager that manages nonvolatile data that must persist across power cycles. Nonsensitive data can be stored in plaintext; secrets can be protected with confidentiality, integrity, and anti-replay. The embedded applications that invoke the storage manager are free to apply one or more of these protection options for their data. The data is stored on the flash device in a special partition. The same flash also stores the BIOS, the embedded engine's binary image, as well as other system firmware.

Now that nonvolatile data can be stored on the flash, why the field programmable fuses? When comparing the field programmable fuses with the flash storage, anti-replay becomes an interesting aspect. Two anti-replay mechanisms are supported by the storage manager: native monotonic counter and RPMC (replay-protected monotonic counter) flash:

- *Native monotonic counter*: The monotonic counter resides in the chipset's RTC (runtime clock) power well. Upon RTC power loss, for example, due to coin battery removal, all anti-replay blobs managed by the engine are invalidated by the storage manager. Because of this limitation, the applications must be able to re-create the blobs in case they are lost.

- *RPMC flash*: The flash device natively mitigates anti-replay attacks. The advantage is the independence of the RTC power well. The disadvantage is the cost of the RPMC flash. Not all OEMs use RPMC flash parts for all products.

The field programmable fuse scheme provides anti-replay protection that completely eliminates the dependency on RTC well or RPMC flash. Thanks to its nature, writing a fuse is a one-time operation. That is, once a fuse has been burned (its value changing from 0 to 1), the operation cannot be reversed, and the fuse will assume the value of 1 from then on. This characteristic makes field programmable fuses especially suitable for holding data that requires certain properties:

- The data must survive flash wipe or corruption. Such data includes platform state information, OEM programmable confidential information, and so forth. The security and management engine's verified boot architecture uses the field programmable fuses for OEMs to program digests of their public keys.

- The data is used to support security claims; loss of the data may result in security vulnerabilities. For example, the fuses can be used to permanently record the fact that a security enhancement feature, such as anti-theft or TPM, has been enabled for this platform. If an attacker (owner of the device) intends to bypass specific restrictions by reflashing the firmware image with another version that does not support the security enhancement, then the image replacement will be caught by the fuses.

The storage manager is not able to provide this level of protection with its anti-replay mechanisms.

In addition to anti-replay, the fuse block is hidden inside the security and management engine and invisible to the outside of the engine. In other words, confidentiality and integrity are native characteristics of the field programmable fuses, without having to apply encryption and hashing algorithms.

The main drawback of field programmable fuses is the relatively small number of fuses available on die. For a typical configuration of the engine, there are 1024 programmable fuses in a 32×32 array layout. About one in every four fuses is reserved for locking, repairing, and redundancy check purposes, leaving only a few hundred fuses for applications to program. As such, the uses of the field programmable fuses are not a runtime matter, and must be predefined and allocated carefully on a case-by-case basis.

Field Programmable Fuse Task

From the firmware architecture perspective, the field programmable fuse manager is implemented in its own *task* (container). See Chapter 4 of this book for more information about the security and management engine's task isolation infrastructure. Being a dedicated task, other tasks are not able to penetrate the field programmable fuses. Firmware modules that own fuses can program or sense the fuses by calling the field programmable fuse task via the intertask calling mechanism supported by the kernel.

The flow for programming a fuse is depicted in Figure 6-2. The figure does not detail steps for the fuse manager to burn a fuse; for example, a valid bit check, a redundancy check, and so forth. The flow for sensing the value of a fuse is similar and is not shown in this figure.

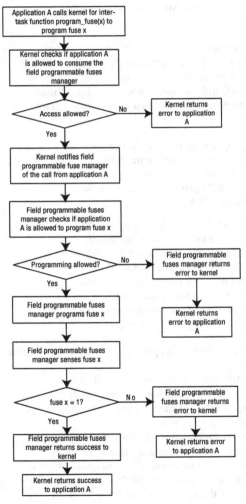

Figure 6-2. *Flow for application A to programming fuse x*

Depending on the nature of the data, there are five usage models of the programmable fuses:

- *Single-bit one-time programming*: The data is of Boolean type. Once programmed, the change becomes permanent and it can no longer be reverted. This usage requires only one fuse. For example, once the OEM finishes the manufacturing process, it programs a single-bit one-time fuse to show that manufacturing is completed. Certain configurations of the security and management engine are intended for only OEMs to use; it is not supposed to be touched by end users. The firmware logic for handling such configurations consults this "end of manufacturing" indicator fuse, before proceeding with the configuration manipulation.

- *Single-bit multiple-time programming*: The data is of Boolean type. It may change a limited number of times, say n, during the lifetime of the platform. In this case, n fuses are necessary for storing the data, and one of the n fuses is programmed every time the value of the data flips. Take the anti-theft technology for example. Once enrolled, the anti-theft technology automatically shuts down the platform per the user-configured policy if it detects that the system is in a stolen state. The shutdown is performed only if the platform is enrolled, therefore the enrollment status is critical for enforcing the shutdown. Users are free to opt out after enrollment or enroll again (that is, changing the enrollment status) for a limited number of times. For a single-bit multiple-time programming fuse, the field programmable fuse manager counts the number of the n fuses that have been burned. If the number is odd, then the data is assumed to be *true*, implying, for example, the anti-theft is currently enrolled; if the number of is even or zero, then the data bit is assumed a value of *false*.

- *Multiple-bit one-time programming*: The data consists of multiple bits. It cannot be changed once programmed. For this usage, the number of fuses required is equal to the bit size of the data. For example, in Intel's verified boot architecture, the OEM programs its 256-bit hash of OEM's RSA public key to field programmable fuses during the manufacturing process. The OEM also programs its secure boot policies to designated fuses. Once done, the value cannot be erased or updated during the lifetime of the platform.

- *Multiple-bit multiple-time programming*: The data consists of multiple bits. It may change for a limited number of times. For this usage, the number of fuses required is equal to the data's bit size multiplied by the number of times the data is allowed to change during the lifetime of the platform.

- *Incremental integer*: The data is a non-negative integer that assumes values from 0 to *m*, inclusive. The data assumes an initial value of 0 and can only be updated from smaller to greater; for example, from 1 to 3, but not from 3 to 2. A set of *m* fuses are required for this usage model. The number of burned fuses represents the value of the data. A typical usage is the version number of a firmware component. When vulnerabilities are fixed in a firmware patch, the version number of the new release will be incremented by one from the previous vulnerable version. The latest version number is recorded in the fuses. When the embedded engine loads the firmware, it checks the firmware's version number and compares with what is shown by the fuses. If the former is greater, the fuses are updated with the new version number; if the former is smaller, then the system concludes that it is under a rollback attack and proceeds accordingly.

Intel Boot Guard

Intel Boot Guard technology provides hardware-based boot integrity protection that prevents malicious firmware and software from taking over boot blocks. It does so by detecting an unauthorized boot block and disallowing it to execute. The Boot Guard is a hardware and firmware solution that does not depend on any software.

Intel released the authenticated code module, or ACM, for OEMs to enable the Intel Trusted Execution Technology[8] (TXT) and the Boot Guard feature. As will be described later in detail, the ACM plays a pivotal role and carries critical tasks in the Boot Guard solution. Digitally signed by Intel, the ACM component is stored on the flash together with BIOS and other firmware components. The public key for verifying the signature on the ACM is hard-coded in Intel's CPU. There is a security version number associated with the ACM module, which is used to identify and revoke vulnerable ACM releases and stop the system from booting.

To take advantage of the Boot Guard technology, the OEM must implement a new firmware component to the boot flow, called the *initial boot block*, which is loaded before the BIOS. The initial boot block is responsible for checking the integrity of BIOS, initializing memory, and loading BIOS into the system memory. Just like the ACM, the initial boot block is stored on the flash chip. The boot flow is shown in Figure 6-1, and the additions of the ACM and the initial boot block are shown in Figure 6-3.

CPU reset → bootrom → ACM → initial boot block → BIOS → boot loader → operating system → applications

Figure 6-3. Boot flow with ACM and initial boot block

Note that this is a simplified boot flow. The boot flow with the TXT is more complicated. Intel Boot Guard technology defines three boot configurations:

- *Measured boot*: Measures the initial boot block into the platform's secure storage device, such as a TPM.

- *Verified boot:* Cryptographically verifies the integrity of the initial boot block using a digital signature scheme. The verified boot reduces material cost because it offers boot protection without a TPM device.

- *Measured boot + verified boot*: Measures and verifies the initial boot block.

But, why is it necessary to introduce the initial boot block? Why can't the Boot Guard directly verify the BIOS? Here are a couple reasons.

- *Size*: The size of today's BIOS image is in the scale of megabytes and increasing. However, the initial boot block is desired to be small enough to fit in the on-die memory of Intel silicon in all compatible platforms. In other words, the architecture must work with fixed and limited memory size. This is not scalable for a BIOS whose size may increase.

- *Flexibility*: Modularity in design provides flexibility and the ease of changing only parts of the product. Also, an OEM can use one private key to sign the initial boot block and another key to sign the BIOS. Even in the event the private key for signing the BIOS image is leaked or compromised, there is no need to recall hardware.

Operating System Requirements for Boot Integrity

Microsoft's Windows Certification Program[9] specifies a requirement for boot integrity. Intel's Boot Guard technology helps OEMs meet this requirement for their Windows-based systems:

> *Boot Integrity: Platform uses on-die ROM[ii] or One-Time Programmable (OTP) memory for storing initial boot code and initial public key (or hash of initial public key) used to provide boot integrity, and provides power-on reset logic to execute from on-die ROM or secure on-die SRAM.[iii]*

Google does not pose requirements for boot integrity for Android-based systems. In fact, most Android device manufacturers do not implement a secure boot, and intentionally allow a custom operating system to be loaded.[10] CyanogenMod is one of the most famous customized mobile operating systems derived from Android. Tutorials and materials for rooting Android devices are publicly available.

[ii]Read-only memory
[iii]Static random-access memory

OEM Configuration

The Boot Guard configurations set by the OEM slightly vary among different products. In general and at a minimum, the OEM is responsible for configuring its public key hash for a verified boot, and the boot policies via the security and management engine.

The security of a verified boot is rooted to the OEM's asymmetric keypair. The OEM generates a 2048-bit RSA keypair as its root key for signing manifests for the initial boot blocks. The private portion of the root keypair must be kept securely, and signing manifests for initial boot blocks shall be its sole usage. On the other hand, the SHA-256 hash of the public key is programmed to the field programmable fuses during the manufacturing process. The public key hash consumes 256 fuses that belong to the *multiple-bit one-time programming* category, which cannot be updated once written. Because of the one-time programming limitation, the OEM will not be able to renew the root key or update the hash, even if the private key is compromised. Therefore, the OEM must protect its root private key in a signing server with strong protection from attacks or leakage.

In addition to programming its public key hash, the OEM is also responsible for defining its boot policies and saving them in the field programmable fuses. The boot policies are also a one-time configuration that cannot be revised. The policies instruct the Intel hardware with regard to the following:

- What boot protections are enabled—that is, measured boot only, verified boot only, neither, or both

- What actions to take upon ACM failure

- What action to take upon initial boot block failure

In the scenario that the CPU is unable to load the ACM from the flash or the digital signature of the ACM fails to verify, the CPU may either (based on the OEM's setting for the second bullet in the preceding list) enter the shutdown state or proceed with booting from the legacy vector. Although the instant shutdown option offers the highest level of integrity protection, it is generally not recommended because it may potentially lead to a large number of customer support calls. And problems are extremely difficult to debug if the system powers itself off at a very early stage of the boot process.

After the ACM is checked out successfully, the initial boot block becomes the next subject of interest. Recall that the security and management engine is capable of triggering instant shutdown of the platform (see Chapter 4 for details). When a boot integrity-check fails, it is the engine's responsibility—according to the OEM's set policies—to shut down the platform and terminate the boot process. The OEM can determine when the shutdown should happen upon failure. A few options are available:

- *Unrestricted*: Do not shut down the system; let it boot and run normally as if the failure did not occur.

- *Remediation*: Let the system continue to boot but shutdown ungracefully after a certain amount of time. The amount of time (for example, 30 minutes) should be enough for a repair technician to perform basic remediation work, such as updating the initial boot block or BIOS from the operating system. Yet, the time before shutdown should not be too long; otherwise, the boot policy becomes meaningless.

- *Diagnostics*: This is similar to the remediation option, but the timer is set to a much smaller value, such as one minute. This option allows the manufacturer's support engineers to retrieve debug information from the system.

- *Zero-tolerance*: Shut down the platform immediately upon a boot integrity failure. Similar to the case of ACM failure, this option is generally not recommended.

The security and management engine offers two methods for the OEM to program its public key hash and the boot policies to the designated field programmable fuses. In both cases, the configuration is allowed only before the end of the manufacturing process:

1. *Through HECI[iv] commands sent from the host operating system*. The commands are honored by the engine only before the "end of manufacturing" HECI message is received and recorded. This method is not available for production parts.

2. *Through image building*. Intel provides OEMs with a software program called *firmware image tool* to build a flash image from various components, such as binaries of BIOS, the security and management engine, and so on. The tool allows an OEM to configure the engine for Boot Guard support, including setting its public key hash and boot polices. These values will be automatically programmed to the field programmable fuses by the engine's firmware as soon as the "end of manufacturing" HECI message is received and recorded.

The boot policy configuration applies to both the measured boot and verified boot.

Measured Boot

The measured boot mechanism is made possible by the Intel TXT. The Intel TXT is designed to harden platforms at the hardware level, from hypervisor, firmware (BIOS, root kit, and so forth), and other software-based attacks.

The Windows Certification Program requires measuring all boot components using a TPM. Intel's measured boot meets this requirement because the initial boot block is measured as the first boot component:

> *During the boot sequence, the boot firmware/software shall measure all firmware and all software components it loads after the core root of trust for measurement is established. The measurements shall be logged as well as extended to platform configuration registers in a manner compliant with the following requirements.*

[iv]HECI, or host-embedded communication interface, is the two-way communication channel between the security and management engine and the host operating system. Refer to Chapter 3 for more information about the HECI.

The Intel TXT works by creating a measured launched environment (MLE), which enables precise comparisons between the current state of the platform and known-good references for all components of the boot process. The measurements (extended hashes of components) are stored in the platform's secure storage device, usually a TPM, and are available for local or remote attestation. If measurements match known-good configurations, then the TXT marks the system *trusted*; otherwise, the TXT marks the system *untrusted* and follows defined fallback policies. It can either abort the boot process or let the platform continue to operate—but with degraded functionality, such as forbidding it from running sensitive tasks, for example.

For the measured boot, the CPU loads the ACM after verifying the signature associated with it. The ACM calculates the hash of the initial boot block and stores the measurement in a PCR slot of the platform's discrete or firmware TPM device. The measurement is available for attestation later.

Verified Boot

The measured boot mechanism relies on a dedicated storage device, typically PCR slots of a TPM, to securely store measurements of the initial boot block and other components involved in the boot process. Unfortunately, a TPM may not be available on all form factors. This is especially the case for low-cost mobile devices. Specifically, for systems in which TPM is not required for other functionalities, adding a TPM merely for the purpose of safeguarding the boot integrity increases not only the BOM (bill of materials) cost but also development and integration effort, which may not yield a good return-on-investment. However, the boot integrity can still be a critical requirement for those devices. The verified boot mechanism provides an alternate approach without relying on a TPM or other devices. Notice that the verified boot mechanism by itself does not measure all boot components. Therefore, without a measured boot, it may not satisfy the Windows Certification Program requirements.

Cryptographically, data integrity is achieved by employing either a hash (including a keyed hash and a plain hash) or a digital signature as a "measurement." Without an independent and trusted reference, the "known good" measurement must be kept within the platform and intact from unauthorized alteration. The verified boot features a hardware-based root of trust for verifying the integrity of the initial boot block. Next, the initial boot block verifies the integrity of the BIOS, the BIOS verifies the integrity of the boot loader, and the boot loader verifies the integrity of the operating system, and so forth. The integrity of successive components loaded following the initial boot block is guaranteed by a chain of trust.

Manifests

The initial boot block binary is associated with a manifest, called the *initial boot block manifest*, or IBBM for short. The IBBM contains the following fields:

1. The security version number of the IBBM

2. The SHA-256 hash of the initial boot block

3. The RSA signature on (1) and (2)

4. The RSA public key that is used to verify (3), referred to as the *IBBM public key* onward

The IBBM 2048-bit RSA keypair is also generated by the OEM, but it is different from the OEM root RSA keypair introduced earlier; although an OEM is free (but not encouraged) to utilize the same keypair for both. The only usage of the IBBM RSA keypair is to sign IBBMs. The IBBM RSA private key must be kept securely by the OEM. The OEM root public key hash is stored in the security and management engine's programmable fuses. In contrast, the IBBM public key appears only in the IBBM.

The IBBM is not the only manifest in the picture. The OEM uses its root keypair to sign another manifest, namely the *key manifest*, which contains the following fields:

5. The security version number of the key manifest

6. The SHA-256 hash of the IBBM public key

7. The RSA signature on the (5) and (6)

8. The OEM root public key, used to verify (7)

The hash of the OEM root public key (8) is stored in the programmable fuses. Both the IBBM and the key manifest are stored on the flash. The relationships among the root key hash, two manifests, and the initial boot block are better explained graphically in Figure 6-4.

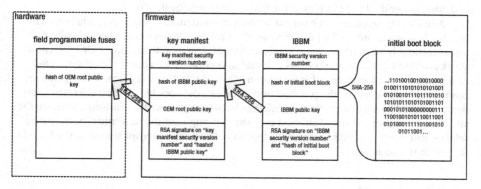

Figure 6-4. *Using the OEM public key hash to verify the initial boot block via the key manifest and IBBM*

As Figure 6-4 depicts, the root of trust is the OEM root public key hash located in the fuse hardware and handled by the security and management engine. This makes the verified boot a hardware-based scheme that is significantly more difficult to compromise than software solutions.

The key manifest seems an unnecessary middleman sitting between the OEM root public key hash and the IBBM. Why not just use the OEM root key to sign the IBBM directly? The indirection introduced by the key manifest is desirable for OEMs that manufacture multiple product lines. With the key manifest, the OEM can use a single root key for all its products, but different IBBM keys for different product lines.

For the sake of revocation, both manifests are versioned.

- The security version number of the key manifest enables the OEM to revoke the IBBM keypair should it be compromised. If the IBBM keypair must be replaced, then the OEM will generate a new IBBM keypair and place its public key hash in a new key manifest, and at the same time increment the security version number of the key manifest.

- The security version number of the IBBM covers the initial boot block, and it allows the OEM to revoke and patch a vulnerable initial boot block. When a new initial boot block is released, the security version number of the IBBM must be incremented accordingly.

The two version numbers are examined by the security and management engine during the verified boot process. If the engine finds that the version number of a manifest being loaded is greater than the corresponding value recorded in the field programmable fuses, then it programs a certain number of fuses to reflect the greater version number. The fuses reserved for the security version numbers belong to the category of *incremental integer*. The version number of a manifest being loaded being smaller than the corresponding value recorded in the fuses is an indicator of a rollback attack, where an attacker unlocks the flash part and replaces a good and later version of the manifest with a vulnerable and older version. In this situation, the embedded engine will react accordingly per the boot policies in the fuses configured by the OEM.

Admittedly, revocation relying on security version numbers has its limitations. The mechanism works only if the platform has already run, at least once, a later manifest or an initial boot block with a greater version number, and then the manifest or initial boot block is rolled back to an earlier and vulnerable version. If the attacker blocks manifest or initial boot block updates (this is rather trivial to do) in the first place, so the platform has no chance to ever see the patched manifest or initial boot block, then the revocation design backed by security versioning will not be able to protect the platform. To make the situation worse, an advanced attacker may reverse-engineer the new initial boot block release and figure out the security bugs that were fixed, and attempt to exploit the bugs in the old initial boot block.

Verification Flow

The verification of the initial boot block is a collaborative effort by the security and management engine and the ACM running on the CPU. The ACM is responsible for the following:

- Loading the initial boot block firmware and the two manifests from the flash

- Retrieving the OEM's public key hash, boot policy, its own security version number, and the security version numbers of the two manifests from the engine

- Verifying the integrity of the initial boot block using the manifests and OEM's public key hash.

- Notifying the engine of updating the security version numbers if necessary

- Enforcing boot policy in the event of a communication error or a time-out with the engine

The security and management engine is responsible for the following:

- Reading OEM's public key hash, boot policy, ACM security version number, and the security version numbers of the two manifests from field programmable fuses, and sends to the ACM

- Incrementing security version numbers of the ACM and the two manifests in the fuses upon requests from the ACM

- Enforcing boot policies in the event of a communication error or time-out with the ACM

- Performing appropriate actions upon failure of verification, per the boot policies

Figure 6-5 presents the high-level sequence diagram. In the figure, the security version number check performed by the ACM is against three elements: the ACM, the key manifest, and the IBBM. For the boot process to succeed, all three values seen by the ACM must be equal to or greater than the respectively referenced values reported by the security and management engine. If one or more of the security version numbers need updating, then the ACM notifies the engine after all checks have passed.

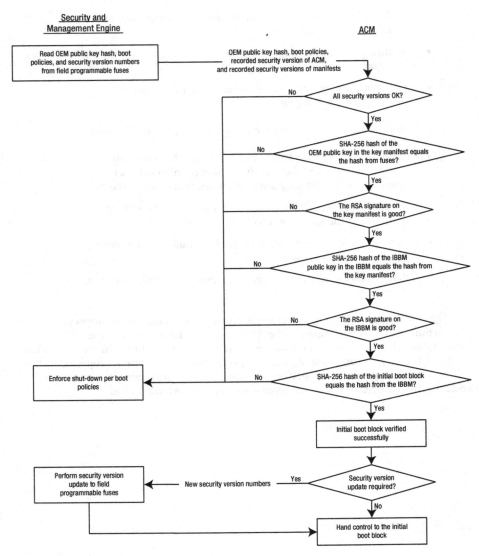

Figure 6-5. *The initial boot block verification flow for the verified boot*

References

1. Joanna Rutkowska, "Evil Maid Goes After TrueCrypt," http://theinvisiblethings.blogspot.com/2009/10/evil-maid-goes-after-truecrypt.html, accessed on March 20, 2014.

2. J. Alex Halderman, Seth D. Schoen, Nadia Heninger, William Clarkson, William Paul, Joseph A. Calandrino, Ariel J. Feldman, Jacob Appelbaum, and Edward W. Felten, "Lest We Remember: Cold Boot Attacks on Encryption Keys," *Proc. 17th USENIX Security Symposium*, San Jose, CA, July 2008.

3. Unified EFI, Inc., "Unified Extensible Firmware Interface Specification," www.uefi.org, accessed on March 20, 2014.

4. John Heasman, "Implementing and Detecting an ACPI BIOS Rootkit," Black Hat Europe, March 3, 2006, Amsterdam, the Netherlands.

5. Anibal Sacco and Alfredo Ortega, "Persistent BIOS Infection," CanSecWest, March 19, 2009, Vancouver, BC.

6. Rafal Wojtczuk and Alexander Tereshkin, "Attacking Intel® BIOS," Black Hat USA, July 30, 2009, Las Vegas, NV.

7. Trusted Computing Group, "Trusted Platform Module Library," www.trustedcomputinggroup.org, accessed on March 20, 2014.

8. Intel Trusted Execution Technology, www.intel.com/txt, accessed on January 30, 2014.

9. Microsoft Corporation, *"Windows Certification Program: Hardware Certification Taxonomy & Requirements—Systems,"* December 16, 2013, pp. 125.

10. N. Asokan, Lucas Davi, Alexandra Dmitrienko, Stephan Heuser, Kari Kostiainen, Elena Reshetova, and Ahmad-Reza Sadeghi, *"Mobile Platform Security,"* Morgan & Claypool Publishers, 2013, pp. 40.

■ ■ ■

CHAPTER 7

Trust Computing, Backed by the Intel Platform Trust Technology

Love all, trust a few, do wrong to none.

—William Shakespeare

In recent years, computing devices such as laptops, smartphones, tablets, and so forth, have become very functionally powerful. These devices have deeply penetrated into people's daily lives in many ways. To take advantage of all the convenience that the advanced technologies have to offer, it is almost impossible for a regular user to avoid giving personal data and confidential information to these intelligent machines. A computer probably knows more secrets of its owner than the owner's best friend. A user, implicitly, trusts his computers just like he trusts his family and friends.

For financial applications, shoppers input their credit or debit card numbers to purchase from online retailers; bank customers deposit checks using mobile devices by taking pictures of the checks and uploading to the bank's server; financial institutions often require a social security number for the purpose of authentication; investors buy and sell stocks through electronic brokers. For personal applications, most people store all their photos, videos, and documents in local storage or upload to the cloud; in addition, users' private information exposed in e-mails and social networking sites is handled completely by computers.

As you enjoy the convenience, a trust relationship is established. You are willing to give out the secrets because you trust the computers, not only your personal devices, but also the remote web sites and servers they interact with. You believe they are reliable and accountable and they will protect your sensitive information and use it legitimately.

Consumers need to trust the devices, and so do the service providers. The owner of a platform is not always the one to protect. For example, one of the biggest concerns of any content provider is its for-profit contents being transmitted to a rogue device that has been hacked by the owner. If the provider was not able to identify compromised devices, hackers could happily consume the received contents for free or even share with more people, resulting in direct profit loss for the provider.

The reliance on computers in the sectors of governments and large businesses is even more vital. Computer security for those highly sensitive domains is not merely about preventing loss of revenue or privacy, but also safeguarding national secrets and security. When the specification for the Trusted Platform Module[1] (TPM) was introduced more than a decade ago, it was found especially useful for defense and intelligence agencies and other organizations where critical data must be stored and safeguarded from compromise.

For any new technology to be valuable, the benefit of applying the technology must exceed the expenses of initial deployment and continuous management. Ten years ago, the cost of TPM deployment was relatively high; consumer usages were not depending on computer security as heavily as today. In other words, the expenses incurred to users outweighed the benefit of utilizing hardware-based security, making TPM not a popular consumer feature. In contrast, TPM was financially meaningful for governments and large enterprises and organizations.

But the situation has gradually changed over time. On one hand, today's personal computing devices are managing and processing critical assets for individuals, and compromise of security and the loss of such assets can result in a tremendous impact. Considering the ever-increasing threats from advanced attacks, protecting personal devices with a more robust technology is now inevitable. On the other hand, the cost of deployment and administration for TPM has reduced significantly and become more affordable, thanks to the improved manufacturing processes and cutting-edge embedded designs for TPM. Given these considerations, it makes sense, economically, to install TPM in consumer devices. For example, select tablets and desktops built with Intel's Bay Trail SoC (System-on-Chip) are shipped with integrated TPM capability; Google's Chromebook that sells for $250 also has TPM built in. These are lower-cost consumer-grade products.

TPM Overview

What does "trusted" mean in the context of computing? A trusted or trustworthy platform is *a platform that behaves in a manner that is expected for its designated purposes*. A platform is trusted if and only if the integrity of its hardware, firmware, and software components is proven to be intact. That is, the platform is operating in a state that is identical to what is configured by its manufacturer and other authorized entities.

For a consumer device, there are three angles of *trust*, depending on the identities of the trusting entity and the adversary, respectively:

- *The owner of the platform needs to trust the platform* in order to let it perform sensitive operations. In this case, the adversary is a remote or local attacker, for example, an evil maid[2] (see Chapter 6 of this book for a description of the Evil Maid attack).

- *A remote server needs to trust the platform* in order to grant it access to premium services. In this case, the adversary is the owner of the platform. For example, wireless carriers may refuse to deliver feature updates or honor a warranty for rooted phones; many companies do not permit employees' rooted devices to be used for Bring Your Own Device (BYOD) purposes; content providers may ban transmissions of paid contents to devices for which integrity cannot be verified.

- *In a distributed system, a node computer needs to be trusted by its peers.* Sensitive operations should not be assigned to a node for which integrity cannot be verified.

The TPM covers these scenarios by employing a dedicated security processor that is isolated from the host firmware and operating system. The TPM device acts as *the* root of trust for the platform. A trust that is rooted in separate and shielded hardware is generally believed to provide more robust protection and expose a minimal attack surface compared to a software-based root of trust. Notice that the TPM itself is just a library and does not provide security per se; the host firmware and software must invoke the TPM to benefit from its functionalities and establish the trust.

The TPM specification is created and maintained by the Trusted Computing Group (TCG), a not-for-profit organization formed to develop, define, and promote open, vendor-neutral, global industry standards, supportive of a hardware-based root of trust, for interoperable trusted computing platforms. Its members include major hardware and software vendors, such as Intel, IBM, Microsoft, HP, Lenovo, and so on. The first version of the TPM specification was released in 2003. The latest published version is 1.2. The TPM version 1.2 is also published as ISO/IEC standard 11889. The next version is 2.0, which is under public review as of April 2014. The TPM specification is intended to define a standardized interface for hardware-based root of trust for all form factors of computing systems, so that users and remote servers can trust the integrity of the systems with a high level of confidence. In addition to attestation, a TPM also provides fundamental cryptography functionalities, such as random number generation, hashing, key management, and so forth. Since its release, over two billion end-point devices have been shipped with TPM.

It is worth pointing out that there is no such thing as 100% trustworthy computing. Given sufficient time and resources, even hardware such as TPM may be broken by skilled hackers with special tools and applying, for example, side channel attacks and cold boot attacks. However, it is commonly accepted that hardware-based security mechanisms are much harder to defeat than software solutions. The difficulty is due to equipment and skills required for finding and exploiting hardware vulnerabilities. One other important consideration is that it almost always requires a physical presence to compromise hardware. This means that it is rarely possible for remote attackers to infect a large number of devices through widespread viruses. This also means that it is unlikely that an average user can hack his own device by simply following step-by-step instructions or installing malware that is published on the Internet. This limits the scope of impact, even if vulnerability in hardware is found and exploited.

After all, the robustness of the trust protection only has to be such that the expense associated with the effort exceeds the benefit that the attacker may gain from successful exploitations. For most cases, especially consumer applications, a well-designed TPM implementation would satisfy this requirement.

Cryptography Subsystem

The TPM 1.2 specification involves a limited set of cryptography algorithms:

- *Hash and HMAC family:* SHA-1 and HMAC-SHA-1.

- *Symmetric encryption family:* Vernam one-time-pad[3] or AES.

- *Asymmetric encryption and digital signature family:* RSA.

- Random number generator.

The draft of the TPM 2.0 specification published in March 2014 defines a much larger set of cryptography capabilities for its cryptography subsystem:

- *Hash and HMAC family:* SHA-1, SHA-256, SHA-384, SHA-512, SM3,[4] and their HMAC. The SM3 is the cryptographic hash standard published by the State Encryption Management Bureau of China.

- *Symmetric encryption family:* AES and SM4.[5] The SM4 is the block encryption standard of China. The Cipher Feedback (CFB) mode is required by the TPM specification, whereas other modes are optional. Note that the CFB mode does not require the size of the plaintext or ciphertext be a multiple of the block size.

- *Asymmetric encryption family:* RSA and ECC.

- *Digital signature family:* RSA, ECC, and SM2.[6] The SM2 is the elliptic curve cryptography standard of China.

- *Key derivation family:* NIST (National Institute of Standard and Technology) SP800-56A[7] and the counter mode of SP800-108.[8]

- Random number generator.

Readers who are not familiar with these algorithms may refer to Chapter 3 of this book for detailed information. A TPM can choose to implement only necessary cryptography algorithms that are applicable to the platform's use cases. Most cryptography algorithms used by the TPM specification follow existing government and industry standards, such as AES, HMAC, RSA PKCS, and so forth. However, besides leveraging existing cryptography standards, the TPM specification also defines additional cryptography schemes, for example, the modified Schnorr digital signature based on ECC.

For certain standardized cryptography algorithms, the TPM specification may specify additional restrictions and requirements. This deserves special attention from implementers who intend to deliver compliant TPM products. Here are two examples:

- TPM's ECC key pair generation should follow NIST's FIPS (Federal Information Processing Standard) 186-3: *Digital Signature Standard*, with a small modification. Per FIPS 186-3, the value of resulting private key d should be between 1 and n inclusively, where n is the order of the base point of the selected curve. However, the TPM specification mandates that the lower bound of d be $2^{nLen/2}$ instead of 1, where $nLen$ denotes the order of n. This is equivalent to saying that the most significant $nLen/2$ bits of d cannot be all zeroes.

- When generating a k-bit RSA key pair, the TPM is required to set the most significant two bits of the two $k/2$-bit prime candidates p and q to 1, respectively. This is to assure that the bit length of the resulting modulo $n = p \times q$ is not shorter than k. Although this is in fact common practice exercised by many implementations, it is not explicitly required by the RSA PKCS standard.

■ **Note** For cryptography algorithms, pay attention to specific requirements mandated by the TPM specification on top of the corresponding cryptography standards.

Storage

In addition to the cryptography subsystem, the TPM is also equipped with volatile and nonvolatile memory. The most critical volatile data on the TPM is the PCR (platform configuration register), which stores the platform measurements and is read only to the host. The PCR should not be persistent. Furthermore, secure internal memory is used for runtime operation and must not be visible to the host.

The nonvolatile memory is used for storing TPM secrets, such as primary seeds, endorsement key pairs, and persistent objects created by TPM callers. It must be protected against external access.

Endorsement Key

Unique to the TPM device, an endorsement key is an identity for the *Root of Trust for Reporting*. The private portion of the endorsement key is stored securely in the TPM's nonvolatile memory and is never exposed externally. The TPM 1.2 specification requires the endorsement key be used only in two operations—namely, establishing the TPM Owner and establishing Attestation Identity Key (AIK) values and credentials, and it prohibits using the endorsement key for other purposes. Per the TPM 2.0 draft, it is the *privacy administrator*'s responsibility to control the uses of the endorsement key. The specification still recommends restricting the use of the endorsement key, due to potential privacy concerns. Generally, if a public key is not vouched for by a certification authority, then the privacy concerns are not material. A TPM implementation may create multiple asymmetric key pairs descended from the endorsement key.

The TPM 1.2 specification requires a preinstalled 2048-bit RSA key pair as the *endorsement key*. The 2.0 version allows multiple endorsement keys to be derived from the *endorsement primary seed*. For TPM 2.0, the endorsement key can be either RSA or ECC.

Attestation

The TCG defines *attestation* as "the process of vouching for the accuracy of information. External entities can attest to shielded locations, protected capabilities, and Roots of Trust. A platform can attest to its description of platform characteristics that affect the integrity (trustworthiness) of a platform. Both forms of attestation require reliable evidence of the attesting entity." The TPM provides a way to establish the "reliable evidence."

As briefly discussed in Chapter 6, the PCR carries a critical role in platform integrity measurements, especially during the boot process. A PCR stores the accumulative cryptographic hash of platform components, using the "extend" operation defined as follows, where || means concatenation:

$$\text{digest}_{new} := H_{hashAlg}\left(\text{digest}_{old} \| \text{data}_{new}\right)$$

Starting from the Core Root of Trust for Measurement (CRTM), the boot process traverses a series of platform firmware and software. Each component measures the successive component and extends the results to the designated PCR. The control is transferred to the next component after the measurement.

There are two types of measurements using PCR: static and dynamic, as defined by individual platform specifications. PCRs that are configured to hold static measurements are cleared upon only platform power-up and hard reset, whereas PCRs for dynamic measurements may be cleared by the TPM2_PCR_Reset command.

For example, in the server environment, Intel Trusted Execution Technology (TXT) securely measures the following components during boot in seven static PCRs.[9] The operating system may use the remaining PCRs of the TPM to perform software measurements specific to the operating system.

- *PCR0*: BIOS (basic input/output system) code

- *PCR1*: BIOS settings

- *PCR2*: Option ROM (read-only memory) code

- *PCR3*: Option ROM settings

- *PCR4*: Boot sector—master boot record (MBR)

- *PCR5*: Boot configuration

- *PCR6*: Platform state changes

The entity that requests the attestation may choose to examine any of the defined PCRs according to its usage model and trust policies, but PCR0, which proves the BIOS integrity, is usually examined.

The TPM reports the platform state by quoting PCR values. The platform state report is available to local and remote entities. To assure that the PCR values in a report actually reflect the state of the platform, it is necessary to bind the report to the platform. A common approach is to have the TPM digitally sign the report with one of its asymmetric keys, for example the AIK, for which the associated public key is present in its corresponding certificate signed by a trusted attestation authority. The requesting entity can then use the subject public key in the certificate to verify the TPM's signature on the state report. The TPM specification encourages the use of domain-specific signing keys for the purpose of signing reports.

Binding and Sealing

Binding refers to the operation of encrypting a caller's data using a TPM trusted key, which is descended from the endorsement key. Because the TPM that encrypts the data is the only entity that possesses the trusted key, only the same TPM is able to decrypt and retrieve the data, and the data is essentially bound to the platform.

Sealing is similar to binding but poses an additional condition for decryption. The "unseal" (decrypt) operation is allowed only if the platform is in a specified state identified by values in PCRs. The specific state is usually the state when the "sealing" of the data was performed.

A famous example of sealing is full disk encryption. The symmetric key for encrypting the disks can be sealed in the TPM, and unsealed during the boot process only if the integrity of the boot path is verified by measurements in the PCRs. If malware such as a boot kit is detected, then the platform state will be incorrect and the TPM will refuse to decrypt the disk encryption key. The encrypted data on the disk is safe from, for example, the Evil Maid attack.

Intel Platform Trust Technology

The security and management engine shipped with recent Intel platforms, such as Haswell ULT multichip packaging and Bay Trail SoC, features the Intel Platform Trust Technology (PTT). The PTT implements a firmware-based TPM that is compliant to version 1.2.

From an architecture perspective, the TPM is an application running on the embedded engine's core and communicates with the external world, for example the Windows 8 operating system, through an I/O driver in the embedded kernel. As part of the security and management engine, the firmware-based TPM is inherently isolated from the host. The TPM also benefits from all the security hardening countermeasures implemented on the security and management engine. These hardening features are discussed in Chapter 4. The engine serves as the *Shielded Location*, as defined in the TPM specification, for the firmware-based TPM.

As described in earlier chapters of this book, the security and management engine runs a collection of firmware applications. Although the actual set of applications installed on the engine varies from product to product, so far, there is no product that hosts only TPM. As a result, to minimize the trusted computing base of the TPM, it is necessary to protect the TPM from being attacked by other internal firmware applications, such as AMT (Advanced Management Technology), in case they are compromised. To achieve this goal, the TPM is placed in an isolated process or task, and covered by the task isolation mechanism. Figure 7-1 illustrates the high-level architecture. Note that the TPM uses internal memory and does not rely on the embedded engine's capabilities of using the system DRAM (dynamic random-access memory).

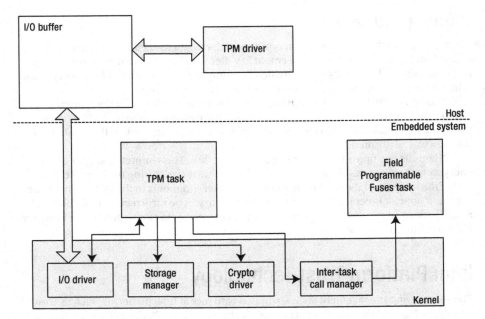

Figure 7-1. *Block diagram of the firmware-based TPM architecture and its communication with the host*

As depicted in the figure, the TPM application consumes and relies on other elements of the security and management engine:

- *Kernel*: For nonvolatile secure storage, cryptography algorithms, I/O driver, and security fuse access for endorsement key derivation. The kernel also handles intertask calls from the TPM to the field programmable fuses task.

- *Field programmable fuses task*: For programming and sensing a fuse allocated for recording whether the endorsement key in the fuse has been revoked or not. This programmable fuse is a *single-bit one-time programming* fuse. See Chapter 6 for details.

The TPM is not consumed by other processes or tasks, although this may be supported in the future.

To establish the communication channel between the host and the firmware-based TPM, the BIOS reserves a dedicated I/O buffer during boot. Command calls to the TPM are signaled through system interrupts. The I/O buffer is not protected for confidentiality or integrity.

The design of BIOS setting up the I/O buffer for TPM input and output does not sacrifice security. This is because the I/O buffer is not considered part of the shielded location, and information handled by the TPM is not disclosed to the I/O buffer unless the disclosure is the intent of a *Protected Capability*. The worst damage that a rogue BIOS can achieve is denial of service, rendering the TPM unusable. However, this does not benefit the host in any way.

Cryptography Algorithms

All algorithms of the TPM's cryptography subsystem are implemented by the embedded kernel's cryptography driver. For algorithms on which the TPM specification has special requirements, the TPM module is responsible for satisfying the requirements. For example, when invoking the cryptography driver for generating an ECC key pair, the TPM must test the significant half of the resulting private key d. If the most significant $nLen/2$ bits of d are all zeroes, a new key pair will be generated and tested.

The RSA key pair generation is a time-consuming operation on the embedded engine. For a 2048-bit RSA, a generation takes an average of 30 seconds. To avoid timing out key generation commands, the TPM implements a cache in volatile memory that holds up to five pregenerated key pairs. When a key pair is consumed, a new key generation will be kicked off in a low-priority thread and the resulting key will fill the empty slot.

Endorsement Key Storage

The TPM on the security and management engine features a preinstalled endorsement key (2048-bit RSA). The endorsement key is required to be unique per hardware part. Because of its uniqueness, the endorsement key cannot simply be hard-coded in the firmware, which is the same on all parts. Instead, hundreds of millions of endorsement keys are pregenerated. During Intel's manufacturing process, different key materials are burned to the platform's security fuses for all parts, respectively. Note that *key materials* are not the key value.

The security fuses are the highest-valued assets of the engine and they can be accessed only from the kernel of the engine. Consequently, the TPM task has to call the kernel's cryptography driver to retrieve fuse values for the endorsement key materials. The kernel, upon receiving the call, verifies the caller is indeed the TPM task, before fulfilling the request.

Without applying lossless data compression, it takes at least 2080 bits of space to express a 2048-bit RSA key pair—32 bits for public exponent e, 1024 bits for private component p, and 1024 bits for private component q. The value of e can be a constant, say 65537, for all keys and hence hard-coded in the firmware, reducing the number of bits to 2048. Other key components, including the 2048-bit modulus n and the 2048-bit private exponent d, can be calculated from e, p, and q. 2048 is a really large number for the fuse array, which is a constrained resource. Unfortunately, lossless compression can hardly yield satisfying results due to the semi-randomn nature of cryptographic keys. Is there a more efficient approach to store the unique endorsement key in fuses? Intel's firmware-based TPM uses a patented technique[10] to lower the required fuse space.

As described in Chapter 3, the RSA key generation works by generating two large pseudo-random numbers and testing their primality, until two probably primes, p and q, are found. A pseudo-random number generator (PRNG) works by taking a seed and running deterministic heuristics in a loop, until the requested number of bits has been output. The seed is usually much smaller in size than p or q. Therefore, p or q can be represented by the seed and the number of iterations (an integer) that has been run to yield p or q.

Algorithm 7-1 shows the pseudo code for generating a probable prime of 1024 bits using the PRNG proposed in ANSI X9.31 Appendix A.2.4.[11] This PRNG is recommended by NIST. This algorithm is implemented by the key generation facility and not the TPM firmware.

Algorithm 7-1. Generation of 1024-bit Probable Prime

```
Input: None
Output: Key (128 bits), Seed (128 bits), DT (DT < 65536)

Begin:
Key := rand(128);
Seed := rand(128);
DT := 0
ANSI_PRNG_INIT(Seed, Key)

Block_0 := ANSI_PRNG(DT++)
Block_1 := ANSI_PRNG(DT++)
Block_2 := ANSI_PRNG(DT++)
Block_3 := ANSI_PRNG(DT++)
Block_4 := ANSI_PRNG(DT++)
Block_5 := ANSI_PRNG(DT++)
Block_6 := ANSI_PRNG(DT++)
Block_7 := ANSI_PRNG(DT++)
Block_0_fixup := Block_0 | C0000000000000000000000000000000h
Block_7_fixup := Block_7 | 00000000000000000000000000000001h

While DT < 65536
   If (isPrime(Block_0_fixup || Block_1 || Block_2 || ... || Block_6 ||
Block_7_fixup))
      Break
   Else
      Block_0 := Block_1
      Block_1 := Block_2
      Block_2 := Block_3
      Block_3 := Block_4
      Block_4 := Block_5
      Block_5 := Block_6
      Block_6 := Block_7
      Block_7 := ANSI_PRNG(DT++)
      Block_0_fixup := Block_0 | C0000000000000000000000000000000h
      Block_7_fixup := Block_7 | 00000000000000000000000000000001h

If (DT == 65536)
   Goto Begin
Else
   Output Seed, Key, and DT
```

The purpose of `Block_0_fixup` is to set the most significant two bits of the candidate. The purpose of `Block_7_fixup` is to make sure the candidate is odd. `isPrime(candidate)` denotes the Miller-Rabin primality test. `isPrime()` returns true if candidate is a prime number with high probability, and false otherwise. Function `rand(size)` returns a random number of `size` bits. Function `ANSI_PRNG_INIT(Seed, Key)` initializes an instance of the ANSI X9.31 PRNG in the AES mode with 128-bit Key as *K and Seed as V. Function `ANSI_PRNG(DT)` runs the PRNG for one iteration and returns a 128-bit random value. After iterating the PRNG once, the value of DT is incremented by one. Essentially, the algorithm attempts to find consecutive 1024-bit number output by the PRNG that is a probable prime after fix-ups.

Note that the *preliminary primality test* introduced in Chapter 3 for expediting the prime search is not applied to Algorithm 7-1. To take advantage of the preliminary primality test, an extra value, *delta*, must also be output from the algorithm and stored in fuses for the firmware to recover the generated prime. Because the endorsement key generation is not an online operation, its velocity is not a concern.

The size of integer DT is limited to 16 bits in order to conserve fuse space. Experiments for a large amount of prime generation show that the value of DT output by Algorithm 7-1 rarely exceeds 2000h. The Seed, Key, and DT together can be used to derive the probable prime. The three values are burned to security fuses during manufacturing. The total storage is only 128+128+16 = 272 bits, realizing a saving of as many as 752 bits compared to storing the 1024-bit prime itself. To generate an RSA key pair, the algorithm is executed twice to generate *p* and *q*, respectively.

Algorithm 7-2 gives the pseudo code for recovering the probable prime from Seed, Key, and DT. The algorithm is implemented by the TPM firmware. The values of Seed, Key, and DT are read from security fuses by the kernel and provided to the TPM.

Algorithm 7-2. Retrieval of 1024-bit Probable Prime

```
Input: Key (128 bits), Seed (128 bits), DT
Output: Prime (1024 bits)

i := 0
ANSI_PRNG_INIT(Seed, Key)

Block_0 := ANSI_PRNG(i++)
Block_1 := ANSI_PRNG(i++)
Block_2 := ANSI_PRNG(i++)
Block_3 := ANSI_PRNG(i++)
Block_4 := ANSI_PRNG(i++)
Block_5 := ANSI_PRNG(i++)
Block_6 := ANSI_PRNG(i++)
Block_7 := ANSI_PRNG(i++)

While i < DT
  Block_0 := Block_1
  Block_1 := Block_2
  Block_2 := Block_3
  Block_3 := Block_4
```

```
Block_4 := Block_5
Block_5 := Block_6
Block_6 := Block_7
Block_7 := ANSI_PRNG(i++)

Block_0_fixup = Block_0 | C000000000000000000000000000000h
Block_7_fixup = Block_7 | 0000000000000000000000000000001h

Output Prime = Block_0_fixup || Block_1 || Block_2 || ... || Block_6 ||
Block_7_fixup
```

Endorsement Key Revocation

The endorsement key initially placed in security fuses may be revoked by the TPM2_ChangeEPS command introduced in TPM 2.0. In this case, the TPM must generate a new endorsement key pair, store it in nonvolatile memory, and remember not to use the one in the security fuses in the future. The TPM task uses a field programmable fuse for the purpose of saving the revocation status of the endorsement key in fuses.

Endorsement Certificate

The public portion of an endorsement key can be published in an endorsement certificate that is vouched for by a trusted certification authority. The certificate may be shipped together with the endorsement key. Size-wise, a typical X.509 certificate with a 2048-bit RSA subject key and a 2048-bit signature can be as big as approximately 1KB. An ECC certificate is smaller but its size is still in the scale of a few hundred bytes. Some TPM implementations do not have the luxury of storing the endorsement certificate on the device.

Fortunately, the TPM specification does not mandate the endorsement certificate be installed on the device. An alternative design is to have the external requesting entity (for example, operating system, service provider, and so forth) obtain the endorsement certificate from an online server. The server is linked to a database where all TPM endorsement certificates are stored. When an endorsement key is revoked, its certificate will no longer be available from the server. Notice that this flow is between the requesting entity and a server, and does not involve the TPM device at all.

■ **Note** For a pregenerated and preinstalled endorsement key, the corresponding endorsement certificate does not have to be stored on the TPM device.

Supporting Security Firmware Applications

For TPM, *locality* is defined to be the privilege level of a command. When a TPM session is established, the locality associated with the session is specified. Future access to the object must be made at the specified locality. The TPM version 1.2 defines five localities 0–4. The TPM 2.0 draft introduces extended localities 32–255. The TPM interface is responsible for determining the locality each time the TPM is accessed.

For the security and management engine, the extended localities are useful for identifying communications between the TPM task and other firmware applications that may benefit from the TPM capability. The communication is through the kernel's intertask manager and the call can be placed at locality 32 from the TPM's perspective, for example.

Figure 7-2 illustrates the conceptual idea of using extended localities to support internal firmware applications. Let us see a hypothesis example. A secure server encrypts a secret with one of the firmware-based TPM's asymmetric public keys and sends the encrypted secret (a data object) to the TPM at a basic locality. The data object will be accessed from locality 32. The TPM imports the object, performs decryption, and now possesses the clear secret. The firmware task designed to process the secret can then retrieve the secret from the TPM task at locality 32. The TPM interface for extended localities is guarded by the kernel's intertask call manager. Intertask calls are internal to the security and management engine, and the host has no way to peek. Also, only TPM, the consuming task, and the kernel are involved in the process. Other firmware tasks are not able to steal the key, thanks to the task isolation mechanism.

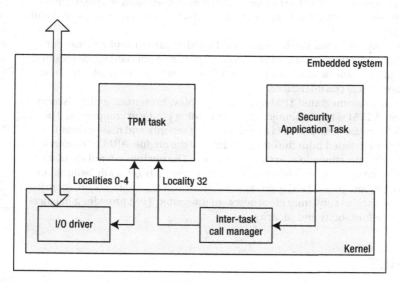

Figure 7-2. Using extended localities for internal security applications

Integrated vs. Discrete TPM

Traditionally, the TPM is implemented as a physically discrete hardware component and connected to the platform via a hardware bus; for example, the LPC (low pin count) bus or SPI (serial peripheral interface). Many personal computers and laptops feature discrete TPMs. The following are two benefits of using a discrete TPM:

- *Easy integration and maintenance*: A discrete TPM can be physically disconnected from the platform for debugging and testing. A malfunctioning TPM device can be replaced without impacting the rest of the platform.

- *Better security*: The isolation between the TPM and the host is physical, and the TPM device is not co-located with any other devices or functionalities. Compared to an integrated TPM, a well-designed discrete TPM can be certified at a higher FIPS 140-2[12] level and the Common Criteria's evaluation assurance level[13] (EAL).

Contrary to popular belief that discrete TPM provides better security, older versions of discrete TPM are vulnerable due to dependencies on the physical bus. For example, the LPC bus reset attack[14] against TPM version 1.1 demonstrated by researchers of Dartmouth College works by resetting the LPC bus and clearing the PCRs of the TPM on the LPC bus, without resetting the platform. This flaw that allows a simple hardware attack was addressed in TPM 1.2, for which a similar attack would require expertise and special hardware.

In addition, discrete TPMs also have drawbacks with regard to deployment—for example, development effort, BOM (bill of materials) cost, and onboard space required for installation, just to name a few. For small form factors such as a smartphone, these shortcomings are critical considerations.

In recent years, the integrated TPM has come into play. In contrast to the discrete TPM, an integrated TPM is implemented inside an existing platform component. For example, Intel's firmware-based TPM is a module of the security and management engine, and logically isolated from the other modules of the engine. ARM's TrustZone may also realize TPM functionalities in its secure mode. The obvious advantage of an integrated TPM is the virtually zero BOM cost. Security-wise, it is generally believed that the robustness of an integrated TPM is not as good as a discrete one. That said, for price-sensitive markets, such as consumer electronics, an integrated TPM provides a balanced solution between affordability and security.

References

1. Trusted Computing Group, "Trusted Platform Module Library," www.trustedcomputinggroup.org, accessed on March 20, 2014.

2. Joanna Rutkowska, "Evil Maid goes after TrueCrypt," http://theinvisiblethings. blogspot.com/2009/10/evil-maid-goes-after-truecrypt.html, accessed on March 20, 2014.

3. Gilbert S. Vernam, "Cipher Printing Telegraph Systems for Secret Wire and Radio Telegraphic Communications," *Journal of the IEEE 55*, pp. 109–115, 1926.

4. State Encryption Management Bureau of China, "SM3 Cryptographic Hash Algorithm," standard publication GM/T 0004-2012, www.oscca.gov.cn/UpFile/20101222141857786.pdf, accessed on April 15, 2014.

5. State Encryption Management Bureau of China, "SM4 Block Cipher Algorithm," standard publication GM/T 0002-2012, http://gm.gd.gov.cn/upfile/2009113105257460.pdf, accessed on April 15, 2014.

6. State Encryption Management Bureau of China, "Public Key Cryptographic Algorithm SM2 Based on Elliptic Curves," standard publication GM/T 0003-2012, www.oscca.gov.cn/UpFile/2010122214822692.pdf, accessed on April 15, 2014.

7. National Institute of Standards and Technology, "Recommendation for Pair-Wise Key Establishment Schemes Using Discrete Logarithm Cryptography," http://csrc.nist.gov/publications/nistpubs/800-56A/SP800-56A_Revision1_Mar08-2007.pdf, accessed on April 15, 2014.

8. National Institute of Standards and Technology, "Recommendation for Key Derivation Using Pseudorandom Functions," http://csrc.nist.gov/publications/nistpubs/800-108/sp800-108.pdf, accessed on April 15, 2014.

9. William Futral and James Greene, *Intel Trusted Execution Technology for Server Platforms: A Guide to More Secure Datacenters*, Apress, 2013.

10. Daniel Nemiroff, "Cryptographic Key Generation Using a Stored Input Value and a Stored Count Value," US patent 20100329455 A1.

11. American National Standards Institute, "Digital Signatures Using Reversible Public Key Cryptography for the Financial Services Industry (rDSA)," ANSI X9.31-1988, September 1998.

12. National Institute of Standards and Technology, "Security Requirements for Cryptographic Modules," http://csrc.nist.gov/publications/fips/fips140-2/fips1402.pdf, accessed on April 15, 2014.

13. Common Criteria, www.commoncriteriaportal.org/cc/, accessed on April 15, 2014.

14. Dartmouth College, PKI/Trust Lab, "TPM Reset Attack," www.cs.dartmouth.edu/~pkilab/sparks/, accessed on April 15, 2014.

CHAPTER 8

■ ■ ■

Unleashing Premium Entertainment with Hardware-Based Content Protection Technology

If there's content that can only be there if it's rights protected, we want to be able to have that content available to you... So in no sense are we hurting you, because if they're willing to make the content available openly, believe me, that's always the most wonderful thing. It's the simplest.

—Bill Gates

Fast-developing technologies have gradually changed many aspects of people's lifestyle, including the way we enjoy video and audio entertainment. Computers, from stationary workstations to mobile handhelds, are used increasingly as multimedia players. Readers have switched from paper books to e-books and audio books; CD, DVD, and Blu-ray rental and sales numbers have been declining in the last ten years because more and more people rent and purchase titles from the Internet.

Compared to traditional media, user experience for the new digital entertainment is not by any means worse: a lot of premium content is available at online stores at the same time or before the CD/DVD/Blu-ray releases; the picture quality of downloaded and streaming content is equal or higher than that of the disc; video and sound can be echoed from computers to big-screen TVs. What's more, the digitization of content further benefits consumers in several ways:

- *Convenience*: It is a human-oriented design for the users to sit comfortably on a couch in his living room, browse catalogs of thousands of titles, and watch interesting ones immediately. It saves the room that is needed for storing physical discs; digital contents can be stored on the cloud rather than local hard drives; sharing content with friends and family takes just a few clicks.

- *Lower cost*: Data transmission eliminates the material, manufacturing, and logistics expenses of discs, and eventually reduces the costs of content and benefits consumers. More flexible purchase options are now available. For example, instead of having to buy an entire music CD at a higher price, a music lover can pay for the individual songs of her choice.

- *Easy management*: Searching for specific content in a large collection is fast and accurate. No more worries about physical damages to a disc due to, for example, temperature and relative humidity.

Rights Protection

Alongside the widespread deployment of the entertainment feature on all forms of computers is the problem of copyright protection from diverse types of piracy, such as sharing, downloading, and counterfeiting. In the case of content protection, the device user is untrusted, and the content provider wants assurance from the device manufacturer that a user cannot bypass protections. This increases the scope of threats and attacks that have to be defended against, primarily physical and side-channel attacks.

It is commonly accepted that general-purpose computers with an open operating system and using software to handle content are not as robust as closed systems (for example, a dedicated Blu-ray player) because of inexpensive approaches that have been developed by researchers and hackers to defeat software protection schemes without involving advanced expertise or special equipment.

Obviously, profit loss because of piracy on computers is one of the biggest concerns of content providers (such as writers and film studios). Therefore, the content owners have to decide whether to demand rights protection for their content, and if so, what assets of the content shall be protected and at which level.

For example, most 4K ultra and 1080p high-definition movies sold at online stores today require the purchaser's device to feature appropriate hardware-based protection for rights management and playback of the content. Software-based protection measures may be deemed insufficient for such content. In other words, if the hardware of the user's computer does not meet minimum requirements, then the content owner and the service provider that distributes the content will not sell the title to the platform. On the other hand, the content of standard-definition formats usually requires only software-based protection or does not require protection at all. There also exists content that is free of any rights management, allowing consumers to make unlimited copies and share with others.

In any case, the choice and decision is solely the content owner's. Before buying or renting content, the customer should be well aware of all restrictions posed by the content.

■ **Note**   The content provider decides the types and levels of rights protection that are required for its content.

Regarding what assets to protect for content, there are several considerations. Here are just a few examples:

- How many times can the content be played back?

- Can the consumer keep the content for good, or for only a limited period?

- Is the content permitted to be played back on the user's other devices in the same *domain*? If so, what is the maximum number of devices allowed?

- Is the user allowed to share the content with others? If so, what is the limitation? Is there a limitation on the number of times it can be copied and shared? What is the rights policy for the copied version of the content?

- Can the content be displayed on an external monitor or TV? If so, what type of protection is required on the link between the computer and the monitor or TV?

Such policy restrictions are recorded in a *license* (or *rights object*) file that is transmitted together with the content to the end user during a transaction.

It appears that the rights policy tightens what the user can do with the content. Why would software and hardware vendors spend resources to enforce them?

As a matter of fact, content right protection mechanisms implemented on a computer is *for*, and not against, users' interest, because they are necessary to satisfy people's raising demand for entertainment. It should be emphasized that, on Intel platforms, for example, the protection mechanisms

- Do not touch users' personal files

- Do not introduce constraints to content that does not come with rights protection mandated by the provider

- Do not enforce policies that have not been accepted by the user

- Do not impact or change anything the user would normally do with his computer

The protection mechanisms do one thing and only one thing: increase the difficulty and cost of unauthorized activities that violate the terms and conditions associated with the content to a level that meets the robustness requirements determined by the content provider, so that the content can be made available to end users. If a user is not happy with the content's terms and conditions, then he should not obtain the content, and the protection schemes simply will not be functioning at all.

It would be an annoying experience for a user to encounter an error window saying that the computer cannot play the movie because it lacks necessary hardware. Therefore, most modern computers today support the types and levels of protection mandated by the content providers. A platform without such capability will significantly limit what users can do for entertainment and degrade the user experience. To this end, Intel platforms shipped with the embedded management engine and select core processors feature a hardware-based content protection infrastructure that is able to satisfy the most stringent protection requirements. This technology enables consumers to enjoy their favorite content seamlessly on Intel products and do not need to worry about compliance problems that prevent the content providers from delivering the content.

DRM Schemes

Digital rights management (DRM) controls the use of digital content. Discussions in this chapter will focus on video and audio content, but the protection mechanisms largely apply to rights management for textual publications and still images as well.

A number of DRM schemes exist in the market today. Content owners and distributors choose the desired schemes used for protecting their content. Many vendors support more than one scheme, so their content can be distributed on various types of systems and platforms. The following is a list of most popular DRMs used for online media:

- *Widevine*: The Widevine DRM was designed by a company of the same name, which was acquired by Google in 2010. Widevine is supported by Google TV, Google Chromecast, Google Play, and other media players on Android and other Google products.

- *PlayReady*: Microsoft first introduced PlayReady in 2007. It is widely used by Windows applications. In May 2010, Microsoft announced that Netflix had chosen PlayReady as its primary DRM technology.[1]

- *FairPlay*: Created by Apple, FairPlay is a built-in component of the QuickTime software, which is installed on all lines of Apple devices, such as iPhone, iPod, iPad, Apple TV, and iTunes.

- *Marlin*: The Marlin DRM is developed and maintained by the Marlin Developer Community, with founding members including Intertrust, Panasonic, Philips, Samsung, and Sony. Marlin is mainly deployed in the smart TV market. Especially popular in Europe and Asia, it is used by the national IPTV standard of Japan, as well as major online video streaming web sites in China, such as Baidu and PPTV.

- *OMA DRM*: OMA is an acronym for Open Mobile Alliance, created by major mobile phone manufacturers and carriers for developing open DRM standards to enhance interoperability among mobile devices.

This is not a complete list and there are other smaller DRMs too. These competing schemes realize, to a certain extent, similar rights management capabilities with distinct design details. In general, the three main elements of a DRM scheme is device key management, rights management, and content encryption.

The main building blocks of a platform's DRM implementation are graphically presented in Figure 8-1, where TRS is short for *tamper-resistant software*. The cryptography block includes a pseudorandom number generator (PRNG).

Not all components in the figure are applicable to all DRMs, and a DRM may support additional value-add features. The DRM client is responsible for performing device key provisioning and storage, enforcing rights management, and securing playback flows, per the defined policies.

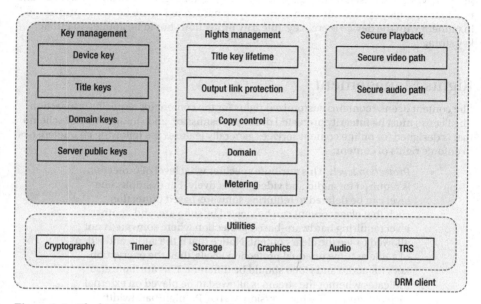

Figure 8-1. *The building blocks of a typical DRM client*

Owners of some DRM schemes release specifications with corresponding software development kits (SDKs) that contain reference code. Usually, SDKs implement DRM-specific functionalities, such as key management and rights management, and leave the utility implementations to adopters. An SDK not only remarkably simplifies the adopters' efforts for integration, but also unifies behaviors of different products on different systems, and hence reduces the chance of incompatibility.

Device Key Management

The device secret key is a critical asset for a content protection scheme. It can be a random AES[2] (*advanced encryption standard*) key or an asymmetric key pair. The device secret key is provisioned to each individual device during the manufacturing process, or remotely with a server before the DRM is invoked for the first time in the field. For most DRM schemes, the secret key on a specific device is unique, although a small number of DRMs still use global keys. Using unique keys makes it easier to implement revocation for compromised devices.

Once provisioned, the device secret key must be stored with confidentiality in nonvolatile memory of the device and never exposed in the clear or shared with other devices. A compromised device secret key could be used to decrypt content keys in licenses, retrieve the decrypted content, and distribute or playback freely. Therefore, the key is more valuable than any single title. Compromising the key may result in the device being revoked and no longer eligible for content playback.

Besides the device secret key, a device is also provisioned with a content provider's public key, which is used in, for example, verifying digital signature of licenses. A content provider's public keys are not secrets and may be hardcoded in the device or provisioned in tandem with the device secret key. Integrity protection should be applied to public key storage.

Rights Management

The content license contains customized rights for the content for a specific transaction. The license must be integrity protected during transmission and storage. A DRM scheme that is designed for online content services generally features the following characteristics to enforce rights of content:

- *Protection levels*: This attribute specifies what level of protection is required for audio and video, respectively. For example, one level can be defined to requiring software-based protection such that clear content can be viewed by software, and another level requiring hardware-based protection where software is not allowed to see the clear content. Notice that if the audio and video of a title assume unequal protection levels, then the encryption keys for audio and video should be different. This attribute also indicates whether the stream is allowed to be played on external displays, and if so, which version of HDCP[3] (high-bandwidth digital content protection) is required.

- *Domain*: A user can create a domain on the server and enroll all his devices in the domain. Content may be copied from one device to another of the same domain. The domain members then share the content and a domain key, which is used to, for instance, securely transport title keys between two devices in the same domain.

- *Secure timer*: A DRM may leverage the system's trusted clock and secure timer to enforce playback duration. For example, a movie rental may expire after 24 hours after the first playback begins.

- *Playback metering*: A DRM may measure durations of the user's playback of content and report to the server. For example, a user earns free credits toward the purchase of premium movies after he has watched a certain amount of commercials, metered by the DRM.

- *Transaction tracer*: After downloading the content, the transaction tracer allows the user to start playback even if the computer is offline. The platform will record and report offline playback events to the rights server once network connection is resumed.

Notice that the rights policies are generated for each transaction, depending on the options selected by the customer.

Playback

The main goal of securing content playback is to protect clear content keys, as well as the video and audio paths. The content keys are sent to the platform encrypted with the device key or its derivative. The algorithm for encrypting the content key is DRM specific. The other attributes of the license should be at least integrity protected.

The entire flow of the content, especially after it is decrypted on the platform, must be safeguarded according to requirements specified in the license. A license should define the following policies:

- Whether the content keys (for video and audio, respectively) may be handled by software

- Whether clear compressed and uncompressed video data may be processed by software, respectively

- Whether clear compressed and uncompressed audio data may be processed by software, respectively

- What protection mechanism should be applied to the connection between the platform and an external display

Apparently, these playback requirements are specific to the title rather than individual transactions—they are the same for all issued licenses of the content.

UltraViolet

In early 2011, Intel announced the new digital media services[4] with the second-generation core processor family (code name "Sandy Bridge"). The services feature innovative hardware-based content protection mechanisms that enable consumers to enjoy UltraViolet[5] content "anytime and anywhere." Intel has partnered with content providers such as Best Buy CinemaNow and Walmart VUDU for UltraViolet content distribution. The security and management engine is one of the main elements of the solution.

UltraViolet is developed and maintained by the Digital Entertainment Content Ecosystem (DECE), an alliance of companies that include film studios, consumer electronics manufacturers, and vendors that form the ecosystem. In contrast to common misunderstandings, UltraViolet is, in fact, not a DRM. Instead, it is a free cloud-based content rights library that encompasses several existing DRMs, such as OMA. The ultimate goal of UltraViolet is allowing users to *buy once, play everywhere*, regardless of the DRM scheme of the title and the device on which the purchase was made.

The coexistence of multiple DRM schemes in the market today is good for competition, but in the meanwhile results in inconvenience for consumers. Say, someone who owns an Android smartphone, an iPad tablet, and a Windows 8 laptop is not able to watch the TV programming he purchased from Google Play on his iPad or Windows laptop because Apple's FairPlay and Microsoft's PlayReady are not compatible with Google's Widevine. UltraViolet aims at resolving this problem by unifying content encoding and format used by various DRMs and storing the proof-of-purchase on a centralized location—the UltraViolet cloud. Besides online content, new releases of DVD and Blu-ray discs from participating film studios are also UltraViolet-enabled. Once a user buys an UltraViolet-enabled disc, he can register with the cloud server and stream the same title on all of his UltraViolet-capable devices.

End-to-End Content Protection

The journey of protected content begins at the server that creates the encrypted content and finishes at a screen that displays the content. A number of steps and components are involved in the flow, as shown in Figure 8-2. They work together to realize complete end-to-end protection.

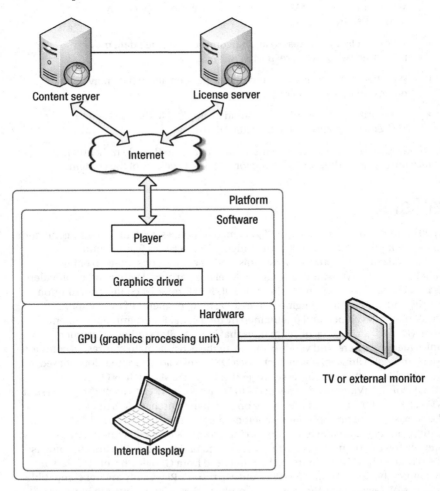

Figure 8-2. *End-to-end flow of content with software-based protection*

In a nutshell, the encrypted media and its license are delivered to the platform through open networks. The player receives them, installs the license, and performs operations per the license's permissions. For playback, the player produces the decrypted content and passes it to the graphics driver (user mode and kernel mode) for displaying on either the internal screen or an external device.

To guard the content from end to end, every link and every component must apply proper protections. This is because an attacker only needs to circumvent the weakest point in the path to acquire the protected content. The entire ecosystem is broken if one link or component is compromised, no matter how robust the others are. Let us first take a look at a few components, and then identify the weakest.

Content Server

A content server is responsible for encrypting clear encoded titles with the defined cryptographic algorithm and delivering encrypted content to users' platforms. Different schemes may deploy different algorithms. The most popular choices nowadays are AES in counter mode, CBC (cipher block chaining) mode, and CBC-CTS (ciphertext stealing) mode with 128-bit keys. Few DRM schemes also support 256-bit keys. Refer to Chapter 3 for an introduction on AES and these modes.

Notice that a long title (such as a 120-minute movie) may be divided into multiple sessions that are encrypted with different keys, respectively, with a key rotation algorithm. Also, different resolutions of a title should be encrypted with separate keys, because their desired rights managements may vary. In most cases, the title encryption is performed only once and the encrypted content will be consumed by all customer platforms. Re-encryption of a title is required under certain scenarios, such as compromise of the key.

The transmission from the content server to the platform's software is through an open Internet connection. Essentially, encrypted content alone is not a secret because it is useless without the decryption key. The content delivery may be real-time streaming as the consumer is watching, or the user can download the entire title and save it in local storage beforehand. Some distributors let clients proactively download content before viewing. Such options allow users to enjoy the entertainment even without high-speed network, such as when traveling on a plane.

License Server

A license server maintains databases for encryption keys of all titles and issues rights for content transactions. A license defines the use policies associated with the underlying content. Attributes regarding secure playback are the same for all users, for example, requiring HDCP when the content is sent to an external device for display; whereas other restrictions described in the license vary depending on the consumer's preference at the time of purchase. Naturally, if a user is willing to pay more, then the policy will generally enable more rights, such as sharing. The license server generates customized licenses for different transactions on the fly and transmits to end users' platforms.

Licenses must be integrity protected during the transmission for obvious reasons. The license server owns an asymmetric key pair, where the private key is used for signing licenses and the public key is for DRM clients to verify the signature.

The license server and the content server must be always in sync about the keys and initialization vectors used in title encryption. Although they are logically separate modules, in reality the two servers can be implemented on the same machine.

Software Stack

Besides implementing fundamental playback functionalities (such as start, stop, pause, fast-forward, slow motion, scene selection, and so forth) with the graphics driver, the player software also downloads content from the content server and, for rights-protected content, interacts with the license server to receive the license.

For content that does not mandate hardware-based protection, the player is also responsible for handling the device key, installing licenses, managing secure playback, and enforcing rights. This was the common practice before hardware-based content protection architectures were born, and it is still used today for nonpremium content. For example, Windows Media Player is able to enforce rights for Microsoft's PlayReady scheme. This includes unwrapping the content key in the license and decrypting the encrypted media file with the content key. In other words, the player has access to the entire clear compressed content. Additionally, a user's operation requests on the content are examined by the software and allowed only if permitted by the installed license.

To achieve meaningful protection, most software-based solutions utilize antitampering techniques, such as TRS, which make reverse-engineering and code modification harder. However, TRS is a type of security through obscurity and obfuscation with no provable robustness. What's worse, TRS not only enlarges the size of the software but also raises power consumption. Notice that both nonvolatile storage and battery life are critical performance vectors for mobile systems.

For hardware-based content protection, the player does not handle the processing of the license or decrypting of the content. Instead, it acts as a proxy and relies on the hardware infrastructure for enforcing the rights and decrypting the media for playback. As a result, there is no longer a necessity to apply TRS to the player because it has no secrets to hide.

External Display

Most rights management schemes require protection of the data transfer from the display controller to external display devices with the HDCP protocol, proposed by Intel in 2000. The protocol applies encryption on the link between the source (transmitter) and the sink (receiver or repeater). The link can be wired, for example, with an HDMI (high-definition multimedia interface) cable, or it can be wireless, such as through Intel's Wireless Display.[6]

Weak Points

From Figure 8-2 and the accompanying analysis, one may conclude that, for software-based content protection, the weakest points are on the client. For example, the player and the graphics driver on the platform's open operating system both possess plaintext content without provable security.

To harden the weak points to some extent, many DRM schemes require integrity assurance for the operating system by securing the boot process, so the platform is running in a known trusted state when it is playing premium content. Intel's Boot Guard technology introduced in Chapter 6 is used to satisfy such requirements.

Intel's Hardware-Based Content Protection

To robustly harden the weak points, the content protection mechanisms on the client side must be implemented in hardware, for all three aspects of the problem:

- Playback protection

- Device key management

- Rights management per policy

Figure 8-3 illustrates the high-level block diagram for Intel's hardware-based solution. The player software communicates with the embedded engine through the HECI (*host embedded communication interface*; see Chapter 3 for details) driver and offloads sensitive operations to the engine. Note that the engine does not use a network stack and it does not interact with remote servers directly. The graphics driver collaborates with the engine and GPU (graphics processing unit) for PAVP (*protected audio and video path*) session establishment and management.

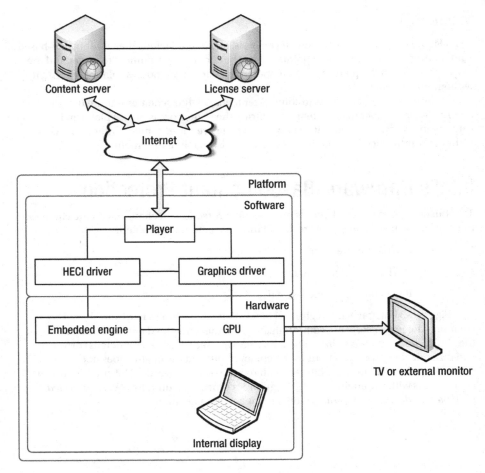

Figure 8-3. End-to-end flow of content with Intel's hardware-based protection

The embedded engine's firmware implements content protection functionalities in a dedicated *task*, logically isolated from other applications running on the engine. Refer to Chapter 4 for the task isolation mechanism of the firmware.

Intel's digital media services and the UltraViolet feature are backed by the hardware-based protection. However, notice that the solution is not specific to UltraViolet. It provides a generic foundation that is able to support any content protection schemes on any operating systems.

Protected Audio and Video Path (PAVP)

For a secure playback session, the player should not be in charge of content processing. The software stack on the host operating system, including ring-0 drivers, must not be able to access clear content or the content encryption key, and the clear content shall not be present in memory that is visible to the host. The PAVP technology is designed to meet these requirements with native hardware blocks, so the capability can be invoked with minimum software development and integration effort.

The PAVP is an Intel proprietary technology that protects the audio and video flows in the GPU. The main idea is to have the GPU take encrypted content and the content key as input, perform decryption of the content in the hardware, and then display the content on screen. The security and management engine and graphics driver also participate in the flow. The embedded engine is responsible for finding out the content key and injecting it through an internal bus to the GPU; the graphics driver is responsible for programming frame metadata and initializing playback.

Figure 8-4 depicts the building blocks of PAVP and their connections. MMIO stands for memory-mapped input and output. For SoC (system-on-chip) platforms, the embedded engine, and the GPU communicate through the IOSF (Intel on-chip system fabric) sideband. For non-SoC, the channel is the DMI (direct media interface).

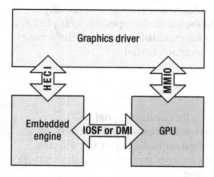

Figure 8-4. *The building blocks of PAVP*

The protection of the link between the platform and the external monitors is also managed by the embedded engine and the GPU using HDCP protocols. With this architecture, the entire content path, from the content server to the display, is protected with provable security.

Device Key Provisioning

For protection with a hardware root of trust, the device secret key must be secured by hardware and never exposed to the software stack. The security and management engine offers several approaches for device key installation. The computer manufacturers, after obtaining device keys from the DRM authority, can choose an appropriate installation process based on the requirements of the DRM scheme.

If the factory environment is trustworthy, then a device key may be provisioned in cleartext to devices and locked down before the conclusion of the manufacturing. The embedded engine's kernel provides a method for manufacturers to store nonvolatile data to the engine during manufacturing. The engine's firmware will convert secret nonvolatile data to secure blobs. It is also possible to send the clear device key to the engine through HECI and have the engine store in a secure blob.

Alternatively, if secure provisioning of the device key is required after the product leaves the factory, then the EPID (*enhanced privacy identification*; refer to Chapter 5 for technical details) algorithm can be leveraged. In this scenario, the platform and a remote provisioning server mutually authenticate each other and establish session keys that are then used to protect the device key when it is transmitted from the server to the platform. Note that the platform remains anonymous during the procedure. Also, recall that the EPID involves heavy mathematical calculations and may be slow on some platforms. The EPID-based provisioning can also be deployed in the factory environments, if necessary, so end users do not experience extra delays caused by device key initialization when they launch playback for the first time on new computers.

The EPID method is also advantageous in that the device does not have to be returned to the factory for refurbishment when its device key is lost (but not compromised). Reprovisioning of a new device key can be done remotely and conveniently by invoking EPID again.

The embedded engine saves device secret keys in its assigned partition of the system's flash memory, with protections for confidentiality, integrity, and optionally, anti-replay. The keys for protecting the device key blobs are device-specific, so copied blobs do not work on other platforms. See Chapter 3 for more information on the secure nonvolatile storage mechanism implemented by the engine's kernel.

Rights Management

The security and management engine is an ideal place for conducting rights enforcements for several reasons: first, it is equipped with necessary utilities, such as hardware-based PRNG, a cryptography driver, protected nonvolatile storage, a secure timer, and so forth; second, as discussed in previous chapters, its unique isolation nature makes it immune from attacks and threats from the host.

Intel Wireless Display

The HDCP is a specification developed by Intel to protect audio and video entertainment over digital interfaces. Today, HDCP protocol has become a popular choice across the industry for guarding the content transmission from a computer to a repeater or a receiver (a display device such as monitor or TV). A repeater functions as both a receiver and a transmitter for downstream HDCP repeaters and receivers. The latest HDCP version, 2.2, is an interface-independent specification that can be applied to any interface.

The Intel Wireless Display (WiDi) is a proprietary interface that adopts HDCP 2.2. It allows streaming movies or anything on the computer's screen from a WiDi-capable Intel platform to a TV or projector that supports WiDi or Miracast (requires WiDi 3.5 or newer). When the transmitted content requires link protection, HDCP 2.2 is the core on which the security of WiDi is built.

In the WiDi setup, the Intel platform is the HDCP transmitter. The transmitter side of the protocol is implemented jointly by WiDi software, the graphics driver, the GPU, and the security and management engine. The WiDi software running on the host talks with the receiver through the operating system's Wi-Fi stack. The embedded engine sits behind the software and communicates with the software via HECI.

A transmitter does not receive content; hence it does not hold a device private key or certificate. A receiver (or repeater) owns a 1024-bit RSA (*Rivest, Shamir,* and *Adleman*) key pair. The receiver's unique device ID and RSA public key $kpub_{rx}$ are digitally signed by the HDCP governing authority, Digital Content Protection (DCP) LLC, in a certificate hardcoded in the device together with the device's RSA private key. Notice that the certificate is a binary format defined by the standard and not a generic X.509 certificate, and no intermediate certification authorities are involved.

Revocation for compromised receivers is realized by a system renewability message (SRM), which is a structure that comprises an SRM version number, the list of IDs of repeater and receiver devices that have been revoked, and the authority's signature. Because HDCP is designed to be an offline protocol that does not depend on Internet connectivity to function, the SRM is delivered to transmitters together with the content, if and only if the content mandates HDCP protection. A transmitter is required to reserve at least 5KB of nonvolatile memory for SRM storage, and the transmitter must keep the latest version of the SRM that it has ever encountered in its secure storage.

The HDCP 2.2 protocol is comprised of four stages:

1. *Authentication and key exchange (AKE)*: The transmitter verifies that the receiver has a valid RSA key pair endorsed by the DCP LLC, and it is not one of the devices revoked in the SRM. A master key *Km* is also exchanged in this phase if one does not exist on the transmitter for this receiver. The master key is specific for this pair of transmitter and receiver and it is used in lieu of the RSA key to expedite future HDCP handshakes between these two devices.

2. *Locality check*: The transmitter enforces the locality of the receiver by making sure that the time elapsed between sending a message to and receiving the response from the receiver is no longer than the specified duration.

3. *Session key exchange*: The transmitter generates a session key and initialization vector (IV) and sends securely to the receiver. The content is encrypted using a salted version of the session key and the IV with a 128-bit AES counter mode.

4. *Authenticating repeater*: If the receiver is a repeater, then the repeater assembles downstream device topology information and forwards it to the upstream transmitter for authentication.

As the root of trust, the security and management engine is responsible for performing all sensitive operations in the HDCP protocol, including but not limited to the following:

- Validating the receiver's certificate and checking its device ID against the revocation list.

- Managing SRM.

- Maintaining a database of master keys and corresponding repeater IDs. The database supports up to ten receivers. The oldest entry will be removed when an eleventh receiver is paired with the transmitter.

- Randomly generating the IV and the session key.

- Securely storing the HDCP global secret constant lc_{128}.

- Injecting the salted session key (session key exclusive-OR'ed with lc_{128}) to the GPU's PAVP block.

- Facilitating locality checks, with or without precomputed L and L'.

The GPU of the transmitter uses the salted session key and IV to encrypt the content before the encrypted content is transmitted to the receiver. On the receiver side, the same key is derived to decrypt and play the content.

Authentication and Key Exchange

To showcase the embedded engine's roles in the transmitter side of the protocol, Figure 8-5 replicates the AKE protocol flow chat (without stored Km) of the HDCP 2.2 specification and describes the operations that are offloaded to the firmware for processing. The firmware must hardcode DCP LLC's root public key and lc_{128}. The symbol $(data)key$ denotes the ciphertext of $data$ encrypted with key. Refer to the HDCP 2.2 specification for meanings of variables such as r_{tx}, r_{rx}, H, H', Kh, and so forth.

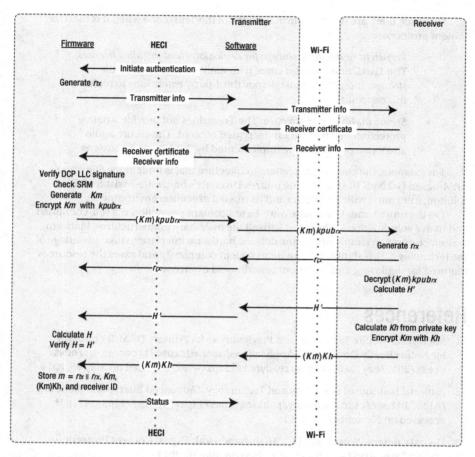

Figure 8-5. *Authentication and key exchange without stored Km; transmitter implemented in firmware*

The HDCP 2.2 protocol is made up of a few flows, and Figure 8-5 exhibits just one of them. Besides AKE without *Km*, the embedded engine participates in all other flows as well, to assure that HDCP's security objectives are satisfied at the hardware level.

Content Protection on TrustZone

The ARM processor architectures with TrustZone support DRM and hardware-based content protection. The TrustZone security framework allows software to execute sensitive DRM operations to the secure mode. The sensitive operations include content key processing and rights management. Conceptually, the separation for nonsecure and secure modes is similar to Intel's solution where the security and management engine handles sensitive operations.

However, there are two notable limitations of the TrustZone when it is used for content protection:

- *Persistent nonvolatile storage for device keys and installed licenses*: The TrustZone does not come with native secure nonvolatile storage. Integrators must deploy third-party extensions to realize this capability.

- *Secure audio and video path*: The Trust does not provide a native protection mechanism for decrypted content. The secure audio and video path has to be implemented by third-party extensions.

For example, the content protection architecture that is built in the Samsung's ARM-based Galaxy S III smartphone utilizes Discretix's hardware-assistant DRM solution, integrated with TrustZone and its trusted execution environments.[7]

On the other hand, Intel's hardware-based content protection is a self-contained and native solution that is equipped with all the necessary infrastructures. Platform manufacturers can simply invoke the defined hardware interface to take advantage of the technology. This significantly reduces system complexity and saves the resources required for deploying and maintaining additional extensions.

References

1. Microsoft, "Netflix Taps Microsoft PlayReady as Its Primary DRM Technology for Netflix Ready Devices and Applications," www.microsoft.com/en-us/news/press/2010/may10/05-25playreadynetflixpr.aspx, accessed on May 25, 2014.

2. National Institute of Standards and Technology, "Advanced Encryption Standard (AES)," http://csrc.nist.gov/publications/fips/fips197/fips-197.pdf, accessed on November 17, 2013.

3. Digital Content Protection LLC, "High-bandwidth Digital Content Protection System," www.digital-cp.com, accessed on May 10, 2014.

4. Intel, Unlock the World of UltraViolet with Intel Devices, www.intel.com/content/www/us/en/architecture-and-technology/intel-insider-for-premium-hd-home-entertainment.html, accessed on May 25, 2014.

5. DECE, UltraViolet, www.uvvu.com, accessed on May 25, 2014.

6. Intel Wireless Display, www.intel.com/go/widi, accessed on May 25, 2014.

7. Discretix, "Hardware-Assisted DRM with ARM TrustZone on the Samsung GALAXY S III Smartphone Secured by Discretix," www.discretix.com/press-release/hardware_assisted_drm_with_arm_trustzone_on_the_samsung_galaxy_s_iii_smartphone_secured_by_discretix, accessed on May 30, 2014.

CHAPTER 9

■ ■ ■

Breaking the Boundaries with Dynamically Loaded Applications

Sometimes we stare so long at a door that is closing that we see too late the one that is open.

—Alexander Graham Bell

In previous chapters, we have studied the firmware architectures and security hardening features of the security and management engine. Let's recap the main design points:

- The security and management engine's firmware starts from boot ROM (read-only memory), which is not erasable and not modifiable.

- The boot ROM is the root of trust of the engine.

- The majority of the engine's firmware, including all applications, are stored in a flash device, together with other system firmware such as BIOS (basic input/output system).

- Firmware modules may be compressed with Huffman[1] or LZMA[2] to conserve the flash space. Firmware modules are not encrypted.

- Metadata of all firmware modules (including the kernel and various applications) is put together in a structure called *manifest*, also stored on the flash.

- The manifest contains SHA-256[3] digests for every firmware module. SHA-256 is one of the most frequently used *Secure Hash Algorithms*.

- The manifest is digitally signed by Intel with 2048-bit RSA[4] (Rivest, Shamir, and Adleman). The signature and the public key are both appended to the manifest.

During the boot process:

- The ROM verifies the RSA signature of the manifest. The SHA-256 fingerprint of Intel's public key is hard-coded in the ROM.

- The boot ROM verifies the SHA-256 digest of the first firmware module that is loaded from the flash.

- The integrity of subsequent modules is verified by one of the modules that have been verified and loaded previously in the boot process.

- When being loaded, a module performs the necessary initializations, and then creates a "worker" thread that waits for events. Most common events are system interrupts, HECI (host-embedded communication interface) messages initiated from the host, and service requests of other modules. Upon receiving an event, the module serves the event and waits for the next event.

By design, a module that runs on the engine must be compiled as part of the engine's firmware system, registered in the manifest, and preinstalled on the flash. The set of firmware applications and modules for a given product is determined at the time of compilation and cannot be changed after it leaves Intel's facility. From this perspective, the engine is a self-contained system, and doors are closed against loading new applications.

That being said, the engine is technically not a closed system, because it is capable of exchanging data with the external world at runtime. Notice that what is input to and output from the engine is only data, and may not be executable code. Running unauthorized code is a major violation of the security objectives of the engine.

Closed-Door Model

With the closed-door model, everything that can be executed on the engine is strictly controlled. Thanks to the integrity check mechanisms that are enforced during the boot process and runtime, the boundary of the engine is well guarded. It is very difficult for attackers to inject root kits and other malware to the system. The security architecture does not need to worry about possible vulnerabilities and potential flaws brought into the system by external applications. Therefore, the closed-door model is advantageous for security management.

Product quality-wise, the closed-door model makes validation simpler, because the functional testing is performed on predefined and constant configurations. Some of the common software and system problems, such as integration complexity and component compatibility, are not applicable.

Despite its security and stability, this design has its drawbacks:

- *Expansion of the engine's functionality is restricted by the flash space.* There are multiple products of the firmware, and their sizes vary between approximately 1.5MB and 5MB, which is fairly small considering the ever-growing number of features carried by the engine. Increasing the size limit is not free. In today's fierce competition environment, the BOM (bill of materials) cost is a pivotal consideration for all computer manufacturers. Raising the flash space consumed by the security and management engine requires flash chips of greater capacity, and hence adds the BOM costs for deploying manufacturers. When the size of the firmware binary reaches the maximum, new features can't be rolled out without taking current features out of the firmware.

- *Firmware update can be cumbersome.* Adding new applications to the engine or fixing bugs in existing modules requires more than Intel's development and validation effort. Rewriting firmware on the flash is a very privileged operation, and if done improperly, may render the system unbootable and result in a large number of support calls. Therefore, computer manufacturers have to test new firmware releases with all lines of products respectively and make sure there are no security or compatibility issues.

- *Intel is the sole development owner for the security and management engine.* Independent software vendors cannot build applications that run on the engine.

To address these drawbacks to some extent, newer versions of the security and management engine firmware include a module called the *Dynamic Application Loader*, or DAL for short. As indicated by the name, the DAL allows the engine to dynamically load and execute Java applets at runtime. The applets are not stored on the flash, but on the host's hard drive. With the DAL, the embedded engine is no longer a closed-door realm. The engine is now open to more flexibility and possibilities to be explored.

Meanwhile, more importantly, the security objectives of the engine remain the same and the security protection strength is not degraded because of the DAL.

DAL Overview

The DAL is implemented as an application in its isolated task in the firmware architecture. See Chapter 4 for details on the engine's task isolation design. Because the DAL loads an application from the host, it is active only when the host is awake. The DAL is not available if the host is in the sleep state. The relationships between the DAL task and other firmware components are depicted in Figure 9-1.

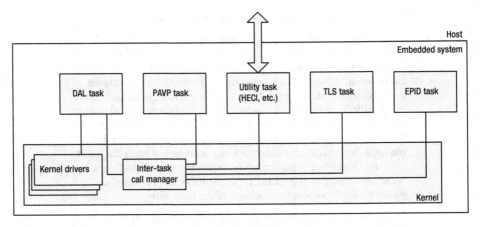

Figure 9-1. *The DAL task and its relationships with other firmware components*

To support functionality requirements of the loaded applets, the DAL task consumes several kernel services and other peer tasks:

- *Cryptography driver*: Provides implementations of popular cryptography algorithms, including AES[5] (advanced encryption standard), SHA, HMAC[6] (keyed-hash message authentication code), RSA, random number generator, and so forth.

- *Storage manager*: Secure nonvolatile storage for DAL management data and applet specific secrets.

- *Protected runtime clock*: Provides secure timer services for applets.

- *Image verifier*: The DAL replies on the kernel to verify the digital signatures on the dynamically loaded applications.

- *PAVP (protected audio and video path) task*: Some applets—for example, the applet that is part of the Intel IPT[7] (identity protection technology) solution—require secure display path that is not visible to software running on the host operating system. See Chapters 8 and 10 for more details on PAVP and IPT, respectively.

- *EPID (enhanced privacy identification) task*: Some applets realize functionalities that require Intel platform's hardware support. The EPID algorithm and SIGMA protocol are utilized to authenticate the platform and establish secure sessions between the host/server application and the loaded applet. Refer to Chapter 5.

- *TLS (transport layer security) task*: Provides applets with secure PKI (public key infrastructure) support.

- *Utility task*: This task implements a number of interesting services, for example, CPU and chipset information, firmware status report, power states, HECI, and so forth. The HECI is the channel for the host to transmit the application's binary image to the DAL firmware task for execution.

Due to these dependencies, the firmware product that features the DAL must also support these tasks. The DAL task is not consumed by any other firmware modules. Note that the DMA (direct memory access) is not used for transmitting applets from the host to the engine. To further minimize security risks, the DMA driver is not available to applets to invoke.

DAL Architecture

The DAL is essentially a Java virtual machine that enables the operation of Java applets in the security and management engine's firmware environment. The Java applets in bytecode implement their designed functionalities that can be executed in the firmware. The components that make up the DAL feature are shown in Figure 9-2.

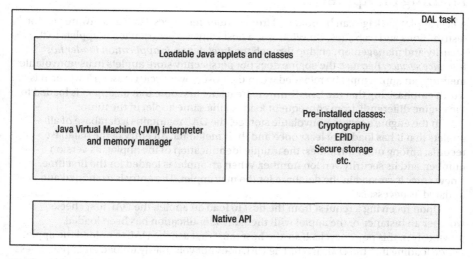

Figure 9-2. Components of the DAL

A service layer (classes) can also be loaded from the host together with the applets. The service layer may realize utilities such as HECI. In addition, the DAL task preinstalls select services, such as cryptography and EPID, without needing to load from the host. Those services are specific to the firmware engine and they are expected to be used by most applets.

The native API (application programming interface) component receives the Java API calls, performs conversion, and in turn calls appropriate kernel API or other tasks. It serves as a proxy so the Java classes do not need to be aware of the engine's specific interfaces.

Loaded Java applets are free to take advantage of various services offered by the engine, but there is no guarantee regarding performance, due to a few facts. Firstly, to save resources, when multiple applets are loaded to the system, the DAL and the installer application may decide to temporarily unload an applet and reinstall it later as needed. This procedure may delay the applet's responses to requests from the host. Secondly, the DAL task shares hardware resources with other firmware capabilities running in the security and management engine. The engine is a multithreaded environment, and the amount of clock cycles allocated to a specific thread is not guaranteed.

With these considerations, the DAL is not intended for loading major features to the engine. Rather, it is designed for offloading critical security components of a consumer solution, for example, the Intel IPT. In contrast, loading the entire or a large part of the AMT (advanced management technology) firmware application from the host at runtime is not an appropriate usage of the DAL.

Loading an Applet

A Java applet package can be obtained from various resources, such as software vendors' distributions and web sites. On Windows, a host software program loads applets to the security and management engine through the *Intel dynamic application loader host interface service*. Because the engine does not persistently store applets in its nonvolatile memory, an applet must be reloaded when the host power cycle is reset. However, it is worth emphasizing that the DAL firmware treats the first time that an applet is loaded to the engine differently from consequent loads of the same applet in the future.

In the engine's secure nonvolatile storage, the DAL maintains a database of all applets that it has loaded at least once and their metadata. An entry of the database records, among other attributes, the unique identification of the applet, its version number, and its security version number. When an applet is loaded for the first time, a new entry is created in the database for the new applet. The entry is examined and updated as necessary.

Upon receiving a request from the host to load an applet, the DAL first checks whether an instance of the applet with the same identification has been loaded previously in this power cycle. If so, the host must first ask the DAL to unload the applet before loading it to the DAL again. The DAL does not voluntarily unload an applet unless the host requests so. The reason for reloading an applet may be to update the applet to a newer version. This is shown in Figure 9-3.

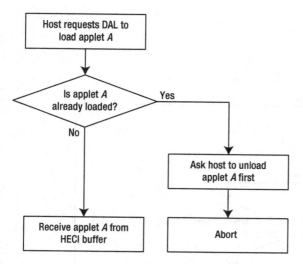

Figure 9-3. *Handling an applet load request*

A loadable Java applet is always packaged with its corresponding manifest. The structure of the manifest is similar to what is shown in Figure 4-1 in Chapter 4. Specifically for security, the following fields are critical in the loading process:

- Applet identification.

- DAL flag, indicating this is a DAL manifest.

- Version number.

- Security version number. A security version is assigned to every applet release. If vulnerabilities are found in an applet, then the new applet release that fixes the vulnerabilities will be assigned an incremented security version.

- RSA signature of the manifest.

- RSA public key.

- SHA-256 digest of the applet.

The applet to be loaded also specifies the minimum version of the engine's firmware that is required to run this applet. Earlier firmware releases may not be equipped with the necessary infrastructures to support the applet. The process of loading an applet is illustrated in Figure 9-4.

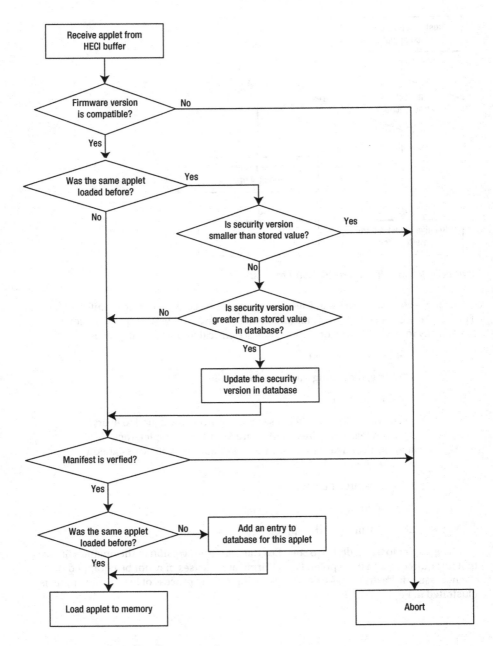

Figure 9-4. Process of loading an applet

The loading process starts from the DAL task receiving the complete applet package, including the manifest, from the host in the HECI buffer. As introduced in Chapter 3, a HECI message has limited capacity, depending on the engine's configuration. If the size of the applet package is greater than the capacity of a HECI message, then the package will be split and come in multiple messages.

After possessing the applet, the DAL first verifies that the firmware currently operating on the engine is capable of executing the applet. The DAL aborts the loading if the firmware is too old to support the applet. A firmware update will not be automatically launched in this case. The user must manually update the engine's firmware in order to run the applet.

If the applet has been loaded before, then the DAL makes sure that its security version is not smaller than the one stored in the database. If this is not the case, then it may be a rollback attack that exploits the vulnerability in an older applet release and the DAL shall reject to load the applet. If the security version is greater than what is shown in the database, then the DAL updates the database with the newer value. If the DAL has never seen this applet before, then it creates an entry for it in the database after the integrity check passes.

The manifest validation is performed by invoking the kernel API. The manifest must be signed with the same RSA key that signs the manifest for the engine's firmware image loaded from the flash.

Secure Timer

The DAL provides applets with secure timer services that measure the time elapsed between a *Set timer* call and a *Get current timer value* call. When multiple applets are running simultaneously, each applet may create one or more independent timers. The timer is useful for applications that must enforce durations—for example, a one-time password that expires every 30 seconds.

Host Storage Protection

The engine is allocated with only limited flash space for its data partition. Therefore, to reduce the flash footprint, it is recommended that the Java applets do not store data on the flash. Instead, applets' nonvolatile data, especially if its size is large, should be placed on the host's hard drive.

To facilitate and protect the host storage mechanism, the DAL provides an encryption key and an integrity key for every applet. A typical usage would be to encrypt data using the encryption key, append an HMAC-SHA-256 signature (generated using the integrity key) to the encrypted data, and then send the blob of encrypted data and the signature to the host for storage. To retrieve the data, the applet simply fetches the blob from the host, verifies the HMAC signature using the integrity key, and then decrypts using the encryption key. Optionally, anti-replay protection can also be applied to data blobs if necessary, to mitigate rollback attacks (replacing a blob with an older version).

The encryption key and the integrity key are persistent for the same applet even if the engine has gone through power cycles. Derived from a bit string that is randomly generated when the DAL is initialized for the first time on a platform and the applet's unique identification, the keys are unique for the applet that runs on the specific platform. In other words, an applet is not able to make use of a data blob that was created by another applet; cloning a data blob from one platform to another would not pass the integrity check. It is up to individual applets to decide the proper reaction to take upon blob failures.

Security Considerations

Naturally, alongside the openness of the DAL come new security concerns. Specific security requirements are set for safeguarding the engine with the existence of the DAL:

- Applets can be executed only after being loaded by the DAL firmware application. Modules in a manifest that is intended for the DAL shall not be executed directly on the engine's embedded processor.

- The DAL shall not load manifests that are intended to be loaded by the engine's regular boot process.

- The DAL shall enforce context separation among distinct applets.

- The DAL shall record the greatest security version numbers for each applet respectively, for rollback attack detection.

- An applet shall follow security design guidelines for regular firmware applications, such as using minimum privileges, minimizing attack interfaces, and so on.

The first two bullets are the most critical requirements. Because the applets' manifests are signed with the same RSA key that signs the firmware image, the architecture must mitigate image replacement attacks where an attacker replaces the firmware image on the flash device with an applet image, which will pass the signature verification conducted by the boot ROM.

The countermeasure employed by the architecture is to introduce a "DAL" flag in the manifest. The firmware's boot process will not load a manifest with a DAL flag set. Conversely, the DAL will not load a manifest if its DAL flag is not set.

Reviewing and Signing Process

Applets may be developed by Intel or third-party software vendors. The process for reviewing and signing an applet is the same regardless of whether Intel or a third-party is the applet developer. The high-level process is described in Table 9-1.

Table 9-1. Applet Reviewing and Signing Process

Stage	Name	Activity
1	Applet creation	Vendor creates the applet.
2	Applet review	Intel reviews the applet for functionality, security, and privacy.
3	Manifest creation	Intel creates preproduction manifest and provides to the vendor.
4	Preproduction testing	Vendor tests and debugs the applet on a preproduction security and management engine. Sometimes a simulator is used instead. Go back to stage 1 if any change is made to the applet.
5	Presigning	Intel makes sure the content of the applet is identical to what is in the final preproduction manifest.
6	Signing approval	Approvers review and sign the manifest. Critical manifest parameters (such as security version number and DAL flag value) are displayed to approvers for a final review.
7	Signing	The signing tool replaces the RSA public key and the signature in the preproduction manifest with a production RSA public key and signature.
8	Production testing	Vendor tests the applet on a production security and management engine.
9	Ready for distribution	Vendor is ready to distribute the applet.

References

1. D.A. Huffman, "A Method for the Construction of Minimum-Redundancy Codes," *Proceedings of the I.R.E.*, September 1952, pp. 1098–1102.

2. Igor Pavlov, "LZMA Software Development Kit," http://7-zip.org/sdk.html, accessed on December 12, 2013.

3. National Institute of Standards and Technology, "Secure Hash Standard (SHS)," http://csrc.nist.gov/publications/fips/fips180-4/fips-180-4.pdf, accessed on November 17, 2013.

4. RSA Laboratories, PKCS #1 v2.1: RSA Cryptography Standard, ftp://ftp.rsasecurity.com/pub/pkcs/pkcs-1/pkcs-1v2-1.pdf, accessed on November 17, 2013.

5. National Institute of Standards and Technology, "Advanced Encryption Standard (AES)," `http://csrc.nist.gov/publications/fips/fips197/fips-197.pdf`, accessed on November 17, 2013.

6. National Institute of Standards and Technology, "The Keyed-Hash Message Authentication Code (HMAC)," `http://csrc.nist.gov/publications/fips/fips198-1/FIPS-198-1_final.pdf`, accessed on November 17, 2013.

7. Intel Identity Protection Technology, `http://ipt.intel.com`, accessed on April 20, 2014.

■ ■ ■

CHAPTER 10

Intel Identity Protection Technology: the Robust, Convenient, and Cost-Effective Way to Deter Identity Theft

People need to be more aware and educated about identity theft. You need to be a little bit wiser, a little bit smarter and there's nothing wrong with being skeptical. We live in a time when if you make it easy for someone to steal from you, someone will.

—Frank Abagnale

Most people have received scam e-mails that prompt them to visit fake web sites that resemble actual bank web sites. If the user is fooled into believing in the "phishing" web site and enters his username and password, then the credentials will be saved by attackers that will later log in to the victim's bank account and drain the account. Besides phishing, an advanced attacker may also infect the victim's computer with key logger malware to capture and record the keystrokes when the victim is typing his username and password for login.

With the rapidly increasing threats of identity theft in today's mobile era, multifactor authentication is deployed more widely than ever. Naïve single-factor username and password combination is likely not secure enough for authenticating access to high-value assets, even though the password is long and complicated.

Multifactor schemes would mitigate phishing and key logging attacks by requiring additional credentials during the authentication process. The username and password compromise the first factor—"something you know." Two other types of credentials are the following:

- *"Something you are"* refers to something that is part of you, commonly your biological characteristics, such as fingerprints. For example, the iPhone 5s is equipped with a fingerprint identity sensor. A user can unlock the phone by scanning his fingerprint.

- *"Something you have"* refers to a physical object that belongs to you. It can be as simple as a "key-card matrix" on which a fairly large number of index-key pairs are printed. During authentication, the web site challenges the user with a randomly selected index, and the user looks up the matrix and enters the corresponding key to sign in. This solution is not ideal, because the same set of keys is repeatedly reused, and may be monitored and replayed by thieves. A more robust "something you have" is a hardware digital token or key fob that displays a one-time password.

The security and management engine is a critical functional component of Intel Identity Protection Technology[1] (IPT). The Intel IPT provides a strong, convenient, and cost-effective solution for multifactor authentication, as well as other features, such as the protected transaction display (PTD). This chapter is dedicated to revealing how the engine takes advantage of its built-in infrastructure to make the IPT possible.

One-Time Password

In contrast to a regular password that is valid for an unlimited number of authentication sessions until it is reset, a one-time password (OTP) is a credential that is used only once. Although the value of an OTP may seem random, it is not randomly generated, but cryptographically derived. A good OTP algorithm shall render it practically infeasible to predict future OTP values based on previous observations. The OTP is usually updated at fixed internals, for example every 30 or 60 seconds, depending on security models of specific applications.

The token (client) possessed by the user and the back-end authentication server are always in sync—they refresh the OTP by performing the same calculation at the same time with the same "derivation materials." In other words, after initialization, the token and the server will both assume the same OTP at any given moment in the future. To prove his ownership of the token to the server, the user types in the OTP value displayed on the token at the time of authentication to satisfy the requirement of second-factor authentication, supplementing other factors (for example, the username and password).

The utilization of OTP significantly increases the difficulty of phishing attacks. The attacker's fake web site has to also collect the OTP entered by the user. Because the OTP is valid for only a small duration, the attacker cannot save the OTP and make use of it later. Instead, the phishing server has to be set up as a real-time man-in-the-middle, where it simultaneously establishes two connections, one with the victim's client platform and the other with the real authentication server. This makes the attack more complex and expensive. Figure 10-1 shows a real-time man-in-the-middle attack scenario.

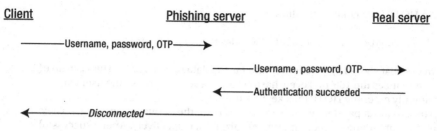

Figure 10-1. Man-in-the-middle attack

An OTP system has two aspects to consider:

- *Secrecy*: With reasonable resources, adversaries shall not be able to calculate or guess OTP values. Theoretically, any collision-free one-way cryptography function with a secret *seed* as input is qualified. The HMAC[2] (*hash-based message authentication code*) algorithm is the most popular choice.

- *Synchronization*: The same OTP value must be known by the server and the client at any given moment, without requiring synchronizations after initialization.

The security strength of an OTP system solely depends on the seed, so the seed must be reliably protected by both the server and the client from leakage. Traditionally, more attention has been paid to designing physically strong and tamper-resistant tokens. However, the server's security hardenings are even more critical because if it is hacked, then likely seeds for all tokens are at risk.

RSA Security, the Security Division of EMC, designs and manufactures a well-known OTP token, SecurID. In March 2011, the company issued an open letter[3] stating that its corporate security systems had identified an "extremely sophisticated cyber-attack" being mounted against it. The letter did not disclose technical details, probably due to the concern of benefiting potential attackers, but it revealed that the attack had resulted in *certain information* specifically related to SecurID being extracted from RSA's systems. In the aftermath, RSA offered token replacements or free security monitoring services to its more than 30,000 SecurID customers. The breach cost EMC $66.3 million, according to the company's earnings.

The most famous OTP standards are the *HMAC-based one-time password* (HOTP[4]) and the *time-based one-time password* (TOTP[5]).

HOTP

The derivation algorithm chosen by the HOTP method is HMAC-SHA-1. The HMAC *key*, also referred to as *seed*, is a shared secret agreed by the server and the client at the time of initialization. The key may be randomly generated or calculated from a master secret of the server. The key is static for the life cycle of the client and it must be kept secret by both parties against tampering.

An HOTP is calculated as follows:

```
HOTP(key, counter) := Truncate(HMAC-SHA-1(key, counter))
```

In the `HMAC-SHA-1()` function, *counter* is the data to be hashed. The `Truncate()` function reduces the 160-bit keyed-hash result to a smaller size so the user can conveniently enter the HOTP on a keyboard.

The two input parameters, *key* and *counter*, are the derivation materials. They are used for providing secrecy and synchronization, respectively. After a successful authentication, both the server and the client increment the *counter* by one, hence the *counter* should always be in sync. The server automatically increments the *counter* once it verifies the HOTP. On the client side, for a connected token (such as via a USB port), the connected computer can programmatically increment the counter.

However, many token products are not equipped with connection capability. The advantage of a connection-less token is obviously its simple hardware and low BOM (*bill of materials*) cost—it needs only small tamper-resistant storage for the *key* and *counter* and an HMAC-SHA-1 logic; it does not require circuits for USB or clocking. The tradeoff is that the user has to, after a successful authentication, manually notify the token and have it increment the *counter* and generate the next HOTP. The notification is usually realized by the user pushing a button on the device. This manual step introduces uncertainty and potential problems for synchronization. For example, the user may accidentally push the button twice, resulting in the token's counter value being more advanced than the server's. To take care of such issues, the HOTP protocol defines a "look-ahead window," where the server calculates the next *s* HOTPs. The authentication is accepted as long as any of the *s* HOTP matches the HOTP received from the client. The window size *s* cannot be too large, otherwise security may be compromised.

But this mechanism does not completely resolve all potential synchronization issues. Imagine the user's three-year-old child plays with the token and pushes the button countless times. The server's look-head window will not cover this case, and the token must be returned to factory for reinitialization.

TOTP

The TOTP scheme is a variant of HOTP that replaces the *counter* in the HOTP with a time value, *time*:

```
TOTP(key, time) := Truncate(HMAC(key, time))
```

The HMAC function may be HMAC-SHA-1, HMAC-SHA-256, or HMAC-SHA-512. The *time* is equal to the Unix time or Epoch time (number of seconds that have elapsed since midnight UTC (coordinated universal time) of January 1, 1970) divided by a predefined interval, with the default floor function. The `floor(x)` function represents the greatest integer that is not greater than fraction *x*. The recommended interval is 30 seconds:

```
time := floor(Unix_time/interval)
```

Compared to the HOTP, the TOTP scheme uses *time* as the counter for synchronization, which eliminates the problems of incrementing the counter for connection-less tokens. The TOTP scheme requires a token to have clocking capability by embedding an oscillator in the device. A token's clock drift needs to be considered and accommodated accordingly by the server. The protocol also recommends the server to implement "look-ahead" and "look-behind" windows to for resynchronization when a tolerable amount of clock drifts have occurred on the token.

The TOTP scheme is the cornerstone of the reference architecture of OATH[6] (*Initiative for Open Authentication*), an industry-wide collaboration to promote the adoption of strong authentication.

Transaction Signing

The OCRA[7] (*OATH* Challenge-Response Algorithm) is an authentication and signing mechanism created by the OATH. The OCRA algorithm is based upon HOTP with extension to including various types of information in the calculation of the OCRA.

In a nutshell, the calculation of OCRA uses the following formula:

```
OCRA := CryptoFunction(Key, DataInput)
```

The same formula is applicable to both the server and the client. The CryptoFunction defines the HMAC algorithm (HMAC-SHA-1, HMAC-SHA-256, or HMAC-SHA-512) and the result size after truncation. *Key* is a preshared secret, like in the HOTP scheme. The value *DataInput* is a concatenation (denoted by symbol "||") of the byte arrays of a number of variables:

```
DataInput := OCRASuite || Counter || Q || P || S || T
```

Here's what these variables mean:

- *OCRASuite*: Represents the suite of operations to calculate the OCRA. The OCRASuite string describes the selection of CryptoFunction and the list parameters that are included in the DataInput following OCRASuite.

- *Counter*: A 64-bit unsigned integer that is initialized to 0. It is incremented by both the server and the client after every successful authentication session.

- *Q*: The 128-byte challenge sent from the other party.

- *P*: Digest of a password preagreed by the server and the client. The hash algorithm can be SHA-1, SHA-256, or SHA-512.

- *S*: Contains application-specific information of the current session, up to 512 bytes.

- *T*: Current timestamp.

The *Counter* is optional. Some other parameters (*P*, *S*, and *T*) may also be absent as defined by the OCRASuite. A typical OCRA authentication session in which the server verifies the client's identity is a three-way handshake, as shown in Figure 10-2.

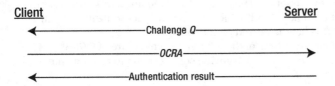

Client   **Server**

←————————————————Challenge *Q*————————————————

————————————————*OCRA*————————————————→

←————————————————Authentication result————————————————

Figure 10-2. *Three-way handshake for one-way OCRA authentication*

Four modes are defined for OCRA:

- *One-way authentication*: The server verifiers the client's identity by sending a challenge *Q* to the client and verifies the OCRA value received from the client. This is the usage depicted in Figure 10-2.

- *Mutual authentication*: The server and the client verify each other's identity by exercising the one-way authentication in both directions. The client verifies the server's identity first. See Figure 10-3 for the four-way handshake flow.

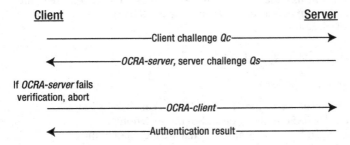

Client   **Server**

————————————————Client challenge *Qc*————————————————→

←————————————*OCRA-server*, server challenge *Qs*————————————

If *OCRA-server* fails
verification, abort

————————————————*OCRA-client*————————————————→

←————————————————Authentication result————————————————

Figure 10-3. *Four-way handshake for mutual OCRA authentication*

- *One-way signature*: Similar to one-way authentication, but session information *S* is not used in calculating the OCRA.

- *Mutual signature*: Similar to mutual authentication, but session information *S* is not used in calculating the OCRA.

Besides OCRA, it is also possible to employ asymmetric-key cryptography and public key infrastructure (PKI) to achieve the same authentication and transmission integrity. The advantage of OCRA is its simper cryptography logic (HMAC) and faster computation. Public key algorithms require more gates to implement and more clock cycles to compute, which poses challenges for BOM cost and performance for small form-factor client devices. Now that the server and the client already have a shared secret, the OCRA makes use of it to avoid the higher-cost and inefficiency of PKI.

Using OCRA, the man-in-the-middle attack presented in Figure 10-1 is no longer a threat, because the transaction, including the session-specific information (for example, the recipient of a money transfer), is signed with a key that is known by only the server and the client. Consequently, the attacker is not able to alter a legitimate user's transactions or initiate his own transactions, because he cannot forge signatures without knowing the correct *key*.

OTP Tokens

Numerous two-factor authentication solutions that deploy OTP as the second factor are on the market today. An OTP token can be implemented in software or hardware.

Functioning as an OTP client, a software or virtual OTP token is a program installed and executed on a desktop computer or a mobile device. The software OTP has a number of pros:

- *Low cost*: No hardware purchase required.

- *Convenience*: No hassle of carrying physical tokens. No worries about replacing the token when its battery runs out.

- *Transparency*: In most cases, the user does not need to type in the OTP. The software automatically calculates and transmits it to the server.

- *Reliable synchronization with server*: Clock drifting on a computer is much less of a concern than clock drifting on a small token device, because the computer's clock always synchronizes with the time server over the network.

- *Easy reinitialization*: When reinitialization is necessary for any reason, there is no need to return the token to the vendor. Reinitialization with the server can be done remotely.

While enjoying these advantages, the software solution has a key drawback—it is more vulnerable. Generally speaking, because software OTP may be compromised by malware installed by viruses or remote attackers, the robustness of software OTP cannot match that of well-implemented hardware OTP systems. Physical access and special equipment are required to tamper a hardware OPT device, making the attack more difficult and costly to mount. For enhanced security, hardware OTP clients are deployed by many large enterprises and government agencies. The pros of the software tokens are exactly the cons of hardware tokens.

Is it possible to feature the pros of both software and hardware OTPs? The security and management engine provides such a solution for the Intel IPT.

Embedded OTP and OCRA

The second factor in multifactor authentication—"something you have"—does not have to be a separate object. It can be the computer that the user is operating on. In Intel's IPT solution, the security and management engine that is built in an Intel platform is the second factor. Security-wise, the engine is physically a hardware device that the user carries with his computer; therefore, its protection strength is comparable to hardware OTP tokens. On the other hand, thanks to its embedded nature, it has all the desirable properties of software OTP as well.

The OTP scheme supported by the engine implements the TOTP algorithm and the OCRA protocol. The solution is compliant with the OATH standard. This standard-based model that Intel IPT uses simplifies interoperability with other third-party components.

Token Installation

The installation (also referred to as *provisioning*) of a token on the embedded engine is equivalent to a hardware token's manufacturing process. As required by the TOTP, two pieces of information are delivered to the client from the server during the installation process:

- *Key*: As defined in the TOTP calculation formula.

- *Time baseline*: The Unix time at the moment of installation.

Obviously, the transmission of *key* must be encrypted because it is the root of security for all upcoming authentication sessions. The transmission of *time baseline* and encrypted *key* should be integrity protected to prevent unauthorized alternation by denial-of-service attacks.

As discussed in Chapter 3, the engine's kernel lacks the knowledge of wall-clock time, but it is capable of securely tracking time that has elapsed for individual applications. Therefore, the server has to send *time baseline* to the engine during provisioning. The OTP application calls the *set time* kernel function immediately upon receiving the baseline from the server. When an authentication is requested, the OTP calls the kernel's *get current time* function and uses the returned value to calculate the TOTP.

Recall the EPID (enhanced privacy identification) algorithm and the SIGMA (SIGn and Message Authentication) protocol introduced in Chapter 5. They are the backbone of the OTP provisioning process. In the SIGMA session, the authentication server is the verifier and the OTP client is the prover. The service provider must be issued a verifier certificate beforehand. The server's certificate chain is verified by the embedded engine during the SIGMA session. The conceptual provisioning flow is illustrated in Figure 10-4.

Client   **Server**

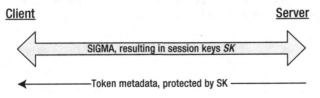

Figure 10-4. Conceptual OTP provisioning flow

Refer to Figure 5-7 in Chapter 5 for details on the SIGMA messages. At the end of a successful SIGMA session, the server has assured that the client is an IPT-capable Intel platform and the client has confirmed that the server is a valid authentication server that supports Intel IPT. Both parties also have derived the shared session keys (SK), including an encryption key and an integrity key. The token metadata, including OTP *key* or *seed*, choice of the HMAC algorithm, current time, and so forth, is delivered from the server to the client securely with the protection of *SK*. The client saves the metadata in secure nonvolatile storage. It can either store the data on the flash chip by invoking the kernel's secure storage capability, or it rewraps the data using DAL (*dynamic application loader*; see Chapter 9 for details) application-specific keys and sends to the host for storage. In the latter case, the data is transmitted back to the engine when an OTP is requested.

Although the provisioning can ideally be a once-in-a-lifetime event, it is necessary to reprovision the token under certain circumstances. For example, if the platform's RTC (real-time clock) well is reset due to reasons such as a drained coin-cell battery, then the secure timer installed by the OTP application will be lost. The OTP firmware has to request the server to install the token again. On the other side, the server may also request reprovisioning; for example, in case the *seed* is compromised. The easy provisioning process is a major advantage of the Intel OTP solution, compared to physical token systems.

TOTP and OCRA Generation

The TOTP and OCRA generation flow is straightforward. After receiving a generation request from the host via HECI (host-embedded communication interface), the firmware reads the current time from the kernel and performs the calculation using *time* and *key*. For OCRA, data input parameters such as the server's challenge and session information are provided by the host to the firmware together with the generation request.

The resulting TOTP or OCRA is sent to the host in the clear for authentication with the server. Note that if the token metadata is stored on the host, then it must be loaded to the embedded engine first. The firmware has no direct connection with the server, and all communication is proxied by the host application.

Highlights and Lowlights

Let's summarize the attractions of Intel's embedded OTP solution:

- *Strong protection*: As a module of the security and management engine, the OTP inherently benefits from the comprehensive hardening measures (refer to Chapter 4) implemented on the engine. The protection is rooted in tamper-resistant hardware, meeting or exceeding the security of consumer-grade hardware tokens.

- *Low cost*: To benefit from the technology, the user does not need to purchase new hardware or software. Almost all service providers support the feature at no cost to customers. Compared to using hardware tokens, the cost of initial setup and continuous management for Intel's OTP is considerably less, which is an incentive for deployment.

- *Multiple tokens in one device*: No more physical tokens. No worrying about damaging or losing your tokens. Token theft is also a much lesser risk now because stealing a computer is more difficult than stealing a small token device. Furthermore, more than one token can be built in a single device—your computer. It is unimaginable to carry many tokens with you all the time.

- *Transparency*: After the initial setup, the second-factor authentication happens in the background without human interaction. The user signs in to web sites or networks by entering merely a username and password combination, just as he did before.

- *Revocable server*: The EPID infrastructure, backed by the engine and Intel's back-end server, ensures that a compromised authentication server can be revoked. Besides compromise, the authentication server may be revoked due to other predefined reasons.

In the meantime, because the tokens, once provisioned, are tied to the hardware of a specific platform, it is impossible to invoke the same token on different devices. As a result, if the user needs to log in to his bank account from more than one device (for example, from both his laptop and tablet), then all devices must register with the bank's web site and install a token, respectively. Fortunately, the inconvenience is trivial, because the provisioning is supposedly a one-time procedure for a device.

However, when the user occasionally has to log in from a public or someone else's computer, an alternate second factor must be utilized in lieu of the Intel OTP token. Service providers must offer feasible backup approaches for the second factor; for example, sending a verification code to the user's cellphone or e-mail address and having the user enter it for authentication.

Protected Transaction Display

The PTD is another critical ingredient of Intel IPT. It is introduced for a different usage model from the OTP and can be incorporated with the OTP. The PTD is designed to enable reliable collection of the user's confirmation or PIN (personal identification number) entry, and detection of malware's falsification of the user's input. The PTD can also ensure that a PIN entry is securely transmitted from the Intel platform to the authentication server, shielded from illegal eavesdropping.

The uniqueness and core innovation of the PTD that distinguishes it from other solutions is that it leverages the PAVP (protected audio and video path; see Chapter 8 of this book for details) technology of Intel platforms to display the authentication sprite, such as the PIN pad, on the user's monitor. Because the PAVP isolates the sprite and protects it from being accessed by the host, malware running on the host operating system is not able to see the sensitive overlay area. As a result, software cannot fake a user's mouse clicks or scrape the screen. Figure 10-5 shows what a user sees during a PTD session.

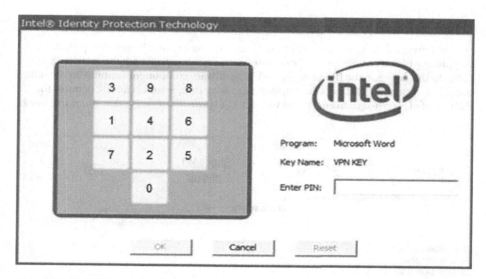

Figure 10-5. PAVP-protected PIN pad on the end user's screen

The user uses his mouse to click the secure PIN pad to enter the PIN. An entry is represented by an asterisk. To further enhance security, the location of the dialog box overlay is randomized for an authentication session; the positions of the ten digits of the PIN pad are also randomized every time. The PIN pad area is not visible to the host. Figure 10-6 shows what an attacker's screen scraper would capture.

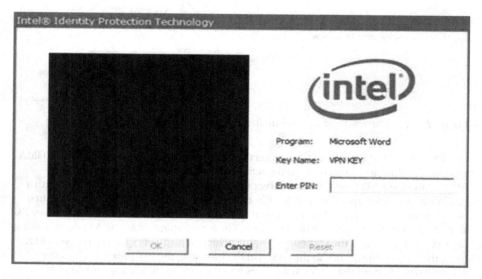

Figure 10-6. PIN pad captured by a screen scraper

Drawing a Sprite

Several flows and designs can be utilized when drawing a sprite. Figure 10-7 presents a sample in which a remote authentication server draws the sprite with the assistance of PAVP. In the diagram, the IPT proxy is the IPT's software component running on the host operating system. GPU stands for *graphics processing unit*. Symbol $(data)k$ denotes the ciphertext of cleartext *data* encrypted with an AES[8] (*advanced encryption standard*) key k.

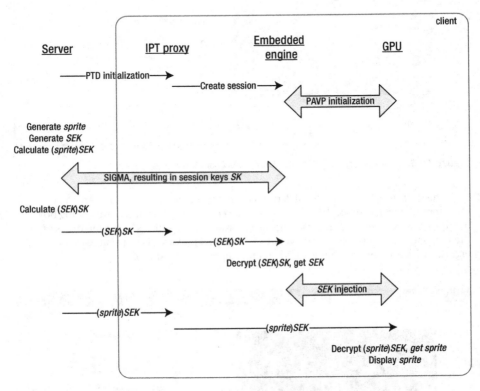

Figure 10-7. *Authentication server drawing a secure sprite*

Similar to OTP, the authentication server must be an endorsed verifier of the SIGMA protocol. To draw a secure sprite on the screen, the server starts with requesting the IPT to initialize a PAVP session. The server then creates the sprite and encrypts it with a randomly generated sprite encryption key or *SEK*. Next, a SIGMA session is established between the server (verifier) and the client (prover). The SIGMA yields the session key *SK* shared between the server and the firmware. The server wraps *SEK* with *SK*. The resulting $(SEK)SK$ is delivered to the embedded engine, which in turn decrypts and recovers *SEK*. Next, the engine injects *SEK* to the GPU. On the host side, the IPT proxy receives the encrypted sprite from the server and passes it to the GPU for rendering and display.

The sequence assures that the clear sprite is never exposed during the entire transmission path from the server to the GPU. Attackers hidden on the Internet or the host can see only the encrypted version of the sprite; they cannot access the encryption key, thanks to the security provided by the SIGMA protocol. The graphics kernel code, like shaders, loaded by the host driver, cannot access sprite frames either. The security is safeguarded at the hardware level.

Gathering the User's PIN Input

The IPT proxy is responsible for collecting the user's clicks on the secure PIN pad. Notice that, as software, the IPT proxy has no knowledge of the position of the PIN pad or its digit button layout, hence it is not capable of calculating the user's PIN input. The proxy records the coordinates of the clicks and reports to the authentication server. The server is the only entity that is able to interpret the user's input. It does so by comparing the click coordinates with the sprite it created.

Optionally, the coordinates may be encrypted using a SIGMA session key before transmission. Figure 10-8 shows a sequential diagram of this flow.

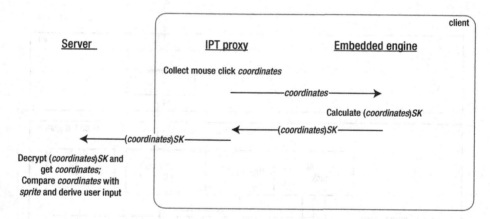

Figure 10-8. *Authentication server gathering coordinates of mouse clicks and deriving user input*

Firmware Architecture

Depending on product, the IPT may be implemented as an applet for the engine's DAL feature, or a native firmware module on the engine. If the firmware supports DAL, for example, on most Intel Ultrabook models, then the IPT implementation will be distributed in a Java applet. On certain smartphones and other products where the DAL is not built into the engine's firmware, the IPT will be a native firmware ingredient that is loaded from the system's flash chip. The firmware design and functionalities of the IPT component are identical for both variants.

Figure 10-9 illustrates the high-level firmware architecture. Internal to the security and management engine, the IPT, together with the DAL that loads it, reside in a dedicated task. The IPT/DAL task is not consumed by any other components of the firmware. The IPT/DAL task consumes the following components of the engine to realize its IPT functionality:

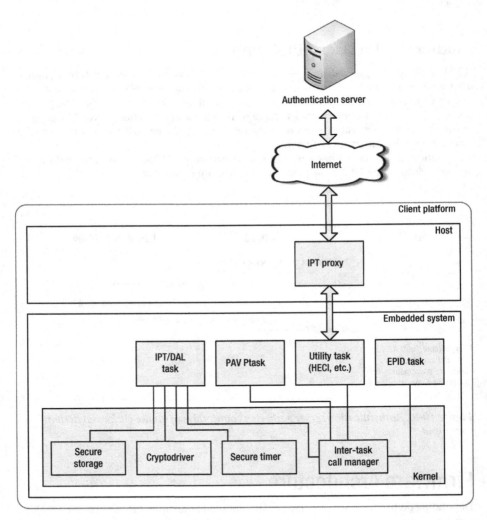

Figure 10-9. *Architecture of the embedded IPT*

- *Storage manager*: The metadata of installed tokens can be stored on the flash device in the engine's data partition. If the metadata is stored on the host, then the application-specific encryption and integrity keys for protecting the metadata are stored on the flash.

- *Cryptography driver*: The TOTP and OCRA calculations use HMAC; the PTD uses AES and HMAC. Additional IPT features may use other cryptography algorithms, such as RSA[9] (*Rivest, Shamir, and Adleman*) digital signing.

- *Protected runtime clock*: The TOTP calculation requires a timestamp.

- *PAVP task*: The PAVP is used by PTD for displaying secure sprites.

- *EPID task*: The provisioning of a token and the session initialization for PTD require EPID and SIGMA's prover functionality.

- *Utility task*: For the HECI communication with the IPT proxy running on the host. Note that HECI is the only interface of the IPT firmware. The IPT does not consume DMA (direct memory access) or network interfaces.

Embedded PKI and NFC

Intel continues to develop innovative technologies to safeguard users' identity. Recently, to further enrich IPT, two new members, PKI and NFC (near-field communication), have joined the IPT family.

The PKI feature supports secure nonvolatile storage for users' asymmetric private keys, such as an RSA key, in the security and management engine. Equipped with this solution, computers can be seamlessly integrated with existing usages, such as VPN (virtual private network) authentication, e-mail and document signing, and so on. Once a private key is imported to the engine or generated by the engine, it will never be exposed in the clear to the external world and all cryptography operations with the private key are performed inside the engine.

The NFC feature enables a user to pay for his online purchases by simply tapping an NFC-capable credit card against the NFC sensor and the secure element chip in the computer, and completing the transaction with positive identity authentication. Thanks to NFC, the customer no longer has to manually type in the long 16 digits of the credit card number. The solution is not only more convenient and user-friendly but also more secure. Key logger malware is not able to steal the card number because it is not entered through a keyboard. The credit card information is processed by the security and management engine and securely transmitted to the server, with robust hardware-level protection.

For more technical details of Intel IPT's PKI and NFC features, refer to the white paper[10] "Deeper Levels of Security with Intel Identity Protection Technology." More information about Intel IPT can be found on the official web site (http://ipt.intel.com/).

References

1. Intel Identity Protection Technology, `http://ipt.intel.com/`, accessed on April 20, 2014.

2. National Institute of Standards and Technology, "The Keyed-Hash Message Authentication Code (HMAC)," `http://csrc.nist.gov/publications/fips/fips198-1/FIPS-198-1_final.pdf`, accessed on November 17, 2013.

3. RSA, the Security Division of EMC, "Open Letter to RSA Customers," `www.sec.gov/Archives/edgar/data/790070/000119312511070159/dex991.htm`, accessed on May 10, 2014.

4. Internet Engineering Task Force, "HOTP: An HMAC-Based One-Time Password Algorithm," *Request for Comments 4226*, `http://tools.ietf.org/html/rfc4226`, accessed on May 10, 2014.

5. Internet Engineering Task Force, "TOTP: Time-Based One-Time Password Algorithm," *Request for Comments 6238*, `http://tools.ietf.org/html/rfc6238`, accessed on May 10, 2014.

6. Initiative for Open Authentication, `www.openauthentication.org/`, accessed on May 10, 2014.

7. Internet Engineering Task Force, "OCRA: OATH Challenge-Response Algorithm", *Request for Comments 6287*, `http://tools.ietf.org/html/rfc6287`, accessed on May 10, 2014.

8. National Institute of Standards and Technology, Advanced Encryption Standard (AES), `http://csrc.nist.gov/publications/fips/fips197/fips-197.pdf`, accessed on November 17, 2013.

9. RSA Laboratories, "PKCS #1 v2.1: RSA Cryptography Standard," `ftp://ftp.rsasecurity.com/pub/pkcs/pkcs-1/pkcs-1v2-1.pdf`, accessed on November 17, 2013.

10. Intel Identity Protection Technology white paper, "Deeper Levels of Security with Intel Identity Protection Technology," `http://ipt.intel.com/Libraries/Documents/Deeper_Levels_of_Security_with_Intel%c2%ae_Identity_Protection_Technology.pdf`, accessed on May 10, 2014.

■ ■ ■

CHAPTER 11

Looking Ahead: Tomorrow's Innovations Built on Today's Foundation

Creativity is not the finding of a thing, but the making of something out of it after it is found.

—James Russell Lowell

Up to this point, this book has revealed the technical details of Intel's security and management engine, with the focus on the architecture and design of its firmware infrastructure. For the past several years, the engine has been serving as the trusted computing base of many state-of-the-art security technologies delivered by Intel platforms. Looking ahead, more innovative creations are to be done on the engine to make the most out of it. What are the next big things to come?

This chapter wraps up the book by first reviewing the critical building blocks of the engine and then briefly brainstorming next-generation technologies that can be built on the engine to further improve the security computing experience for people.

Isolated Computing Environment

The embedded engine was initially introduced by Intel in the south bridge as a *management* engine to resolve the hard problem of enterprise network administration. Managing, maintaining, and supporting network computers in organizations used to be stressful and expensive. For example, when an end-point computer has crashed, the information technology technician often has to make an onsite visit and debug the issue. Furthermore, monitoring statuses of all computers on a network is a difficult task.

Various software and hardware management solutions come with their advantages and disadvantages. To summarize, the cost of software tools is relatively low; however, software suffers constraints that cannot be easily overcome, such as security and dependency on the operating system. On the other hand, hardware methods are stable, more robust against attacks, and independent of the system under debug, but unfortunately, their higher price tags have prevented them from widespread deployment.

Intel's AMT[1] (advanced management technology)—built on the management engine and a key feature of Intel vPro—is both hardware and software. The AMT is hardware because it is natively embedded as part of the computer's chipset; it operates independently of the host operating system; and more importantly, its security is rooted in the hardware. The AMT is also software because the majority of its functionalities are realized by specific software programs that are compiled into the platform's flash device. Thanks to its dual identity, the AMT enjoys both the stability, security, and independency of hardware solutions, and the flexibility and affordability of software solutions at the same time.

The security and management engine features a dedicated processor, backbone hardware, fuse blocks, memory, and nonvolatile storage. It is designed to run normally, regardless of the state of the host. It can communicate with the host operating system and access the host's physical memory (with certain exceptions). The engine's isolation nature makes it significantly less vulnerable to threats and attacks from the host. Therefore, it is an ideal location for not only platform-level management and security solutions, but also those security applications that require the root of trust to be protected in hardware.

Nothing is perfect, and the engine has its disadvantages and limitations. For instance, to save power and prolong battery life, its clock frequency is set to hundreds of megahertz, much lower than that of processor cores on the main host system. The slower speed disallows the engine to meet performance targets of certain operations (for example, video gaming) that require extremely high throughput. Also, the engine has been designed to execute Intel-signed programs only. In the current architecture, it cannot yet be utilized as a generic trusted execution environment.

Security-Hardening Measures

The engine's capability of safeguarding itself and the sensitive data it handles is critical because of its assigned tasks and deep privileges, especially the right to read and write the host memory and its responsibility in processing high-value assets for many applications.

In order to safeguard it from being compromised, comprehensive hardening measures are applied during boot-time and runtime. The following describes a few examples at a high level:

- *Hardware root of trust*: Binary code and the data of firmware components are stored in the flash memory in the clear. Encryption is not used because the security architecture does not rely on security through obscurity. The concept of hardware root of trust contains two folds: first, the root of trust for integrity is a hardware ROM (read-only memory). Unlike the firmware in the flash memory, the binary of ROM by design is not available externally. Although, even if the code of ROM is leaked, the security of the engine should not be impacted; second, the EPID (*enhanced privacy identification*; see Chapter 5 for details) private key and other chipset keys are burned into the engine's security fuse block in Intel's factory. These keys comprise the root of trust for confidentiality and privacy for the engine.

- *Signed firmware*: Intel digitally signs the firmware image that is loaded by the ROM from the flash. The ROM verifies Intel's signature during the boot process. The hash of the public key for signature verification is hardcoded in the ROM. Applets loaded by the dynamic application loader (DAL; see Chapter 9 for details) are also signed by Intel with the same key and verified when being loaded to the engine.

- *Intact internal memory*: The engine's internal memory is intact from probing from the external world.

- *Protected external memory*: Due to the limited capacity of the internal memory, some versions of the engine require a reserved region of the host DRAM (dynamic random-access memory) to function. Because the DRAM is not in the engine's trust boundary, before being swapped to the DRAM, data pages are encrypted; both data and code pages are integrity protected. There is no point in encrypting code pages because they are available in the clear from the flash memory at rest.

- *Protected nonvolatile storage*: The engine's firmware may store secrets in the flash memory with protection for confidentiality, integrity, and/or anti-replay. The cryptographic keys utilized in these protections are derived from unique security fuses that differ from part to part.

- *Restrictive DMA (direct memory access) control*: The engine can access the host operating system's memory via its DMA devices. This powerful ability may be leveraged by malicious firmware applications to bypass memory protection mechanisms of the host. To reduce the possibility of abuse, DMA operations with the host memory are stringently controlled by a small privileged component in the engine's kernel.

- *Task isolation*: The number of the engine's firmware modules has been growing over the years. To preclude one compromised module from attacking other innocent modules, an embedded task isolation mechanism is applied. Essentially, the isolation architecture places a module in its own container and restricts its penetration into peer containers. Assets that are protected against being accessed by other containers include hardware devices, runtime memory, nonvolatile data, synchronization objects, and so forth.

- *Page attributes*: All pages of the engine's logical memory are tagged with attributes that are configured by the kernel during the boot process. The attribute entries are whether a page is code (executable) or data (nonexecutable), read-only, read-and-write, or no-access, the task it belongs to, and so on.

- *Return address scrambling*: For a function call, the return address that is stored in the stack is "scrambled" (exclusive-OR'ed) with a secret value that is randomly generated during the boot process and stored in a protected register. The prologue function calculates the scrambled return address and places it in the stack. Accordingly, the epilogue function first performs unscrambling and then jumps to the unscrambled address, if and only if the unscrambled address looks valid. With the return address scrambling in place, malware cannot easily take advantage of stack overflow bugs and instruct the processor to execute attacker's code that is located at a specific address.

- *Stack DMZ (demilitarized zone)*: Stack overflowing is commonly used by attackers. When creating the stack for a thread, the engine's kernel reserves extra pages (analogous to a DMZ) that are marked as "no-access" in the page attribute table. The attack of overflowing a stack will trigger an access violation exception if it lands on the DMZ.

The engine's reaction upon detection of a security violation varies depending on the presumed nature of the event. Minor violations may be logged and then ignored quietly. Some violations that can be a result of firmware bugs would trigger a self-reset of the engine. If a certain number of resets happen within a certain number of seconds, then the engine will enter a recovery mode and stop functioning. The engine responds to security violations that are very likely due to active attacks with ungraceful global reset in order to terminate the attack immediately. Figure 11-1 summarizes the aforementioned countermeasures into categories.

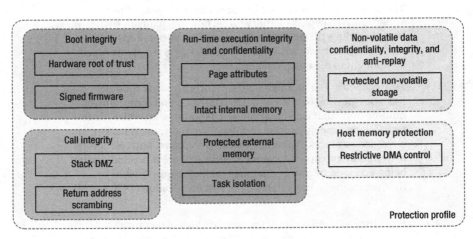

Figure 11-1. *The engine's security-hardening features*

As you can see from the list and Figure 11-1, the philosophy of *defense in depth* is exercised when designing the protection profile of the security and management engine. This means that the security of the engine tries not to rely on any single hardening measure. Consequently, a successful invasion must manage to turn down multiple fortifications, which considerably raises the difficulty of attack attempts.

For example, to install a rootkit that intends to access the host's system memory from the engine, an attack has to circumvent integrity protection, inject malicious code to one of the firmware modules, avoid being caught by runtime integrity checks, and then bypass the kernel's DMA permission filter. It is definitely a tremendous task to go through all of these defenses without triggering the alarm of the engine's security infrastructure.

■ **Note** Try to avoid relying on single hardening measures; always exercise defense in depth when architecting security solutions.

Another example of exercising the philosophy of defense in depth is reflected in the well-known FIPS (Federal Information Processing Standard) 140-2 standard[2] published by the NIST (National Institute of Standards and Technology). For a software or firmware module, the standard requires, among other things, a series of self-tests during the boot process:

- *An integrity test* using, for example, a digital signature to make sure that the module's binary image has not been altered.

- *Known-answer tests* for all cryptography algorithms supported by the module, minus the algorithm that was just checked in the integrity test. A known-answer test calls the underlying cryptography method with hardcoded input vectors and verifies that the output from the method matches the hardcoded expected result.

One can argue that the known-answer tests are redundant because, in theory, once the integrity test passes, the sequential known-answer tests that follow are impossible to fail. However, from a different angle, this double-insurance requirement can also be interpreted as a defense-in-depth strategy. For example, buffer overflow vulnerability or the like may exist in the integrity self-test implementation. An attacker that has intentionally modified the module to his benefit can possibly exploit such a bug and bypass the integrity self-test. The known-answer self-tests offer secondary defense to defeat the attack.

Basic Utilities

The following lists the majority of the engine's fundamental and generic functions that are widely needed by many applications. These have been discussed in previous chapters:

- Most standard cryptography algorithms

- Big-number arithmetic

- Secure timer

- Monotonic counter (increments by one when instructed, never decrements)

- Secure nonvolatile storage

- DMA with the host (limited to select modules only) and within the firmware memory

- HECI (host-embedded communication interface)

- Network interface, limited to select modules only

- Field programmable fuses (FPF)

- Secure firmware update

In addition, the infrastructure supports runtime debug for applications on both preproduction and production configurations. On production parts, variables that hold secret data or keys are replaced with zeroes or test values by the kernel as soon as the debug port is enabled.

Besides these basic methods, the security and management engine is equipped with several useful utilities in its extended infrastructure that are exclusively available on the engine for supporting platform-specific functions of upper-layer applications.

Anonymous Authentication and Secure Session Establishment

The EPID is an anonymous attestation and authentication scheme. It allows a verifier, which may be a local software program or a remote server, to use a group public key to verify a platform's membership of the group by examining the signature generated by the platform using its unique EPID private key. The authentication does not disclose the identity of the platform. The membership of an individual platform may be revoked under predefined circumstances, such as a detected compromise.

The SIGMA (SIGn and Message Authentication) is a protocol for mutual authentication and session key establishment. In the authentication phase, one direction (from the platform to the verifier) uses EPID, which is anonymous; whereas the other direction uses the traditional public key infrastructure (PKI) where a chain of certificates signed by certification authorities and rooted to the EPID authority prove the verifier's identity. For the session key agreement stage, the ECDH (elliptic curve Diffie-Hellman) protocol is employed. To further raise the security bar, the SIGMA protocol can be configured to involve OCSP (online certificate status protocol) for the platform to be confident that the verifier's PKI certificate has not been revoked.

All recent releases of the security and management engine ship with an EPID private key in security fuses. The EPID and SIGMA are building blocks of many attractive features, for example, the Intel Identity Protection Technology[3] (IPT). For authentication, verifying the engine's authenticity is important to applications that take advantage of the engine's built-in functionalities. For session key agreement, the SIGMA protocol provides a convenient and secure approach to protect application-specific communications between a trusted entity and the platform, while maintaining the anonymity and confidentiality of the latter.

One of the potential problems of EPID is the heavy mathematical operations that must be conducted by the verifier and the platform. They slow down the SIGMA protocol execution and arguably worsen the user's experience. One feasible solution without introducing more computing resources is to have both the verifier and the platform save the encryption and integrity keys derived from a successful SIGMA session in their secure nonvolatile storage, respectively. This process is called *pairing*. The session keys resulted from pairing are used in future sessions, even across power cycles. The session keys may be renewed by either side requesting a new SIGMA session once a month, for example, to mitigate attacks against persistent keys and, at the same time, minimize the negative impact of SIGMA to the user's experience.

Protected Input and Output

Input (keyboard, mouse, fingerprint sensor, microphone, and so on) and output (for example, monitor and speaker) devices (I/O devices) constitute the interfaces that connect the human being and the machine. With a user-oriented mindset, safeguarding I/O devices is vital for solutions to any security problems. To realize secure input and output, the I/O devices may be connected with the security and management engine without involvement or interference of the host software. The host cannot access the clear I/O data because it is encrypted, and the decryption key is known to only the processing device and the engine.

Intel's PAVP (protected audio and video path) initially invented for supporting Blu-ray playback is a prototype for protected audio and video output. To display a secret frame, the creator encrypts the frame and transmits the encrypted frame to the graphics processor, which then decrypts and displays it on the screen. The key or the clear frame is not visible to the host. The link between the video output port and the monitor is protected by the wired or wireless HDCP[4] (high-bandwidth digital content protection) protocol. Bypassing the entire software stack is the ultimate mitigation against all types of I/O snooping attacks and it renders all malware on the host that aims at stealing the user's sensitive data through I/O ports inoperable.

Dynamic Application Loader

The security and management engine comes with a number of features stored on the flash chip. But they are not nearly enough to make the most out of the engine's rich set of capabilities. The DAL offers desirable flexibility and extends the boundary of the engine by loading Java applets to the engine from the host at runtime. As software, it is easier to create an applet, change its functionalities, and patch bugs. No firmware update is necessary for building new consumer features to the engine.

But some usages are not suitable for loading by the DAL. Generally, if a feature falls into one or more of the following categories, then it should be natively implemented in the firmware:

- Related to platform security, for example, Boot Guard and firmware-based TPM[5] (Trusted Platform Module). The defined objectives of the platform security features include measuring the integrity of the host, thus they must be running before the operating system is loaded.

- Related to system manageability, for example, AMT.

- Must be available even if the host is not running, for example, AMT and Remote Wake.[6]

- Require high data throughput.

- Code size is large.

Despite these limitations, consumer security features that launch on the operating system can still make good use of the engine through the DAL. Intel IPT sets a great example. Running new applets through the DAL, or other similar and better interfaces to be explored, will be one of the main domains for functional expansion of the engine in the future.

Summary of Firmware Ingredients

Figure 11-2 shows a summary of the security and management engine's firmware components. Notice that it is not an exhaustive list. Also notice that the engine may feature different sets of components for different products. As an example, the Bay Trail series tablets do not support AMT.

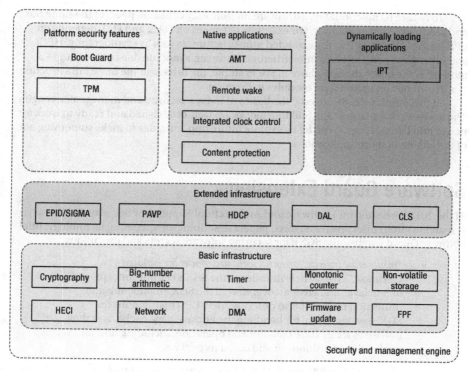

Figure 11-2. *The engine's firmware components*

Most of the firmware ingredients shown in the figure have been discussed in previous chapters. The following have not been mentioned or described in detail.

- *Big-number arithmetic*: Implements signed and unsigned addition, subtraction, multiplication, division, modulo, Montgomery reduction, greatest common divisor, least common multiple, and so forth. These arithmetic operations are extensively invoked by asymmetric-key cryptography, for example, the EPID.

- *Capability licensing service (CLS)*: Allows a remote trusted server to provision platform-specific permits and credentials to the engine. A sample usage of CLS is the Intel Upgrade Service (end of life in 2011) that unlocks advanced CPU (central processing unit) capabilities such as hyperthreading.

- *Integrated clock control*: Supports enablement and configuration of CPU overclocking.

- *Remote wake*: Supports waking up a computer from the sleep or off state from a remote location, so the user can access files on the computer. Network administrators can also use this technology to perform off-hour maintenance.

To realize its functionality, a firmware module may consume peers of the same box and modules in boxes below it. For example, IPT relies on DAL, and DAL depends on EPID/SIGMA and PAVP in the extended infrastructure, as well as cryptography, HECI, and other drivers in the basic infrastructure. However, a module does not consume a module in the boxes that are above it. For example, the drivers in the basic infrastructure box do not rely on upper-layer modules to function.

At this point, we have covered the basics of today's security and management engine. The framework is mature. The building blocks are well-established and ready to work for newer and better things. Next, let us explore future opportunities to make something out of the engine in more applications.

Software Guard Extensions

At the 2013 Workshop on Hardware and Architectural Support for Security and Privacy, researchers from Intel presented three papers describing an upcoming technology, Intel Software Guard Extensions (SGX), for securing software secrets and executions.

- *"Innovative instructions and software model for isolated execution."*[7] This article introduces the SGX's central concept of "enclave" and gives an overview of the SGX architecture and protection model. It also describes new CPU instructions for SGX, new hardware for handling the enclave page cache, and the processes for enclave creation and operation, including how an application transitions in and out of its enclave.

- *"Innovative technology for CPU-based attestation and sealing."*[8] This presentation explains the technical details of provisioning secrets to an enclave, including how to generate hardware-based attestation for software inside an enclave and how software in an enclave seals and unseals secret data.

- *"Using innovative instructions to create trustworthy software solutions."*[9] This paper focuses on the software programming model of SGX. Interestingly, for proof of concept, the authors had built on prototype hardware of SGX three trustworthy applications, namely, one-time password, enterprise rights management, and secure video conferencing. These three are perfect examples for demonstration, because they are highly-demanded real-world applications that exercise many of the SGX's infrastructural capabilities.

In a nutshell, the SGX technology enables software developers to protect sensitive code and data in enclaves that are secured at the hardware level. The protection includes encryption, integrity, and anti-replay. No software on the host, regardless of its ring and privilege, is allowed to touch others' enclaves. Moreover, the hardware can measure the trusted code in an enclave and generate attestation, so that a trusted entity, such as a service provider, is able to confirm the integrity of the code and provide premium services.

Notice the word "innovation" appearing in the titles of all three papers. Running sensitive portions of a software program in the trusted world is not a new idea. However, compared to existing solutions, the SGX's innovation is its capability of managing multiple secure enclaves, mutually untrusted, concurrently in the untrusted world. The CPU-based attestation and sealing are also innovative creations, which function like a dedicated TPM for each individual enclave.

In September 2013, Intel officially announced the SGX feature and published a programming reference manual.[10] The SGX is seemingly a very promising technology that is tasked with resolving long-lasting security problems for the software vendors and consumers. Its design is not trivial. Behind the scene are a number of hardware, firmware, and software components working together to make the SGX a reality. The security and management engine also plays a pivotal role in the solution.

The SGX architecture makes use of the engine through the generic DAL interface. Individual enclaves can invoke the engine's wide range of capabilities, including the cryptography driver, monotonic counter, secure timer, PAVP, and so forth. As the development of SGX continues, other services available from the engine may also be leveraged.

More Excitement to Come

The future development of the security and management engine can move forward in two directions. The first is to expand the family of platform-level features. By their nature, these features cannot be implemented on the host operating system because either the software stack is not trusted or the function must be available even though the host is not active. The engine's unique characteristics of isolation environment should be further utilized to realize security enforcements for the platform, as well as nonsecurity applications that require operations in the sleep state.

Second, the DAL is a milestone development that opens the door of the security and management engine to the external world. It has been used for Intel IPT and will be used for SGX. With the increasing openness of the engine, software vendors and computer manufacturers should be able to develop proprietary and innovative features that make use of the engine's infrastructure.

References

1. Kumar, Arvind, Purushottam Goel, and Ylian Saint-Hilaire, "Active Platform Management Demystified – Unleashing the Power of Intel vPro Technology," *Intel Press*, 2009.

2. National Institute of Standards and Technology, "Security Requirements for Cryptographic Modules," http://csrc.nist.gov/publications/fips/fips140-2/fips1402.pdf, accessed on April 15, 2014.

3. Intel Identity Protection Technology, http://ipt.intel.com/, accessed on April 20, 2014.

4. Digital Content Protection LLC, "High-Bandwidth Digital Content Protection," www.digital-cp.com, accessed on May 10, 2014.

5. Trusted Computing Group, "Trusted Platform Module Library," www.trustedcomputinggroup.org, accessed on March 20, 2014.

6. Intel Remote Wake Technology, www.intel.com/support/motherboards/desktop/sb/CS-032989.htm, accessed on May 10, 2014.

7. McKeen, Frank, Ilya Alexandrovich, Alex Berenzon, Carlos Rozas, Hisham Shafi, Vedvyas Shanbhogue, and Uday Savagaonkar, "Innovative instructions and software model for isolated execution," Workshop on Hardware and Architectural Support for Security and Privacy, Tel-Aviv, Israel, June 2013.

8. Anati, Ittai, Shay Gueron, Simon P. Johnson, and Vincent R. Scarlata, "Innovative technology for CPU-based attestation and sealing," Workshop on Hardware and Architectural Support for Security and Privacy, Tel-Aviv, Israel, June 2013.

9. Hoekstra, Matthew, Reshma Lal, Pradeep Pappachan, Carlos Rozas, Vinay Phegade, and Juan del Cuvillo, "Using innovative instructions to create trustworthy software solutions," Workshop on Hardware and Architectural Support for Security and Privacy, Tel-Aviv, Israel, June 2013.

10. Intel, "Software Guard Extensions Programming Reference," https://software.intel.com/sites/default/files/329298-001.pdf, accessed on May 10, 2014.

Index

■ T, U